Praise for *Immigration*

"The pandemic helped us see many things we must never forget, such as the essential role of immigrants in every aspect of American life. Now that we see, we must act to ensure a future that is fully inclusive of immigrants. This wonderful book tells us how."

—Ai-jen Poo, Director, National Domestic Workers Alliance and Caring Across Generations

"Donald Trump took a hammer to the U.S. immigration system, and in doing so exposed its inhumane and racist scaffolding. The Biden-Harris administration has an unprecedented opportunity to transform the system into one that reflects the best of American values. These thoughtful essays point them—and us—in the right direction."

—Lorella Praeli, President, Community Change Action

"The future of the labor movement—and the country—depends significantly on immigrants and immigration. This crucial collection points the way to a convergence of social movements to achieve lasting power for working people."

—Mary Kay Henry, President, Service Employees International Union (SEIU)

"This volume offers a great wealth of information and analysis about immigration in the U.S.—a moral and practical issue that will become even more important to get right, as this overheated century spins along, producing ever more people with no choice but to move."

—Bill McKibben, author of *The End of Nature*

"Lucid and well-organized. . . . Each essay is packed with useful information and based on decades of experience. Progressive lawmakers and immigration activists will find this to be a valuable resource."

—*Publishers Weekly*

"Bringing together a 'who's who' of thinkers and doers in the immigration space, *Immigration Matters* provides a rich, action-oriented blueprint for reimagining our immigration system. This book is a must-read for policy makers, scholars, and activists interested in a more equitable and just future."

—Lisa García Bedolla, author of *Latino Politics*; Vice Provost and Dean, UC Berkeley

"This is a must-read, comprehensive and deep. In *Immigration Matters*, our nation's most trusted thinkers and advocates ask and answer the hard questions about the future of immigration, one of our most intractable and important policy challenges. They take it on as a moral issue and as a strategic one, suggesting how to bring the center left and progressive left together in a united front for a more just immigration system and a more just America."

—Felicia Wong, President and CEO, Roosevelt Institute

"For progressives to respond effectively to nativism, the fuel for right-wing authoritarian politics, immigrant rights must be a core part of our agenda. This urgently needed book illuminates that progressive vision and lucidly shows how immigrant organizing and coalition-building can power a new generation of social change."

—Katrina vanden Heuvel, Publisher, *The Nation*

"Racism continues to define the shape of American politics, and nativism targeting immigrants of color is one of its principal manifestations. This vitally important book explains why we should lean into a progressive immigration agenda and how we can achieve it by building a broad majority coalition of people of color, immigrants and progressive whites."

—Steve Phillips, author of *Brown Is the New White: How the Demographic Revolution Has Created a New American Majority*

IMMIGRATION MATTERS

IMMIGRATION MATTERS

MOVEMENTS, VISIONS, AND STRATEGIES FOR A PROGRESSIVE FUTURE

Edited by

Ruth Milkman,
Deepak Bhargava,
and Penny Lewis

NEW YORK
LONDON

Requests for permission to reproduce selections from this book should be made through our website: https://thenewpress.com/contact.

First published in the United States by The New Press, New York, 2021
This paperback edition published by The New Press, 2021
Distributed by Two Rivers Distribution

ISBN 978-1-62097-652-4 (hc)
ISBN 978-1-62097-699-9 (pb)
ISBN 978-1-62097-702-6 (ebook)
CIP data is available

The New Press publishes books that promote and enrich public discussion and understanding of the issues vital to our democracy and to a more equitable world. These books are made possible by the enthusiasm of our readers; the support of a committed group of donors, large and small; the collaboration of our many partners in the independent media and the not-for-profit sector; booksellers, who often hand-sell New Press books; librarians; and above all by our authors.

www.thenewpress.com

Book design and composition by Bookbright Media
This book was set in Garamond Premier Pro and Kievit

Printed in the United States of America

10 9 8 7 6 5 4 3 2 1

CONTENTS

Part III: Future Immigration Policy

Part IV: Strategies for Change

PREFACE TO THE PAPERBACK EDITION

In April 2021 the Biden administration instructed all government agencies to stop using the terms "alien" and "illegal alien," a gesture signaling its repudiation of the divisive immigration policies that the previous regime had so vigorously embraced. But meaningful change in immigration policy will require much more than a shift in vocabulary. The scholars and activists whose voices are showcased in *Immigration Matters* dig deeply into the challenges involved from a wide variety of perspectives.

We crafted this book in the summer of 2020, well before the presidential election that ultimately replaced Donald Trump with Joe Biden. Although that outcome was uncertain when we undertook the project, our aim from the outset was to explore the complex terrain that a new administration would have to negotiate if it sought to undo the damage of the Trump years and chart a new course for U.S. immigration policy.

We understood that a Democratic administration would almost surely offer relief from Trump's draconian attacks on immigrants and his efforts to restrict both legal and unauthorized immigration. But we also knew that undoing the damage of the previous four years was only a starting point. Not only was it imperative to resolve the status of the 11 million undocumented immigrants residing in the United States—in most cases for more than a decade. But the nation also faces many other urgent challenges in regard to immigration policy. These include declining population growth, a refugee crisis in our hemisphere, the prospect of explosive increases in worldwide migration in response to climate change, and the ongoing expansion of authoritarian and nativist political forces. With all these issues in mind, this book offers the key elements of a bold, long-term rethinking of immigration with the expectation that the shifts in policy and organizing will play out over many years to come, not only in the early months of a new administration.

The contributors to this volume challenge conventional wisdom about immigration politics and policy in a variety of ways. The opening chapters offer new paradigms for understanding the origins of nativism and the role of immigrants in the U.S. labor market, past and present. The next set of chapters tackles such questions as the optimal level and composition of future migration, border and refugee policy, interior enforcement, and the implications of climate change for migration. The book's final chapters outline organizing, coalitional, and political strategies, documenting both proven models and initiatives that are still at an experimental stage. Taken together, the contributions in this volume offer a transformative vision of reform for the nation's outdated and dysfunctional immigration system, tying that vision to a broader progressive agenda.

We are writing this preface to the paperback edition just after the first hundred days of the Biden administration. Although pandemic recovery and infrastructure proposals are at center stage, immigration is increasingly part of the national political conversation in the post-Trump era. In that context, the fresh thinking featured in this book, grounded in historical perspectives and attuned to emerging economic, political, and environmental realities, is more important than ever.

On his first day in office, President Biden issued a series of executive orders to address the damage Trump's policies had inflicted. Those included measures to:

- Preserve and strengthen the Deferred Action for Childhood Arrivals (DACA) program, which offers protection against deportation and work permits to "Dreamers," the undocumented immigrants brought to the United States as children.

- Rescind the so-called Muslim and African bans, which prevented most immigrants and refugees from over a dozen countries from entering the United States.
- Place a partial moratorium on deportations for one hundred days (an executive order later blocked in the courts) and dramatically narrow the scope of immigration enforcement priorities.
- Revoke Trump's executive order to exclude undocumented immigrants from the census.
- Halt funding for the border wall, the construction of which Trump had sought to achieve by using emergency powers to divert funding from other areas.

Also on his first day in office, Biden sent the U.S. Citizenship Act of 2021 to Congress. If enacted, this legislation would provide a smooth path to citizenship for the 11 million undocumented immigrants currently residing in the United States, along with expedited pathways for Dreamers, farmworkers, and others. Notably, this legislation breaks with previous proposals that conditioned a path to citizenship on increases in border enforcement personnel, detention beds, and border barriers—opting instead for greater use of technology. Indeed, for decades, "comprehensive immigration reform" (CIR) bills linked legalization of the undocumented to ever-tougher enforcement of immigration laws.

The Biden administration's abandonment of this paradigm is a landmark development. The logic behind CIR was that to win bipartisan support for adjusting the status of the unauthorized, ramped-up enforcement would be a necessary tradeoff. Biden's abandonment of this approach reflects two key political developments: first, most of the enforcement elements included in previous CIR bills have been implemented already without the promised quid pro quo of creating a path to legalization; and second, growing opposition to escalating and often draconian interior and border enforcement has pushed Democrats to the left.

Biden's proposed bill includes provisions to increase *legal* immigrant admissions through all four already existing channels: family reunification, employment, humanitarian, and diversity. This marks another significant break from earlier immigration policies that had the unintended effect of increasing undocumented migration because the viable pathways for legal migration were too tightly constricted.

A more limited measure, the "DREAM and Promise Act," which would create a path to citizenship for both Dreamers and holders of Temporary Protected Status who fled natural disasters in their home countries, passed the U.S. House of Representatives in March. At this writing it remains to be seen whether Democrats can overcome Republican opposition to its enactment, given current Senate rules. But Biden's legislative initiatives do expose the new center of gravity in the Democratic Party on immigration made possible by years of movement organizing.

Alongside the executive orders promulgated on Day 1 and the accompanying efforts to advance new immigration reform legislation, the early months of Biden's administration were roiled by a media firestorm about a rise in the number of unaccompanied minors from Central America fleeing violence, extreme weather events, and poverty and seeking asylum at the U.S.-Mexico border. Against the backdrop of the controversy over the border as well as polling data pointing to declining public support for Biden's handling of immigration, he backtracked on his campaign promise to increase the level of refugee admissions from the historically low level set under Trump. That sparked a backlash from congressional Democrats and immigration advocates alike, forcing another policy reversal. The administration's vacillation about the level of refugee admissions, as well as relentless and sometimes inaccurate media coverage of the border situation, distracted attention from the deeper immigration policy issues explored in the following pages.

The administration's unsteady handling of short-term challenges stands in sharp contrast to its decisive early actions to reverse course on Trump's executive orders and to propose sweeping reform legislation. Biden's bifurcated response reflects not only complex and nuanced views among the broader public, but also a limited consensus about immigration reform among Democrats themselves. Although mostly united in their support for a path to legalization for undocumented immigrants, and strongly opposed to many of the racist and cruel policies that Trump adopted, Democrats remain deeply divided on the complex issues of future migration, border policy, and enforcement. Contributors to this volume chart the territory beyond the current consensus.

Immigration repeatedly surfaced as a salient issue in the context of the health and economic crises that roiled the nation in the final year of the Trump administration. Immigrants were disproportionately hit by the COVID-19 pandemic, even as foreign-born farm workers, meatpackers, and health care workers were hailed as "essential workers." Yet under both administrations, every pandemic relief bill passed by Congress excluded undocumented workers and their families, resulting in disproportionate and often extreme hardship. Biden's reversal of Trump's "public charge" rules that made it difficult and risky for even *legal* immigrants to seek help from the government was an important shift. Nevertheless, undocumented immigrants remain ineligible for stimulus checks, child and earned income tax credits, and expanded unemployment insurance.

Blue states have pioneered a far more generous approach. The passage in April 2021 of a $2.3 billion "Fund for Excluded Workers" in New York State was an especially notable breakthrough. The fund provides direct cash assistance to undocumented workers, paid for by higher taxes on the wealthy. (Among the key organizations responsible for the fund's successful passage was Make the Road New York, whose earlier efforts are profiled in this volume.) California created a smaller such fund in 2020, similarly rejecting the tie between immigration status and access to public benefits that has long been a cornerstone of the U.S. welfare state. These initiatives continue the decades-long expansion in state- and local-level immigration policies in the context of stalemate at the federal level: blue states and cities have increasingly promulgated welcoming policies while red states and cities have enacted greater restrictions.

The April 2021 release of preliminary 2020 census data showed that population growth in the United States during the 2010s was the second lowest ever since the first census was taken in 1790. Only in the Great Depression did the nation's population grow more slowly. COVID-19 deaths and long-term fertility decline among the U.S.-born played significant roles, but Trump's restrictive immigration policies were also a key driver of this startling demographic shift. The United States is among the many wealthy nations with aging populations in which the ratio of working-age adults to retirees—what demographers call the "dependency ratio"—has fallen sharply in recent years, posing profound economic challenges.

In response, even some conservative intellectuals and politicians have proposed more generous social welfare policies to address the costs of child-rearing, such as child tax credits. But few have embraced expanded immigration as a solution to population stagnation, partly because pro-immigrant business voices have been sidelined within a Republican Party that has overwhelmingly adopted Trump's nativism.

Yet anyone concerned about the dearth of working-age people in the United States and its implications for both labor supply and tax-based social support systems—that is, its implications for future economic vitality and growth—should embrace expansive immigration policy and recognize the labor and creativity newcomers have brought to this country throughout U.S. history. Indeed, the case for substantially increased levels of immigration is elaborated by several of the contributors to this volume.

The humanitarian case is crucial as well. Today migration is driven by economic opportunities in destination countries, as has always been the case. But "push" factors are also of increasing importance thanks to the havoc wrought by climate change. Recent droughts and devastating hurricanes in Honduras, for example, have led tens of thousands to flee the "dry corridor" of Central America, where subsistence farming has collapsed and crop yields have fallen as much as 70 percent. The ambitious climate agenda embraced by President Biden is surely part of the solution to such devastating crises. But even under the most optimistic climate scenarios, our contributors argue, much higher immigration admissions levels are imperative.

The Biden administration has also responded to a national reckoning with race and racial justice, a matter inextricably intertwined with immigration policy, during its first months in office. Nativism not only has deep roots in American history but provided much of the political fuel for Trumpism, and for the recent surge in white nationalist organizing and hate crimes against people of color, including Asian Americans. The beating heart of conservative politics today is white anxiety about so-called demographic "replacement," fanned by media personalities like Tucker Carlson and finding political expression in an aborted "America First" Congressional Caucus whose organizers infamously invoked the desire to restore an invented Anglo-Saxon national heritage. The January 6, 2021, insurrection at the U.S. Capitol, led by openly white supremacist groups, is best understood in this context, as the most recent chapter in the long history of violent efforts to maintain white political dominance.

These developments have been partly a response to the largest mobilizations in the nation's history under the banner of the Movement for Black Lives, which has forced a renewed focus on the nation's deeply embedded systemic racism. At the same time, political and community mobilizations among immigrants have deepened and spread across the nation. The models of community and labor organizing and coalition building documented in this volume, bringing people together across racial lines with an explicitly political focus, will become increasingly relevant as the 2022 midterm elections loom. Organizing among people of color and immigrants already has transformed the politics of states like Nevada, Arizona, and Georgia, and was a decisive element in the national Democratic trifecta controlling the presidency, the House, and the Senate that emerged from the November 2020 elections.

Those election results also exposed continued and deep polarization along lines of race, ethnicity, and geography, however. A substantial majority of white voters once again supported Donald Trump, particularly white, non-college-educated voters; while overwhelming majorities of African American, Latinx, and Asian American voters backed Joe Biden. Electoral districts with large immigrant populations, urban and suburban, voted overwhelmingly for Democrats, while rural districts and others with few immigrants largely supported Trump.

But demography is not destiny, as the 2020 election also revealed. Many commentators have pointed to wide variations in the Latinx vote by country of origin and by region. Latinx support for Democrats was decisive in states like Arizona and Nevada but proved far weaker in southern Texas and Florida. The deep organizing by community organizations and unions documented in this book is an essential template for translating demographic shifts into political power, and may also offer a path to coalition building in predominantly white, rural areas. The multi-racial state-level coalitions that powered recent electoral shifts also may prefigure a lasting realignment of national politics.

Equally important, now that the immediate threat of Trump's nativist regime is in the rearview mirror, progressives must pivot from opposing to proposing, from resistance to governance. The contributors to this volume took on the ambitious task of looking beyond short-term policy skirmishes to the deeper forces driving—and blocking—change. They outline innovative, imaginative frameworks to power the next generation of research, organizing, and policymaking. Seen from the vantage point of the first hundred days of a new administration, marked by both progress and paralysis, that long-term project of reconstruction is critically important.

Immigration is not a separate track of progressive movement building and policymaking; on the contrary, it is deeply implicated in many of the other challenges that will confront the United States in the years to come. As many of the contributors to this book argue, bold solutions to the nation's immigration challenges may yet prove to be the key we need to unlock the door to broader progressive social change.

Ruth Milkman, Deepak Bhargava, and Penny Lewis
New York City, May 2021

IMMIGRATION MATTERS

INTRODUCTION

Ruth Milkman, Deepak Bhargava, and Penny Lewis

Immigration is among the pivotal, most hotly debated questions of the twenty-first century. Right-wing demagogues have deployed it as the leading wedge issue to rally their base, put the Left on the defensive, and speak to the cultural and economic anxieties of those in the middle. In the United States, the Right—once divided between a pro-immigration corporate bloc and a nativist wing—is now united behind a nationalist, nativist position. It is a motley coalition: avowed racists, strategic racists, people who are not racist but support greater limits on migration, and finally the corporate class, which has surrendered on this issue in order to retain its influence on other matters. The strategy of mobilizing racialized fear and resentment has been used across Europe and the United States to bring right-wing parties to power and to reverse not only pro-immigrant policies but also bedrock labor, civil rights, and social welfare protections. This strategy is formidable, as Trump's victory in 2016 and Brexit (among other examples) demonstrated, and it remains a potent threat.

In the United States, as elsewhere, the nativist turn has been disastrous in its humanitarian impact. Many fewer refugees escaping persecution have been permitted to enter than in the recent past. Families of asylum seekers fleeing violence in Central America have been deliberately separated, with children infamously detained in cages. The 11 million undocumented immigrants present in the United States have been living in fear of a ramped-up interior enforcement apparatus. The Dreamers—young immigrants who entered the country without authorization as children accompanying their parents—were in limbo, as the 2012 program that protects them from deportation and allows them to work legally was threatened with termination. Similarly, hundreds of thousands of Haitian, Central American, African, and Asian immigrants who fled natural and human-made disasters faced possible loss of the Temporary Protected Status (TPS) they were granted long ago. Legal immigrants have had to wait years to become citizens or to be reunited with family members seeking to join them in the United States. And since the COVID-19 crisis began, despite being hailed as "essential," immigrant workers have found themselves shut out of much of the aid provided by the pandemic recovery bills passed by Congress in 2020.

The costs of anti-immigrant policies have not only been borne by immigrants themselves. As racist and nativist rhetoric has escalated, U.S.-born citizens of color also have been victimized by wave after wave of hate crimes. As working conditions are degraded for vulnerable immigrant workers, their U.S.-born co-workers suffer as well, as in the meatpacking industry. The United States is forfeiting the immense economic, cultural, and other benefits that migrants denied entry could have contributed, and the racism and cruelty of U.S. immigration policy have cast a long shadow over the nation's international standing and its very identity.

Nativist attacks have also catalyzed extraordinary reactions, however. Thousands of people—including many non-immigrants who had not previously shown concern—have taken to the streets in response to some of the Trump administration's most egregious anti-immigrant policies, such as the "Muslim ban" and the separation of children from their parents at the border. Opinion research also offers evidence of a backlash to the backlash, with growing sympathy toward immigrants and a modest decline in support for nativism.[1] The Trump era has exposed the nation's contradictory history—its much-vaunted image as a welcoming "nation of immigrants" and a multicultural "melting pot" contrasting with episodes of harsh restrictionism and racialized animosity toward newcomers.

In the twenty-first century, immigrants are central to every aspect of American life. An increasing share of the population is foreign-born or first-generation American, and both groups play a critical role in the U.S. economy. Immigrant organizing is one of the few bright spots in the recent history of the beleaguered U.S. labor movement as well. With foreign-born employment concentrated in both low-wage sectors and high-skill sectors, the immigration question is inextricably intertwined with the debate about soaring economic inequality. Over the past five decades, as Latinx, Asian, and African newcomers have fueled the growth of the non-white population, immigration also has become embedded in discussions of white supremacy and institutional racism. Given the nation's shifting demography, any durable progressive political coalition will have to include immigrants at its center. The contributors to this volume take these developments as a starting point for their analyses of the U.S. immigration system and the politics shaping it, as well as for their proposals for reform.

Historical Background

From the nation's inception, immigrants and their descendants have made up the vast bulk of the U.S. population, with the crucial exception of Native Americans, enslaved Africans, and their descendants. With the exception of the half century between the end of World War I and the late 1960s, the United States has welcomed massive numbers of newcomers throughout its history. Not only has this fulfilled the promise immortalized in Emma Lazarus's famous sonnet, "Give me your tired, your poor, / Your huddled masses yearning to breathe free," emblazoned on a plaque at the Statue of Liberty. Immigration has also fueled U.S. economic dynamism, past and present, both by meeting employers' demand for labor in periods of growth and by continuously attracting talented, creative individuals from across the globe. Indeed, immigrants account for more than one-quarter of all U.S. patents and for one-third of all U.S. Nobel Prize recipients in chemistry, physics, medicine, and economics; both figures are highly disproportionate to the foreign-born share of the nation's population, which has never exceeded 15 percent.[2] Yet nativism also has been a powerful current throughout U.S. history, its ebb and flow reflected in the complex patchwork of immigration laws that have accumulated over the past century and a half.

As Figure 1 shows, the foreign-born share of the population hit a record low in 1970, following decades of severely limited immigration following the passage of restrictive legislation after World War I, most importantly the 1924 Johnson-Reed Act. That marked a historical break from the preceding period of open immigration from Europe, when the foreign-born share of the population hovered between 10 and 15 percent. But the era of restriction was relatively short-lived: with the 1965 Hart-Celler Act, the pre–World War I pattern of mass immigration—although now from Latin America, Asia, and Africa rather than Europe—was gradually restored. More recently, the Trump administration took steps to once again restrict immigration, albeit in the absence of new legislation.

In 2018, the 45 million foreign-born people residing in the United States made up 13.7 percent of the nation's population, only slightly

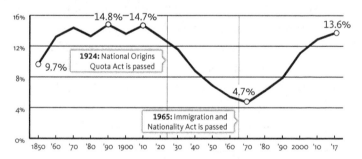

Figure 1: Percentage of U.S. population that is foreign-born, 1860–2017.

Note: Share foreign-born is for the fifty states and District of Columbia.

Source: U.S. Census Bureau, "Historical Census Statistics on the Foreign-Born Population of the United States, 1850–2000" and Pew Research Center; www.pewresearch.org/fact-tank/2019/12 /13/19-striking-findings-from-2019.

below the record high of 14.8 percent, set in 1890.[3] In 2018 there were also 16 million second-generation immigrants—U.S.-born children with at least one immigrant parent.[4] But while the foreign-born share of the population today approximates that of a century ago, immigration is far more regulated in the twenty-first century than it was in the pre–World War I era. Another crucial contrast is that whereas in the earlier period the vast majority of immigrants originated in various parts of Europe, since 1965 most have come from the global South.

Immigration is governed by a crazy quilt of laws and regulations dating back to the late nineteenth century, highlights of which are summarized in Figure 2. The two most important laws, mentioned earlier, were those passed in 1924 and 1965, each of which fundamentally reconfigured the basic architecture of U.S. immigration policy. But in the half century since the 1965 Hart-Celler Act took effect, it has been modified by a series of additional laws and regulations, giving rise to an elaborate and confusing bureaucratic web that is notoriously difficult for immigrants and their advocates to navigate. As a result, well before the Trump era, the system was widely regarded as dysfunctional or "broken" by policymakers across the political spectrum and by the larger public.

Before World War I, the rules were far simpler. There were no numerical limits on overall admissions to the country. Prospective immigrants did not have to obtain visas prior to arrival; they were simply screened by U.S. government officials at Ellis Island and other ports of entry. For Europeans and residents of the Western Hemisphere (unlike Asians, who were targeted by restrictive laws starting with the Chinese Exclusion Act of 1882), this was an era of "open borders." Less than 1 percent of the 25 million Europeans who arrived in the United States between 1880 and World War I were turned away, and deportation was rare. Indeed, in this period the phenomenon of undocumented immigration was virtually unknown.[5]

Figure 2: Milestones in U.S. Immigration Law

THE IMMIGRATION ACT OF 1882 levied a tax of 50 cents for each passenger arriving by ship from a foreign port who was not a U.S. citizen, to be deposited into the U.S. Treasury's "immigration fund," for use in defraying expenses incurred in regulating immigration. The law further established that arriving passengers would be screened and that anyone deemed a "convict, lunatic, idiot, or person unable to take care of himself or herself without becoming a public charge" would not be allowed to land.

THE CHINESE EXCLUSION ACT OF 1882 suspended the immigration of Chinese laborers for ten years but allowed Chinese who were in the United States as of November 17, 1880 to remain. It paved the way for a series of laws passed between 1882 and 1904 that severely restricted Chinese immigration flows and provided for the deportation of many Chinese nationals residing in the United States. Those measures were repealed in 1943.

THE 1924 NATIONAL ORIGINS ACT (Johnson-Reed Act) established immigration quotas, calculated at 2 percent of each nationality's total foreign-born population in the United States in 1890, as indicated in the 1890 census. The law sharply limited admissions of southern and eastern Europeans, who had arrived in largest numbers after 1890. Students, nationals of Western Hemisphere countries, members of certain professions, and the wives and minor children of U.S. citizens were exempt from the quotas.

THE 1942 BRACERO AGREEMENT allowed Mexican nationals to enter the United States as temporary agricultural workers. The agreement, extended in 1949 and 1951, required U.S. employers to pay the transportation and living expenses of Mexican laborers, and to pay them wages equal to those of American farmworkers doing similar work. The agreement was repealed in 1964.

Source: www.migrationpolicy.org/research/timeline-1790.

THE 1952 IMMIGRATION AND NATIONALITY ACT (McCarren-Walter Act) preserved the national-origins quota system, but updated the way in which the quota is calculated. For the first time, Asian nations were assigned quotas allowing their nationals to immigrate to the United States. The law also established that U.S. consular officers would screen foreign nationals for admissibility to the United States.

THE 1965 IMMIGRATION AND NATIONALITY ACT (Hart-Celler Act) abolished the 1924 national-origins quota system and replaced it with a system whereby immigrants are admitted based on family relationships to a U.S. citizen or lawful permanent resident, or to relationships to a U.S. employer. While caps were placed on the total number of immigrants admitted each year in most family-based and employer-based categories, the law provided no cap on the number of "immediate relatives" (spouses, parents, and minor children) of U.S. citizens admitted each year. Immigrants from the Western Hemisphere countries were also exempted from the system of "preference categories" for admissions. However, the law created a 130,000 cap, beginning in 1968, on the total number of permanent residents who could be admitted from the Western Hemisphere (previously there was no such cap).

THE 1986 IMMIGRATION REFORM AND CONTROL ACT (IRCA) provided for a 50 percent increase in Border Patrol staffing and imposed sanctions on employers who knowingly hired or recruited unauthorized immigrants. IRCA also created two legalization programs. One allowed unauthorized aliens who had lived in the United States. since 1982 to regularize their status; the other permitted people who had worked for at least 90 days in certain agricultural jobs to apply for legal permanent resident status. Under these programs, about 2.7 million people who were illegally residing in the United States got legal status.

THE 1990 IMMIGRATION ACT raised legal admissions to 50 percent above the pre-IRCA level (mainly for employment-based immigrants), eased controls on temporary workers, and limited the power to deport immigrants for ideological reasons. It also eliminated discretionary relief for certain aggravated felonies and abolished judicial discretion to grant relief from deportation for criminal offenders.

THE 1996 ILLEGAL IMMIGRATION REFORM AND IMMIGRANT RESPONSIBILITY ACT (IIRAIRA) added new grounds of inadmissibility and deportability, expanded the list of crimes constituting an aggravated felony, created expedited removal procedures, and reduced the scope of judicial review of immigration decisions. The law expanded mandatory detention of immigrants in standard removal proceedings if they had previously been convicted of certain criminal offenses. It also increased the number of Border Patrol agents, introduced new border control measures, reduced government benefits available to immigrants (as did the welfare reform law enacted the same year), increased penalties for unauthorized immigrants, toughened procedural requirements for asylum seekers and other immigrants, mandated an entry-exit system to monitor both arrivals and departures of immigrants, and established a pilot program in which employers and social service agencies could check by telephone or electronically to verify the eligibility of immigrants. It also established a statutory framework for subsequent actions by states and localities, known as 287(g) programs, to take on immigration law enforcement roles that had traditionally been exercised solely by federal immigration enforcement agencies.

THE 2002 HOMELAND SECURITY ACT created the Department of Homeland Security. In 2003 the functions of the Immigration and Naturalization Service (INS)—the Department of Justice agency responsible for provision of immigration services, border enforcement, and border inspection—were transferred to DHS and restructured to become three new agencies: U.S. Customs and Border Protection (CBP), U.S. Immigration and Customs Enforcement (ICE), and U.S. Citizenship and Immigration Services (USCIS).

All of this changed with the passage of the 1924 Johnson-Reed Act amid the nativist upsurge sparked by World War I and the Russian Revolution. One of the legislators for whom the law was named, Albert Johnson, who chaired the Immigration Committee in the U.S. House of Representatives, was an active Ku Klux Klan member. Immigration restriction was at the top of the KKK's political agenda in the 1920s, reflecting the organization's strident anti-Semitism and anti-Catholicism. The 1924 law that the Klan helped pass created national-origins quotas favoring western and northern Europeans and dramatically limiting admissions of eastern and southern Europeans—most of whom were Jews or Catholics, widely viewed not only by the Klan but also by many U.S.-born Protestants as racial and political "others" at the time. The new quotas were determined by each nationality's share of the U.S. population in 1890, just before the massive surge of southern and eastern European immigration had taken off. The 1924 law also effectively barred Japanese from entry (Chinese immigration was already illegal); later it served as a formidable barrier to entry for refugees from Nazism seeking safety in the United States.[6]

As intended, the Johnson-Reed Act slowed new immigration to a trickle. Six years after its passage, the stock market crash and the ensuing surge of unemployment largely eliminated the economic incentive to migrate to the United States as well. Against that background, nativism faded in the New Deal era, especially during and after World War II, when Jews and Catholics were gradually incorporated into the mainstream of American society and came to be seen as "white." That paved the way forward for political efforts to eliminate the discriminatory national-origins quotas established in 1924, which had become anachronistic. After a series of false starts, Congress passed the Hart-Celler Act in 1965, ending the quotas and replacing them with a system that prioritized family reunification and employment needs. This legislation was part of the wave of progressive reforms—including landmark civil rights laws, Medicare, and other Great Society programs—that followed Lyndon Johnson's landslide 1964 electoral victory.

Widely heralded at the time as an anti-discrimination measure, in retrospect the Hart-Celler Act's more notable effect was paving the way for the dramatic increase in immigration shown in Figure 1. The law capped overall legal immigration at 290,000 people per year, with no more than 20,000 from any single country. But admissions soon rose well above that level, as key categories were exempted from the cap and/or authorized by subsequent legislation. The largest such category comprised the immediate family members of U.S. citizens (including naturalized citizens) or legal permanent residents (LPRs). Refugees were also exempt from the cap on total immigration, as were certain types of skilled workers. The cumulative significance of these various exemptions can be seen in data for the fiscal year that ended on September 30, 2017 (before the Trump administration's immigration policies had a significant impact). That year more than a million immigrants became LPRs. Two-thirds of them were family members of U.S. citizens or family members of LPRs, 13 percent were refugees and asylees, 12 percent gained LPR status through employment-based preferences, and 5 percent received that status through "diversity visas" under a program created in 1990.[7]

To be sure, the historical fluctuations shown in Figure 1 reflect not only changes in the law, but also economic and social forces. The primary economic driver of immigration has always been labor demand. In this respect immigrants are distinctly different from refugees fleeing war, natural disasters, political persecution, or discrimination based on religion, ethnicity, or sexual orientation. Refugee flows have grown over recent decades (except under Trump) and will likely expand further with climate change, although historically immigrants have greatly outnumbered refugees. For both groups, "push" factors (some of them results of U.S. foreign policy) explain why migration flows originate in one part of the world rather than another. In contrast, "pull" factors—most importantly labor demand, but also social networks, and especially the presence of family members in the destination country—explain why immigrants are drawn to specific locations. In the past as in the present, few undertake the arduous journey from their country of birth to a new one unless they are in urgent need of refuge from a life-threatening situation or are confident that they can secure a better livelihood on arrival in their chosen destination.

The Browning of America and the Unintended Consequences of Immigration Law and Policy

The political leaders who crafted the 1965 Hart-Celler Act did not anticipate the surge in immigration it unleashed. After he signed the bill at a ceremony in front of the Statue of Liberty, President Johnson confidently declared that "it will not reshape the structure of our daily lives." He was deeply mistaken, however. Not only did the overall volume of immigration rise sharply soon afterward, but the new law also became a key driver of the "browning of America," as most of those who arrived after its enactment hailed from Asia and Latin America. This too was an entirely unexpected development. Attorney General Robert Kennedy predicted an influx of about 5,000 immigrants from Asia during the first year after the 1965 law took effect, "after which immigration from that source would virtually disappear." Instead, starting in the 1970s, Asian immigration spiked upward, and has accelerated ever since (see Figure 3).[8]

Perhaps even more surprising to those who crafted the Hart-Celler Act was the huge increase in migration from Mexico and the rest of Latin America that followed its passage. The law actually limited

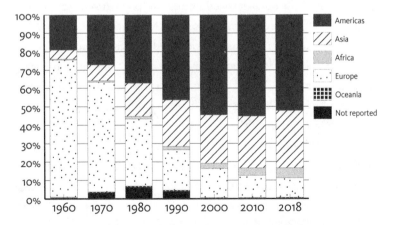

Figure 3: U.S. Immigrant Population by World Region of Birth, 1960–2018.

Source: Migration Policy Institute, www.migrationpolicy.org/programs/data-hub/charts/regions -immigrant-birth-1960-present.

admissions from the Western Hemisphere for the first time in U.S. history, with a cap of 120,000 per year (included in the overall cap of 290,000 per year). This provision was added to the Hart-Celler Act in an eleventh-hour political compromise, with the intent of restricting immigration across the nation's southern border. Instead it had precisely the opposite effect.

A year before passing the Hart-Celler Act, Congress had ended the bracero program, which had been exposed as highly abusive. Originally launched amid the labor shortages of World War II, the program had allowed Mexicans to legally enter the country on a temporary basis as agricultural guest workers. It was abolished in 1964, and yet agribusiness demand for low-wage labor continued unabated. As a result, the introduction of the new cap on legal admissions from the Western Hemisphere in the 1965 immigration law rapidly generated a precipitous rise in unauthorized entry across the southern border by migrant farmworkers who could no longer become braceros. At first, like the bracero program, this was a largely circular migration of single male workers, most of whom returned to Mexico after each harvest. But then a wholly unintended vicious cycle emerged: as U.S. border enforcement ramped up in response to the growth of the unauthorized immigrant population, crossing the border became more expensive for Mexican farmworkers, and circular migration was increasingly replaced by permanent settlement in *El Norte*. In the 1980s, another influx across the southern border developed among Central American refugees fleeing civil wars— wars in which the United States played a significant role.

Latinx immigrants ultimately gained a foothold not only in agriculture but also in urban labor markets, where they found construction, manufacturing, and service jobs. As demand for low-wage labor surged with de-unionization and labor degradation from the late 1970s on, the unauthorized population continued to grow. That in turn led to the passage of the 1986 Immigration Reform and Control Act (IRCA), which like the 1965 law proved to have vast unintended consequences. IRCA's main goal, as its name implies, was to control unauthorized immigration. To that end, it provided amnesty to undocumented immigrants who had been present in the country prior to January 1, 1982 (not coincidentally excluding the many Central American refugees who arrived after that date), while simultaneously tightening border enforcement to prevent a new influx. Once again, the militarization of the border—which was ramped up even further in subsequent legislation—led more and more unauthorized immigrants to abandon circular migration in favor of permanent settlement. Many also arranged for family members to join them, often without authorization. As a result, the unauthorized population mushroomed after IRCA, peaking at 12 million in 2007, when the collapse of labor demand due to the Great Recession brought the influx to a sudden halt.[9]

The Modern Immigrant Rights Movement

Each wave of immigration has spawned new civic organizations attending to the practical needs of newcomers and their U.S.-born children. A century ago these included ethnic and religious groups, labor unions, and the famous settlement houses of the Progressive Era. The post-1965 wave of immigration replicated that same pattern, especially after the passage of IRCA in 1986. In the nation's large urban centers, where the foreign-born population was most concentrated, the amnesty created by that law spurred advocates and organizers to ramp up efforts to help undocumented residents adjust their status—efforts that gradually evolved into the contemporary immigrant rights movement.[10]

That movement, which included organizations that provided direct social and legal services to immigrants as well as those engaged in public policy advocacy and organizing, expanded further in response to a series of anti-immigrant threats. California voters approved Proposition 187 in 1994, with the intent of denying access to public social services to undocumented immigrants, including public schooling for children. Although it was soon struck down in the courts, Prop 187 led to widespread mobilization among immigrants in California, then home to the nation's largest undocumented population. Two years later the U.S. Congress passed two highly punitive laws (see Figure 2) that restricted immigrants' access to public benefits and increased penalties for immigration violations. These measures also profoundly shaped the immigrant rights movement, sparking an explosion of efforts by community-based groups, service organizations, multi-racial community organizations, unions, worker centers, and immigrant rights coalitions to ameliorate the harms. Mirroring the geographical dispersion of immigration beyond the traditional destination states of New York, California, Illinois, Texas, and Florida to the rest of the country, the movement also spread increasingly to new destinations, and a grassroots movement for "amnesty"—later termed "legalization"—began to crystallize, despite the fact that many establishment organizations and politicians initially dismissed it as hopelessly impractical.

Immigrant organizing in the late twentieth and early twenty-first centuries has taken a wide variety of forms. Ethnically specific groups such as Mexican and Central American hometown associations, as well as multi-ethnic coalitions among Latinx, Asian, African, and sometimes even European immigrants, burgeoned in the 1980s and 1990s. In the same period, the Catholic Church and other religious bodies whose congregations included growing numbers of immigrants became increasingly engaged in both service provision and immigrant rights advocacy. A vibrant ethnic media infrastructure of radio stations, TV networks, and newspapers developed to meet the needs of the growing community, amplifying the voices of immigrant rights advocates. Traditional labor unions in sectors such as building services and construction began recruiting immigrant workers into their ranks in the 1980s and 1990s as well, giving the movement a huge boost and sparking the AFL-CIO's historic decision in 2000 to reverse its historically anti-immigrant position. In the same period, non-union organizations known as worker centers began to organize immigrants outside the boundaries of the traditional labor movement, including day laborers, domestic workers, taxi drivers, and restaurant workers.[11]

The immigrant rights movement experienced a major setback after the attacks of September 11, 2001, unleashed a virulent wave of xenophobia, crushing hopes that had been raised shortly beforehand by talks between U.S. president George W. Bush and Mexican president Vicente Fox about a path to legalization for the (predominantly Mexican) undocumented. As that prospect dimmed, the movement increasingly shifted its focus to local and state issues such as access to in-state college tuition and driver's licenses for undocumented residents. In the early 2000s, immigrant rights organizations sponsored the first leadership trainings of a new generation of immigrant youth activists—giving rise to the politically potent Dreamers, who later gave the larger movement an intersectional thrust.[12]

The quest for immigrant rights burst into national consciousness in 2006, when cities across the country witnessed marches of millions of people. This massive mobilization was sparked by legislation sponsored by House Judiciary Committee chairman Jim Sensenbrenner and passed by the U.S. House of Representatives in late 2005. H.R. 4437 never became law, but proposed to criminalize undocumented immigrants as felons, along with anyone who offered them assistance. All the institutions that had begun to support immigrant rights in the preceding years—from community-based organizations to churches to unions—responded in force. Their call to action was amplified by Latinx radio DJs and the wider ethnic media. Protesters poured into the streets, carrying signs saying "We Are America" and "Today We March, Tomorrow We Vote."[13]

The 2006 marches were followed by a less visible but highly effective campaign to encourage eligible immigrants to become naturalized U.S. citizens and to register as voters. That effort soon transformed the political landscape, especially in immigrant-rich California. At the same time, at the national level reformers mobilized a major push for comprehensive immigration reform (CIR), a sprawling grand bargain that aimed to unify a wide variety of interest groups—those fighting for the 11 million undocumented, the Dreamers, labor unions with large immigrant memberships, employers in low-wage or high-skill sectors seeking more access to labor, and constituencies advocating increased family-based migration and expanded admission of refugees and asylees. CIR was proposed in various iterations: in the talks between Presidents Bush and Fox in 2001, and in legislation sponsored by Senators Kennedy and McCain that passed in the Senate (but not the House) in 2006 and then passed in the House (but not the Senate) in 2007. With the support of President Obama, a bipartisan "Gang of Eight" reintroduced CIR proposals in 2013 and 2014, when a bill passed the Senate with sixty-eight votes but never came to a vote in the Republican-controlled House.

Substantively, the various CIR proposals combined provisions for a path to legalization for the undocumented, changes to the family- and employer-based systems for future immigrant admissions, and much greater enforcement of immigration laws—at the workplace, at the border and elsewhere in the interior. The logic behind the enforcement component was to prevent a new influx of unauthorized immigrants like the one that had followed the passage of IRCA in 1986. CIR's delicate balance of expansion and restriction won support from strange bedfellows: the business wing of the Republican Party and a large majority of Democrats. But as that CIR coalition collapsed, an increasingly fierce nativist backlash drove more and more Republicans away, paving the way for Trump to ride the coattails of an energized anti-immigrant movement.

The "grand bargain" embodied in CIR also shaped the Obama administration's policy shifts. After Obama's pledge during his 2008 campaign to move CIR early in his first term, his failure to do so raised the ire of immigrant rights leaders—a sentiment further intensified as deportations soared to record levels. In 2010, the movement organized a mass march on the National Mall in Washington, DC, and an aggressive direct-action campaign. Those efforts generated a variety of reforms, including the signature accomplishment of the Obama years, the 2012 executive action creating the Deferred Action for Childhood Arrivals (DACA) program. Four years later, the Trump campaign's relentless fixation on immigration—including racist scaremongering about "criminals" and "gangs" crossing the border, plus the promise to "build the wall"—took aim at this uneven progress.

Immigration Policy Under Trump

Immediately after taking power, Trump began to deliver on his campaign threats. He quickly issued three executive orders that set the template for the radical policy changes his administration would pursue in the succeeding years. The first two dramatically increased both border and interior enforcement by increasing detention, limiting asylum, and vastly expanding the number and types of immigrants who would be priorities for deportation. The third executive order famously banned travel to the United States from several Muslim-majority countries.[14]

These efforts to deploy the executive branch's vast powers to enforce immigration law were crafted by Stephen Miller, Trump's chief strategist on immigration both during the campaign and within the administration. As one commentator noted, Miller has been "an anomaly in Washington: an advisor with total authority over a single issue that has come to define an entire administration . . . [and as of 2020] Trump's longest-serving senior aide."[15] A leaked email that Miller wrote in 2015, when he was on the staff of then-Senator Jeff Sessions, expressed enthusiasm for a total ban on immigration, "like Coolidge did," an allusion to the 1924 Johnson-Reed Act. Other emails from that period linked Miller to white nationalism, but he remained in the White House.[16]

The Trump/Miller approach to immigration policy was highly reminiscent of the 1920s not only in its restrictive goals but also in its explicit racism, harkening back nostalgically to an era before the "browning of America" began. The president openly embraced white supremacy, as vividly illustrated not only in his comments on the 2017 Unite the Right rally in Charlottesville but also by his query to Senator Lindsey Graham at a White House meeting in early 2018, "Why would we want all these people from shithole countries?"[17]

Prior to Trump's ascent to the presidency, post-1965 immigration policy had been bipartisan in both its punitive and welcoming elements. Democratic administrations had embraced restrictive policies such as the 1996 Illegal Immigration Reform and Immigrant Responsibility Act, passed under Clinton, which dramatically expanded the grounds for immigration detention and deportation (see Figure 2). More recently, many movement leaders lambasted Obama as the "deporter-in-chief." On the other hand, Republican Ronald Reagan had presided over the 1986 IRCA "amnesty," and in his final speech as president had famously invoked immigrants as the crux of America's greatness, declaring, "If we ever closed the door to new Americans, our leadership in the world would soon be lost."[18] Both President Bushes were also sympathetic to immigration reform proposals, in part due to concern about alienating the growing Latinx electorate.

By the Trump years, however, immigration had become a decidedly partisan issue, with nearly all Democrats supporting some version of a more generous and welcoming policy and nearly all Republicans supporting greater enforcement while emphatically rejecting anything that smacked of "amnesty." Trump not only relentlessly demonized immigrants in his speeches but also systematically executed the master plans that Miller had designed to restrict both unauthorized and legal immigration.

Miller convinced Trump to try to end DACA (an effort blocked to date by the Supreme Court's June 2020 decision). The administration also dramatically scaled back the number of refugees admitted to the country to a record low of 18,000 in 2020; Miller reportedly wanted to cut the number to zero.[19] Asylum at the southern border also was effectively halted, even after the huge public outcry about the policy of separating refugee children from their parents. As the 2020 COVID-19 pandemic spread across the country, making immigrants newly visible among "essential workers" in industries such as agriculture and meatpacking, the administration issued a proclamation suspending visas for immigrants who "present risk to the U.S. labor market."[20] Over four hundred anti-immigrant policies implemented by the Trump administration reduced migration to its lowest level since the 1980s.[21]

The old CIR coalition had been pulled apart at both ends, as the Right utterly abandoned support for legalization and the Left rejected as a non-starter the increased enforcement that had been part of previous bills. Issues that had been less central in previous years became increasingly urgent in the Trump era, including refugee and asylum policy and how to regulate the "future flow" of new migrants, with some advocating a shift away from the existing preference for family-based migration in favor of a "merit"-based system.

Among the challenges for progressives that the chapters in this volume engage is how to shape immigration legislation in the post-Trump era. Should progressives reject a comprehensive framework altogether, or construct a radically new version of CIR that reckons with the negative consequences of enforcement and addresses issues such as future migration? What is the right balance among executive actions, piecemeal legislation to address the needs of particular immigrant groups (such as Dreamers or farmworkers), and comprehensive approaches? Before turning to those questions, however, it is crucial to expose and debunk some of the most glaring misconceptions about immigration that have often shaped public discussion in recent years.

Immigration Myths and Facts

Economics

Many Americans believe that immigrants, especially the unauthorized, impose heavy cost burdens on taxpayers. Experts and scholars have repeatedly shown that this is not the case. A 2017 report from the National Academies, for example, documents that immigration has a positive fiscal impact at the federal level, both because immigrants are excluded from many government benefits and because they contribute more to Social Security and Medicare than they receive. At the state and local levels, immigration *does* have a negative fiscal impact: the costs of providing education and social services to new arrivals and their children are not fully recovered by the state and local taxes that immigrants pay. But the children of immigrants pay more than enough in state and local taxes to cover such costs for themselves and their children.[22]

Taxpayer burdens are only one part of the complex balance of costs and benefits. Contrary to popular belief, immigration has a net positive impact on economic growth and on technological innovation. The presence of immigrants reduces the costs of many goods and services (e.g., child care, food processing, and construction), benefiting consumers. In addition, immigration increases demand not only for many goods and services but also for housing, stimulating the real estate industry and other sectors. And despite frequent assertions to the contrary, immigration has only a minuscule effect on the wages of the U.S.-born workforce. Moreover, insofar as the effect is negative, it primarily hurts prior immigrants.[23]

Undocumented Immigrants

"Illegal" immigrants have been front and center in recent political debate. But the size and nature of the unauthorized population are often exaggerated in the public imagination. Consider these facts:

- Unauthorized immigrants made up less than 5 percent of the U.S. workforce in 2016.[24]
- In 2017, just under one-fourth (23 percent) of the foreign-born population was unauthorized, or an estimated 11 million people, including about 700,000 Dreamers protected by the DACA program and another 300,000 individuals with Temporary Protected Status.[25]
- Legal permanent residents—more commonly known as green card holders—make up a larger share of all immigrants (27 percent) than the undocumented.
- Naturalized U.S. citizens account for an even larger group (45 percent of the total).
- Another 5 percent are temporary legal residents.[26]
- In 2017, two-thirds of all unauthorized immigrants were long-term residents who had lived in the United States for ten years or more.[27]

In short, while the public debate about immigration focuses primarily on the undocumented, the vast majority of the nation's foreign-born residents arrived in the United States through legal channels, and nearly half are naturalized citizens.

Other Myths and Facts

The unauthorized may be the least well-understood immigrant group, but many other widely held beliefs about the larger foreign-born population are inconsistent with established facts:[28]

Myth: *Most immigrants today are Latinx.*

Fact: Less than half (44 percent) of the U.S. immigrant population in 2018 was of Hispanic or Latino origin. Since 2007, Asians have outnumbered Latinxs among new immigrant arrivals. In

U.S. government data, "Hispanic" and "Latino" are ethnic, not racial, categories. In 2018, 46 percent of all immigrants self-identified as single-race whites, 27 percent as Asian, and 10 percent as Black. Fifteen percent indicated that they were "some other race," and 2 percent chose two or more races.

Myth: *The vast majority of Latinx people in the United States are immigrants.*

Fact: As of 2018, 67 percent of the nation's Latinx population is U.S.-born.

Myth: *Most immigrants are poorly educated.*

Fact: Thirty-two percent of all immigrants twenty-five years and older had four-year college degrees in 2018, just below the share of U.S.-born adults in that age group who had four-year degrees (33 percent). Immigrants from sub-Saharan Africa, the Middle East (including North Africa), and Asia are *more* likely to have four-year college degrees than U.S.-born Americans. Among those twenty-five years and older, 41 percent of African immigrants, 48 percent of those from the Middle East, and 53 percent of Asians had four-year degrees, compared to 33 percent of U.S.-born adults. The figures are lower for immigrants from Mexico (7 percent) and Central America (11 percent).

Myth: *Most immigrants are employed in low-wage, unskilled jobs.*

Fact: In 2018 the largest share (33 percent) of employed immigrants sixteen years old and up worked in managerial, professional, and related occupations; another 15 percent were employed in sales and office jobs. (Those two white-collar occupational groups accounted for 40 percent and 23 percent, respectively, of all employed U.S.-born workers in 2018.)

One major task for the immigrant rights movement and its allies in the coming years is to help promote wider understanding of these realities in the public square. The movement faces many other daunting challenges as well.

The Future of the Immigrant Rights Movement

Like many social movements, the immigrant rights movement has many competing centers of gravity that engage in passionate debates about goals and strategy. In recent years power has increasingly shifted away from traditional insider organizations focused on Washington, DC, and toward grassroots immigrant rights groups, which have a different perspective. There are other divisions as well. CIR often has been counterposed to narrower strategies to legalize subpopulations among the 11 million undocumented or to reconfigure specific policies, such as family-based migration. Still other debates concern the respective merits of pressing for relief through legislation or through the executive powers of the presidency.

Adult and youth leaders have not always agreed on tactics, with younger activists at times favoring narrower legislation specific to Dreamers, while the broader movement advocated a solution for all undocumented people. Different ethnic groups have had distinct substantive priorities as well, with Latinx immigrants historically pressing most strongly for legalization of undocumented immigrants, while Asian immigrants focused their efforts on increased family-based immigration to reduce the long backlogs in the existing system, and African and Afro-Caribbean immigrants prioritized the diversity visa and TPS. Groups focused on immigration historically were separated from those focusing on refugees and asylees, although more recently that division has faded under a hostile administration that lumps all of them together.

Despite these competing priorities and internal strategic and tactical disagreements, the immigrant rights movement has increasingly united in opposition to Trump's policies. It has also become more tightly aligned with the broader movement for economic and racial justice, which in turn has shown growing interest in immigration as a core priority. As progressives increasingly recognize, a proactive immigration reform strategy is a prerequisite for the success of the larger social democratic project. To neutralize the potency of the nativist appeal—not only in the United States but around the world—requires directly engaging difficult and potentially divisive questions. For example, who should be able to come to the United States, under what conditions, and in what numbers? Liberals and leftists may agree on what they are against—like putting kids in cages or the "Muslim ban"—but not on vision or strategy. Yet without advancing a positive vision of immigration's role in the U.S. economy, society, and culture, progressives risk losing the debate. Nativists have a repugnant but coherent ethno-nationalist vision, and to defeat them pro-immigrant forces must coalesce around a substantive program with a clear vision of immigration policy, its relationship to the larger progressive agenda, and strategies to get from here to there. That is the goal of *Immigration Matters*. The scholars and activists whose voices animate the pages that follow offer alternative visions that directly counter the ethno-nationalist, anti-immigrant agenda promoted by Trump and his counterparts around the world.

The book also aims to move beyond policy frameworks offered in the past, whether from the center or the Left, that have proven politically unworkable, morally reprehensible, or both. Some liberal restrictionists, for example, opportunistically advocate sacrificing admission of immigrants and refugees in the name of "saving" democratic governance; in Australia and Italy this approach has condemned migrants to die at sea or be imprisoned in offshore camps.[29] The "social democracy in one country" approach that views migrants and refugees as tools of capitalists rather than as human beings fleeing desperate circumstances caused by capitalism has similar flaws. One prominent example is German sociologist Wolfgang Streeck's attack on German chancellor Angela Merkel for welcoming millions of Syrian refugees fleeing civil war on the grounds that "it is impossible to protect wages against an unlimited supply of labor."[30] Austria's left-wing Green Party took this approach to its logical conclusion when it entered into a "green-brown" governing alliance with a proto-fascist anti-immigrant party.[31] At the other end of the political spectrum, the "open borders" framework popular on parts of the far left (as well as among free-market libertarians) in the United States rejects all immigration limits without offering any affirmative vision of the role of immigration in society. Although many of its proponents have the best of intentions, this approach may have a boomerang effect, reinforcing the strength of the nativism it seeks to oppose by providing an easily caricatured foil.

What alternatives to nativism and nationalism can reignite the immigrant rights movement and win meaningful, lasting reforms? What coalitions and strategies can pave the way toward a new progressive immigration vision? The chapters that follow present cutting-edge thinking on those questions from academic researchers and from organizers who have been experimenting with new approaches. Taken together, they offer what Perry Anderson calls "a conceptual alternative capable of being articulated across the same range [as conservative approaches], from the philosophical to the technical to the rawly political."[32]

Road Map of the Book

Immigration Matters unfolds in four parts. Part I defines the historical context in which contemporary challenges and opportunities must be understood. Part II focuses on exemplary organizing efforts that have advanced immigrant rights in recent years, offering insights to inform future efforts. Part III offers a series of innovative policy proposals, and Part IV follows up with strategic analyses addressing how to move those proposals forward.

Xenophobic reactions to immigrants are not new. In "American

Nativism, Past and Present," Mae M. Ngai explores the conditions under which nativism has flourished in the past by comparing three historical examples: anti-Chinese sentiment and the Chinese Exclusion Act of 1882, hostility toward eastern and southern Europeans and the restrictive 1924 immigration law, and the anti-Latinx animus that has motivated twenty-first-century restrictionism. Her chapter identifies the economic, ideological, and political factors that facilitate nativism's success, arguing that it thrives in periods of economic expansion, draws on narratives promulgated by influential thinkers, and is mobilized by demagogues to advance their political careers. Ngai is careful to underscore the contingent character of nativist politics, pointing out that immigrants themselves, and their second-generation children, have often exploited such contingency to win struggles for inclusion and to redirect the country toward the best, most welcoming version of itself.

The historical fallacies underlying the "immigrant threat narrative" that blames foreign-born workers for the deteriorating economic status of non-college-educated American workers are the focus of Ruth Milkman's chapter, focusing on the period since the mid-1970s. In "History Shows That the Immigrant Threat Narrative Is Wrong," she argues that the economic woes facing U.S.-born workers were caused not by immigration but rather by de-unionization, de-regulation, subcontracting, and skyrocketing inequality. As employers deliberately degraded pay and working conditions and attacked unions, those U.S.-born workers who could access alternative opportunities abandoned the jobs most affected. Only then were immigrants hired to fill the resulting vacancies. Milkman's analysis suggests that U.S.-born workers should blame employers, not immigrants, for their plight, and that both groups of workers would benefit from stronger unions, workplace protections, and reduced inequality.

The next two chapters in Part I document the history of the modern immigrant rights movement through interviews with prominent leaders. First, in "Stronger Together: Immigrant Workers and the

Labor Movement," Eliseo Medina, a labor organizer who served as a national leader of the Service Employees International Union (SEIU) for decades, recounts the process of building mutual support between the labor and immigrant rights movements through organizing drives such as the SEIU's Justice for Janitors campaign, and culminating in the AFL-CIO's abandonment of support for immigration restriction in 2000. Medina shares insights from his own deep involvement in the movement, including his historic fast on Capitol Hill in 2013 in support of comprehensive immigration reform.

In "From the Ground Up: The Growth of the U.S. Immigrant Rights Movement," Angelica Salas, executive director of the Coalition for Humane Immigrant Rights (CHIRLA), based in Los Angeles, focuses on the community-based sector of the movement. Drawing on her experience in leading mass protests, organizing day laborers and domestic workers, fostering leadership development, and galvanizing immigrant civic engagement and political mobilization, Salas traces the historical arc from local grassroots organizing to building durable national coalitions. She also explores the tense relationship between immigrant rights advocates and the Democratic Party, especially under President Obama. Her reflections illuminate not only the movement's history but also its future prospects.

These perspectives on the history of U.S. immigration dynamics and immigrant rights struggles lay the groundwork for the analysis of successful twenty-first-century immigrant organizing campaigns in Part II. First, in "The Immigrant Youth Movement: Here to Dream and Here to Fight," Cristina Jiménez Moreta analyzes the struggle that led to the creation of DACA in 2012, tracing the evolution and growth of the Dreamers movement of undocumented youth. Jiménez emphasizes the power created when those directly affected by repressive policy lead the fight for change, detailing how immigrant youth shifted strategies and tactics over the decade that led up to winning DACA. As they broke away from the larger adult-led immigrant rights movement, many came to reject the narrative that portrayed undocumented children as innocent victims of their parents' illegal acts, and the Dreamers widened their focus to engage the struggle against deportation and for legalization for all. Yet the movement also acted pragmatically: after repeated efforts to pass immigration legislation failed, they—along with many other parts of the movement—united around a demand for executive action, which secured the DACA victory.

How to build political power to enable such breakthroughs is the focus of "The Nevada Turnaround: Immigrant Workers Build Political Power," an interview with D. Taylor, international president of UNITE HERE, one of the country's most dynamic and militant unions, with a large foreign-born membership. Taylor explains how the rise of immigrant union leadership in Las Vegas led to a political sea change in Nevada, which has shifted from "red" to "purple" to "blue," largely due to the work of the legendary Culinary Workers Union, a local of UNITE HERE. Relentless rank-and-file organizing and willingness to strike in the unlikely setting of "right-to-work" Nevada forged the multi-ethnic and multi-racial union's power in the workplace. Taylor recounts how the union went on to leverage that power politically, helping elect immigrant rights advocates to the Nevada state legislature and to national office.

Campaigns to change the direction of immigration policy must target the private sector as well, given the extensive corporate involvement in immigration enforcement and detention. This is the topic of "Taking on Corporate Complicity in the Trump Era: The 'Corporate Backers of Hate' Campaign," co-authored by Javier H. Valdés, Deborah Axt, Daniel Altschuler, and Angeles Solis, leaders of Make the Road New York (MRNY). Their chapter vividly describes MRNY's successful effort to expose the role of large corporate banks in financing privatized immigrant detention facilities, a campaign that ultimately forced the banks to change their practices. They go on to document another MRNY naming-and-shaming campaign against corporate complicity with the Trump administration, in this case targeting Amazon for its technological assistance to the deportation operations of Immigration and Customs Enforcement (ICE) and for the sale of facial recognition software to the U.S. Department of Homeland Security and to local police precincts. MRNY worked with a broad coalition of progressive community-based organizations on both campaigns, in a model of effective local efforts to challenge corporate power.

These examples of recent organizing victories inform the chapters in Part III, which present a series of cutting-edge policy proposals to build a just and effective immigration system in the years to come. The chapter that opens this section, "Five Freedoms: A Twenty-First-Century Policy Vision for Immigrant Rights," by Marielena Hincapié, executive director of the National Immigration Law Center, summarizes a broad national policy agenda that emerged from the Immigrant Movement Visioning Process that she co-led in 2019–20. The five freedoms of the title are the freedom to stay, the freedom to move, the freedom to thrive, the freedom to work, and the freedom to transform. Hincapié's chapter not only elaborates this agenda and the vision underlying it but also makes the case for a series of short-term immigration reforms, grounded in that long-term vision, that a new administration could rapidly put in place.

Are the Democrats ready for such a challenge, once a new political alignment is in place? Justin Gest's "When Democrats Are Not the Party of Ideas" argues that they have not been thus far. He outlines a path forward in regard to the vexed question of "future flow," that is, how many and which types of immigrants should be offered admission to the United States. Critiquing the nation's current admissions system, he challenges liberals and progressives to consider seriously the alternative approaches embodied in the immigration policies of other wealthy countries. On that basis, Gest makes the case for a "future flow" model based on data-driven predictions of the relative levels of success that different types of immigrants can be expected to achieve once settled in the United States. He argues that such an approach could create political space for a consensus that could finally break the stalemate that made CIR so elusive in recent decades.

The humanitarian dimensions of future flow policies affecting immigrants, refugees, and asylum seekers drive the argument of "Keep It Moving: A 'Future Flow' Agenda for the Immigrant Rights Movement." In this chapter Amaha Kassa makes a powerful case that progressives should not limit the scope of their immigration policy agenda to winning a path to legalization for the undocumented; rather, they should also prioritize refugees and asylees and dramatically expand legal immigration, especially from countries that are underrepresented in the current U.S. foreign-born population. Kassa's pathbreaking policy vision challenges several shibboleths—for example, defending the much-maligned "diversity visa" program. He offers specific proposals for dramatically expanding humanitarian migration. He highlights core principles such as the right to migration and due process and stresses the moral obligation of nations to welcome refugees, as well as the practical economic and social benefits of immigration.

Still another arena that progressives must confront is immigration enforcement. In "Abolish ICE . . . and Then What?" Peter L. Markowitz opens up that crucial conversation. Drawing on a range of international models as well as existing practices in other areas of U.S. law, he argues for a new approach that transcends recent demands to "abolish ICE." Pointing out the irrationality of the existing U.S. system, in which the vast majority of those accused of immigration violations are either deported or legalized, with almost no intermediate options, Markowitz makes the case for a more humane and effective enforcement regime that provides a range of potential consequences for violations, depending on their specific characteristics and severity, and for a radical reduction in expenditures on enforcement, which have exploded since 9/11.

Amid the COVID-19 pandemic, the essential work of immigrants, authorized or not, often made the difference between life and death for millions of U.S. citizens. On that basis, Saket Soni elaborates a paradigm-shifting approach to immigration policy in his lyrical chapter, "Immigrants Are Essential: A Manifesto for the COVID-19 and Climate Change Era." He shows that immigrants were a critical workforce both in the emergency work following disasters such as Hurricane Katrina and more recently in responding to the 2020 pandemic. Soni not only argues that these workers deserve a fast track to legalization but also makes a powerful case for a massive infrastructure-based jobs program, as part of the Green New Deal, to provide the newly legalized with access to high-quality jobs addressing the actual and potential ravages of climate change.

The visionary prescriptions of these chapters beg the question of strategy. How can progressives effectively challenge nativist narratives, build successful coalitions, and win major reforms? That is the focus of Part IV. It begins with a chapter by Representative Pramila Jayapal, a longtime movement organizer who was elected to the U.S. House of Representatives in 2017 and has led congressional resistance to the Trump administration's punitive immigration policies. In "The Progressive Path Forward on Immigration Policy," Jayapal outlines an ambitious blueprint for a progressive comprehensive immigration reform framework. It includes proposals not only to undo the damage from the Trump era but also to radically restructure and break up the out-of-control and sprawling Department of Homeland Security. She sketches the content of a sweeping and long-overdue reform of the nation's immigration laws.

Rational planning is a critical component of strategic efforts, but if advocates fail to recognize the emotional resonance of the immigration issue, their proposals will go nowhere. Cecilia Muñoz's contribution, "The Border and Beyond," reflects on the emotionally charged nature of policy debates about immigration, especially in regard to border politics. A policymaker who helped lead the Obama administration's immigration reform efforts, Muñoz is deeply conversant with the conflicting right- and left-wing approaches to the U.S.-Mexico border. She exposes a range of difficult issues that the Biden administration will have to confront: policies involving migrants (whether individuals, families, or unaccompanied minors) arriving at the border, rules governing asylum seekers, and efforts to address the underlying roots of growing migration from Central America. Muñoz proposes a new strategic scaffolding for border management and outlines potential common ground that can transcend today's polarized debates.

Finding such common ground necessarily involves confronting the xenophobic and racist attitudes that have helped drive increasing opposition to immigration in recent years, reinforced and amplified by the Trump administration. "'We Have Found the Enemy and It Is Not Each Other': Deep Canvassing to Change Hearts and Minds on Immigration in Rural and Small-Town America" documents the social justice organization People's Action's recent efforts to confront and uproot such beliefs, focusing on the key geographical areas that fueled Trump's 2016 electoral victory. In this chapter, Mehrdad Azemun and Adam Kruggel describe the transformative potential of intensive one-on-one "deep canvassing" through a narrative that emphasizes the shared class interests of workers across racial and ethnic lines. People's Action has engaged thousands of rural and small-town Americans in such conversations, and this chapter documents the resulting shifts in attitudes with data from systematic follow-up surveys. These interventions are exemplary efforts to address the mixed and often contradictory white working-class consciousness that right-wing populists have so successfully exploited in recent years.

Finally, building on and expanding the insights of earlier chapters, Deepak Bhargava proposes a long-term vision of a generous and humane immigration policy: to increase admissions dramatically in the coming decades, to transform the United States into the world's most welcoming country for immigrants, and to align the country's actual practices with its most positive self-image. In this concluding chapter, "The Statue of Liberty Plan: Vision and Strategy for the Immigrant Rights Movement in the Twenty-First Century," Bhargava proposes a multi-pronged organizing strategy to advance these goals in the coming years, using a variety of policy levers to build the power of immigrants. He also stresses the centrality of immigration to the broader struggle for racial and economic justice. Bhargava argues that, despite the devastating setbacks of the Trump years, the U.S. immigrant rights movement is poised—with strategic savvy, unity, and discipline—to launch a new era of progressive social change.

While the devastating harms of the Trump administration have dominated headlines in recent years, immigrant rights leaders in the field and immigration scholars in the academy have been working, often out of public view, to develop and nurture imaginative new approaches to meet the challenges facing progressives. The contributions in this volume are a window into their innovative thinking, with research, policy proposals, and organizing strategies that aim to foster a new—and this time positive—chapter in the nation's complex immigration history.

Notes

1. Andrew Daniller, "Americans' Immigration Policy Priorities: Divisions Between—and Within—the Two Parties," Pew Research Center, Nov. 12, 2019.

2. William Kerr, "America, Don't Throw Global Talent Away," *Nature* 563 (2018): 445, www.nature.com/articles/d41586-018-07446-2.

3. Migration Policy Institute, "Frequently Requested Statistics on Immigrants and Immigration in the United States," Feb. 14, 2020, www.migrationpolicy.org /article/frequently-requested-statistics-immigrants-and-immigration-united -states.

4. Second-generation immigrants outnumbered first-generation immigrants in the early twentieth century. That is no longer the case, reflecting a sharp decline in birth rates in the intervening years (ibid.).

5. Mae Ngai, *Impossible Subjects: Illegal Aliens and the Making of Modern America* (Princeton, NJ: Princeton University Press, 2004), 18, 57.

6. For more detail, see Ngai, *Impossible Subjects*; Linda Gordon, *The Second Coming of the Ku Klux Klan* (New York: W.W. Norton, 2017); and Jia Lynn Yang, *One Mighty and Irresistible Tide: The Epic Struggle over American Immigration, 1924–1965* (New York: W.W. Norton, 2020).

7. "Admissions" and LPRs are not totally equivalent, but these data show that the cap is regularly exceeded. The diversity visa program was added in 1990 to offer entry to people from countries otherwise underrepresented in the immigrant population. See Congressional Research Service, "Nonimmigrant and Immigrant Visa Categories: Data Brief," Oct. 2019, fas.org/sgp/crs/homesec/R45938.pdf.

8. Yang, *Irresistible Tide*, 238, 264.

9. See Douglas S. Massey, Jorge Durand, and Nolan J. Malone, *Beyond Smoke and Mirrors: Mexican Immigration in an Era of Economic Integration* (New York: Russell Sage Foundation, 2002).

10. See Chris Zepeda-Millán, *Latino Mass Mobilization: Immigration, Racialization, and Activism* (New York: Cambridge University Press, 2017), 25–40; Walter J. Nicholls and Justus Uitermark, *Cities and Social Movements: Immigrant Rights Activism in the United States, France and the Netherlands, 1970–2015* (Malden, MA: Wiley-Blackwell, 2017), 91–115.

11. See Ruth Milkman, *L.A. Story: Immigrant Workers and the Future of the U.S. Labor Movement* (New York: Russell Sage Foundation, 2006); Janice Fine, *Worker Centers: Organizing Communities at the Edge of the Dream* (Ithaca, NY: Cornell University Press, 2006).

12. Walter J. Nicholls, *The DREAMers: How the Undocumented Youth Movement Transformed the Immigrant Rights Debate* (Palo Alto, CA: Stanford University Press, 2013); Veronica Terriquez, "Intersectional Mobilization, Social Movement Spillover, and Queer Youth Leadership in the Immigrant Rights Movement," *Social Problems* 62, no. 3 (2015): 343–62.

13. See Irene Bloemraad and Kim Voss, eds., *Rallying for Immigrant Rights: The Fight for Inclusion in 21st Century America* (Berkeley: University of California Press, 2011) and Zepeda-Millán, *Latino Mass Mobilization*.

14. Shoba Sivaprasad Wadhia, *Banned: Immigration Enforcement in the Time of Trump* (New York: New York University Press, 2019), 30–32.

15. Jonathan Blitzer, "Get Out," *New Yorker*, Mar. 2, 2020, 44.

16. Katie Rogers and Jason DeParle, "The White Nationalist Websites Cited by Stephen Miller," *New York Times*, Nov. 18, 2019.

17. This was in reference to Haitian and African immigrants. Julie Hirschfeld Davis and Michael D. Shear, *Border Wars: Inside Trump's Assault on Immigration* (New York: Simon and Schuster, 2019), 223.

18. Ronald Reagan, "Remarks at the Presentation Ceremony for the Presidential Medal of Freedom," Jan. 19, 1989, www.reaganlibrary.gov/research/speeches/011989b.

19. Michael D. Shear and Zolan Kanno-Youngs, "Trump Slashes Refugee Cap to 18,000, Curtailing U.S. Role as Haven," *New York Times*, Sept. 26, 2018; Davis and Shear, *Border Wars*, 139.

20. "Proclamation Suspending Entry of Immigrants Who Present a Risk to the U.S. Labor Market During the Economic Recovery Following the COVID-19 Outbreak," Apr. 22, 2020, www.whitehouse.gov/presidential-actions/proclamation -suspending-entry-immigrants-present-risk-u-s-labor-market-economic-recovery -following-covid-19-outbreak.

21. Sarah Pierce and Jessica Bolter, "Dismantling and Restructuring the U.S. Immigration System: A Catalog of Changes Under the Trump Presidency," Migration Policy Institute Report, July 2020; William Frey, "The 2010s May Have Seen the Slowest Population Growth in U.S. History, Census Data Show," Brookings Institution, Jan. 2, 2020.

22. National Academies of Sciences, Engineering, and Medicine, *The Economic and Fiscal Consequences of Immigration* (Washington, DC: National Academies Press, 2017), 11–12.

23. Ibid., 5–6.

24. Jeffrey S. Passel and D'Vera Cohn, "Unauthorized Immigrant Workforce Is Smaller, but with More Women," Pew Research Center, Hispanic Trends, Nov. 27, 2018, www.pewresearch.org/hispanic/2018/11/27/unauthorized-immigrant -workforce-is-smaller-but-with-more-women.

25. Jeffrey S. Passel and D'Vera Cohn, "Mexicans Decline to Less Than Half the U.S. Unauthorized Immigrant Population for the First Time," June 12, 2019, www .pewresearch.org/fact-tank/2019/06/12/us-unauthorized-immigrant-population -2017.

26. Pew Research Center, "Unauthorized Immigrants Are a Quarter of the U.S. Foreign-Born Population," June 12, 2019, www.pewresearch.org/fact -tank/2019/06/12/us-unauthorized-immigrant-population-2017/ft_19-06 -12_unauthorizedimmigration_unauthorized-immigrants-quarter-us-foreign -born-population-2.

27. Jeffrey S. Passel and D'Vera Cohn, "Unauthorized Immigrants Are More Likely to Be Long-Term Residents," Pew Research Center, Hispanic Trends, Nov. 27, 2018, www.pewresearch.org/hispanic/2018/11/27/unauthorized-immigrants -are-more-likely-to-be-long-term-residents.

28. Abby Budiman, "Key Findings About U.S. Immigrants," Pew Research Center, Fact Tank, Aug. 20, 2020; Migration Policy Institute, "Frequently Requested Statistics on Immigrants and Immigration in the United States," Feb. 14, 2020, www.migrationpolicy.org/article/frequently-requested-statistics-immigrants-and -immigration-united-states#Children%20of%20Immigrants.

29. See Tom Farer, *Migration and Integration: The Liberal Case for Borders* (Cambridge: Cambridge University Press, 2019).

30. Aditya Chakrabortty, "Wolfgang Streeck: The German Economist Calling Time on Capitalism," *The Guardian,* Dec. 9, 2016; Wolfgang Streeck, "Between

Charity and Justice: Remarks on the Social Construction of Immigration Policy in Rich Democracies," *Culture, Practice and Europeanization* 3, no. 2 (2018): 3–22.

31. Benjamin Opratko, "Austria's Green Party Will Pay a High Price for Its Dangerous Alliance with the Right," *The Guardian*, Jan. 9, 2020.

32. Perry Anderson, *Spectrum: From Right to Left in the World of Ideas* (London: Verso Books, 2005), 318.

Part I

HISTORICAL PERSPECTIVES

American Nativism, Past and Present

Mae M. Ngai

Nativism was at the very heart of Donald Trump's presidency—indeed, of his entire political career.[1] His campaign for the 2016 Republican presidential nomination kicked off with an attack calling Mexican immigrants "criminals." His first acts as president were to issue executive orders banning Muslims from entering the United States, for the mass roundup of undocumented immigrants and for building a wall on the U.S.-Mexico border.[2] Immigration restriction and trade protectionism, two sides of the same coin and both yoked to white racism, provide the subtitles of Trump's master trope, "Make America Great Again." During the COVID-19 pandemic, the president fanned nativist sentiment with constant attacks against China, aimed at diverting attention from the administration's incompetence during the public health crisis, and in the process encouraged a spate of physical and verbal assaults against Asian Americans.

Yet as much as nativism—virulent opposition to foreigners as dangers to the "American way of life" (however defined)—was a defining hallmark of the Trump presidency, it did not drop from the sky with Trump.[3] Nativism has been a staple of conservative politics since the late twentieth century. It was one of the motors driving the mainstream of the Republican Party rightward. And because not just conservatives but also political moderates and even some liberals support measures to restrict immigration, especially undocumented entry, the boundaries of nativism are blurry. Is nativism the same as nationalism? Or is nativism an extreme nationalism that can be distinguished from other, putatively less harmful forms of nationalism?

How might progressive immigration reformers navigate the politics of nativism and nationalism?

In this chapter I approach these questions from the perspective of history. I examine three major episodes of nativism that led to restrictive immigration policies in American history. I hope a critical historical analysis might inform our approach to nativism and immigration reform in our own time.

John Higham's classic study, *Strangers in the Land: Patterns of American Nativism* (1955), is a useful starting point. The book is a history of the ideological traditions that informed the xenophobia of the late nineteenth and early twentieth centuries, leading ultimately to passage of the National Origins Quota Act of 1924. That law imposed the first numerical ceiling on immigration, discriminated against southern and eastern Europeans, and excluded all Asians. Higham identified three major themes, or patterns, of American nativism, each based on a different mode of difference—religion (anti-Catholicism), ideology (anti-radicalism), and race (Anglo-Saxonism). Each has deep historical roots in Protestant Europe and in the early United States. Higham argued that anti-immigration sentiment at the turn of the twentieth century arose from social, economic, and intellectual changes taking place at the time, especially churning during periods of economic depression and "crises of confidence." The three ideological traditions provided channels through which xenophobia flowed, acquired new meanings, and gained political force. Notably, *Strangers in the Land* was published during the McCarthy era, when communism was defined, above all, as an "anti-American" ideology.[4]

Higham's trinity of religion, ideology, and race is useful because we can see their expression in contemporary hostility toward Muslims, alleged terrorists, and Latinx people. His analysis shows that the construction of the "other" is historically contingent, not simply a "human" reaction to those who are "different" (although Higham did not use the language of social construction). Moreover, nativism is necessarily reproduced according to changing conditions, including the adaptation of older ideas to new contexts. But I disagree with Higham that economic competition and unemployment are the material causes of anti-immigrant politics, which is indeed the conventional explanation for nativism. If we compare the early twentieth-century opposition to southern and eastern Europeans with two other nativist movements, against the Chinese in the late nineteenth century and against Latinx communities in the late twentieth and early twenty-first centuries, a different set of patterns becomes clear.

The first pattern is that nativism emerges not in times of economic contraction but in periods of expansion, especially when expansion is part of large structural transformation, or what political economists call sectoral change. These shifts engendered anxiety as opportunity loomed simultaneously large and elusive for portions of the population. Immigrants generally do not "replace" native-born workers but work in new or expanding sectors and contribute to economic growth. Sectoral changes are evident in the three examples under examination here: the opening of the West and consolidation of a national market after the Civil War; industrialization and urbanization at the turn of the twentieth century; and deindustrialization and the rise of service and finance at the turn of the twenty-first century.

Second, nativism is the combined product of three dynamics: popular anxieties over economic uncertainty; intellectuals and pundits who theorize ethnic or cultural difference as a mode of harm; and politicians who weaponize difference for political gain. This is to say that nativism's force comes more from those who invent and deploy it, rather than being rooted in the experience of aggrieved members of society on whose behalf nativism claims to speak. Nativism is not a "human" reaction to "difference" or "others." Nativism is, above all, a political discourse, which both constructs and critiques difference.

Anti-Chinese racism became prominent in California first in the goldfields in the 1850s and then in the urban workingmen's movement of the 1870s, which finally led to passage of the national Chinese Exclusion Act in 1882. Anti-foreign sentiment during the gold rush was commonly mobilized by white American "forty-niners" as a weapon of competition against foreigners—Mexicans, Chileans, French, Australians. It was a crude expression of Manifest Destiny: "It's all for us, not for you." When Chinese started coming in large numbers a couple of years later, many of the predecessor groups had already been chased from the diggings, so anti-foreign sentiment focused on the Chinese. Moreover, the easy pickings from the rivers were beginning to be depleted, so anti-foreignness combined with the bitterness of dashed hopes.

It was the governor of California, John Bigler, who in 1852 introduced the theory that Chinese were a "coolie race," that is, inherently unfree and incapable of liberal citizenship. In fact, Chinese were not indentured or enslaved but voluntary emigrants. The big lie was a racial shorthand that compared Chinese to slaves in the South. Bigler was the first U.S. politician to weaponize anti-coolieism for electoral advantage.[5]

As anti-coolieism sustained anti-Chinese racism from the goldfields to the cities, it received greater theoretical heft from a young political economist, Henry George, who linked coolieism and monopoly. In a lengthy essay, "The Chinese in California," published in the *New York Tribune* in 1869, George distinguished Chinese labor from other immigrant labor, which also tended to be cheaper than that of native-born white Americans. He assumed that European immigrants would, sooner or later, assimilate into the American working class; that is, their cheapness was a temporary phenomenon. In contrast, George believed Chinese would cause a reduction in wages in a "general and permanent sense." That view was based on the racist premise that Chinese could never be assimilated. George rehearsed the common stereotypes about Chinese, most importantly that they came on a "contract system" enforced by the Chinese merchant elite, which was akin to slavery. This, argued George, made Chinese the ideal labor force—cheap, docile, and virtually unlimited in number—for big capitalists.[6] By yoking Chinese labor to the interests of monopoly, George defined the "Chinese question" as a class interest, which required kicking Chinese out of the working class and imagining class as something subordinate to race and nation, a feat that has had remarkable staying power.

George's article received widespread attention. California papers reprinted it and the Anti-Coolie Association memorialized it. The theory of Chinese as a "coolie race" underwrote the Pacific-coast urban workingmen's exclusion movement of the 1870s, which took off shortly after completion of the transcontinental railroad wrought myriad changes to California. This new national transportation connection brought many migrants from the East Coast to San Francisco, as well as manufactured goods from eastern factories to the West Coast, creating pressure on the high prices and high wages that had previously flourished in a market of scarcity. The railroad had promised untold wealth and development to the Pacific coast, but it also brought joblessness and poverty—the long tail of the national depression of 1873–77. It was not unemployment per se but precarity in a general context of economic expansion and development—first during the gold rush and later in the 1870s—that animated racism against Chinese labor.

Congress passed legislation barring Chinese immigration in 1882, the result of broader political realignments taking place in the post–Civil War years. The Republican and Democratic Parties both included restriction of Chinese immigration in their presidential campaign platforms in 1876. The removal of federal troops from the South in 1877 signaled the North's retreat from Reconstruction and equality for the former slaves and cleared the political space for anti-Chinese racial politics. Anti-coolieism no longer had to answer to abolitionism or to the general principle of racial equality. Exclusion triumphed in Congress in 1882 with a solid bloc of support in the West and the South and a divided North and Midwest.[7]

The national trade union movement, notably the Knights of Labor and the fledgling American Federation of Labor (AFL), also supported Chinese exclusion. The founding convention of the AFL in 1881 voted nearly unanimously for a resolution that called Chinese competition with white labor "one of the greatest evils" and appealed to Congress for "laws entirely prohibiting the immigration of Chinese into the United States."[8]

Samuel Gompers, who served as the president of the AFL from 1886 to 1924, was a steadfast opponent of Chinese immigration. He also opposed immigration from eastern and southern Europe. In this respect Gompers provides a link between the two movements of nativism that illuminates broader continuities. Gompers's background as a German-born cigar maker in New York undoubtedly influenced his politics. At the AFL founding convention he was sympathetic to California's delegate, who cited the use of unskilled Chinese labor in the mass production of cigars as a threat to the skilled artisans who rolled cigars by hand. The same process of de-skilling was taking place in the 1870s and 1880s on the East Coast, where Bohemian and Russian Jewish immigrants were laboring in New York tenement factories for low wages and in horrid working conditions. The large-scale entry of women into cigar production further debased cigar making in the eyes of manly artisans and their unions. Gompers led the AFL in 1891 to call for immigration restriction; within a few years, nativism was embraced broadly within the union movement. Labor nativism also informed the first federal immigration bureaucracy; Terence Powderly, former president of the Knights of Labor, served as commissioner general of immigration during the early twentieth century.[9]

Political scientist Gwendolyn Mink exposed the link between anti-Chinese nativism and immigration restriction in her book *Old Labor and New Immigrants* by modifying the title of Gompers's famous tract "Meat vs. Rice: American Manhood Against Asiatic Coolieism" as "Meat vs. Rice (and Pasta)." Mink argued that in both cases labor nativism "transposed anti-capitalist feeling with anti-immigrant hostility." That is, the embrace of nativism let industrial capitalism and its political representatives off the hook for the harms and displacements caused not by immigrant labor but by industrialization.[10]

These changes were taking place not just in cigar making but throughout the United States. In iron foundries and steel mills, in slaughterhouses and meatpacking factories, and in the manufacture of consumer goods, new technologies and mass production methods de-skilled the crafts and marginalized skilled workers and the control they had had over their labor.[11]

As in the case of Chinese exclusion, organized labor's hostility toward immigrant European workers alone was insufficient to win legislation restricting immigration. Not only did capital exert powerful influence in Washington, but many Americans, themselves only one or two generations removed from immigration, also upheld the country's long tradition of open borders. That policy had facilitated colonial settlement, the slave trade, and the ongoing dispossession of indigenous people with migration and settlement across the continent, but it had also attracted Irish, German, and other European immigrants seeking opportunity and refuge in America.

According to John Higham, religious and ideological difference was too inexact to perform nativism's intellectual and political work at the turn of the twentieth century. German American communities included both Catholics and Jews; while native-born whites could be counted among socialists and other radicals. Nativism thus became energized and theorized through Social Darwinism and scientific racism. Anglo-Saxonism, previously a loose cultural concept, albeit a chauvinistic ethnocentric one, was upgraded into high racial theory, in which "races" were biologically, rigidly, and hierarchically defined. No matter that race science was heterogenous and empirically unsound, ranging the gamut from phrenology to ethnology to eugenics. Anglo-Saxons (or Caucasians) always ranked at the top, Africans always at the bottom. Italians, Russians, Czechs, Serbs, Magyars, and others were classified as the "lesser white races" of Europe. The race schema enabled thinking about "new immigrants" theoretically as a collective group, distinguishable from "old immigrants" from "Nordic" or Anglo-Saxon-Celtic origins (even though Germans continued to be one of the largest immigrant groups in the late nineteenth century). Francis A. Walker, president of the Massachusetts Institute of Technology and head of the U.S. Census Bureau, concisely stated the distinction: he described the new immigrants as "vast masses of peasantry, degraded below our utmost conceptions . . . beaten men from beaten races; representing the worst failures in the struggle for existence."[12]

The culture war ran hard from the 1890s to World War I. On one side stood a coalition of patrician elites including Francis Walker and U.S. Senator Henry Cabot Lodge, prominent leaders of the Immigration Restriction League; eugenicists organized around the American Museum of Natural History; and organized labor. On the other side were arrayed a range of actors, including settlement-house activist Jane Addams, who believed in immigrants' capacity for "Americanization"; cultural anthropologist Franz Boas, who challenged eugenics; and writers Randolph Bourne and Horace Kallen, who sketched out the first ideas about cultural pluralism. Notably, immigrants themselves were but a faint voice in the debate.[13] Nevertheless, industry's voracious appetite for labor and four presidential vetoes forestalled restrictive immigration legislation between 1896 and 1917, when Congress overrode President Woodrow Wilson's second veto to require arriving immigrants to take a literacy test. It was not until the 1920s, during a wave of postwar reaction, that Congress passed laws that set a numerical ceiling on all new admissions and apportioned them in quotas that discriminated by national origin and race.[14]

The hard-core racial nativisms that drove Asiatic exclusion and the national-origin restrictions began to falter during World War II, when the United States fought against fascism. Congress repealed Chinese exclusion laws in 1943, recognizing China as a war ally, although this was mainly a symbolic gesture because it set a Chinese immigration quota of 105 a year. Liberal calls for immigration reform grew during the postwar decades. The second generation of eastern and southern European immigrants—especially American Jews and

Italian Americans—led the movement to repeal the national origin quotas in the 1950s and early 1960s. They conceived of immigration reform as their own civil rights cause, a demand for their full inclusion in American society. Intellectuals and politicians—notably historian Oscar Handlin and President John F. Kennedy—created a new historical narrative, which theorized the United States as a "nation of immigrants," inclusive and assimilating. (John Higham was also part of this trend.) The same Democratic Congress that passed civil rights and voting rights legislation in 1964 and 1965 passed the Immigration and Nationality Act of 1965, also known as the Hart-Celler Act. That law abolished the national origin quotas and established a system based on family and employment preferences and a global ceiling with equal quotas for all countries. This is the system we still have today.[15]

The 1965 immigration act was in some respects a major liberal reform, notably in its repeal of national origin quotas. But it was illiberal in important and arguably more lasting ways, especially in regard to the imposition of numerical quotas on countries of the Western Hemisphere, where none had existed previously. The national origin quotas established in 1924 exempted Mexico and Canada because the State Department wished to maintain good relations with the United States' neighbors. Agricultural interests in the Southwest also did not wish to see their access to Mexican labor impeded.[16]

The 1965 law provided that no country could have more than 7 percent of total immigration, which inevitably resulted in long waiting lists for high-sending countries and a spike in undocumented migration. In fact, the 1965 act was designed as a symbolic reform that highlighted formalistic equality while remaining highly restrictive in practice. The numerical quotas were quite low—overall 290,000 per year, which was a smaller proportion of the total U.S. population than in 1924; and a maximum of 20,000 a year per country. Especially in light of an expanding economy and declining native birth rate, this was a major constraint. Moreover, provisions allocating

80 percent of new green cards to family members (and mostly to those related to U.S. citizens) aimed to perpetuate European immigration, complemented by a 20 percent allocation to employer-sponsored visas that was aimed to keep wages high for U.S.-born workers. If Hart-Celler was a rebuke to nativism, it was still fundamentally nationalist and protectionist. That is to say, it still put the perceived interests of "Americans" and the "nation" in opposition to those of immigrants, who came to join the nation.

Hart-Celler would prove wholly inadequate in the face of the economic trends of the late twentieth and early twenty-first centuries: the rise of the service sector—especially in low-wage industries such as hotels, restaurants, care work, and other jobs providing amenities to the urban upper middle class—as well as industrial agriculture and food processing. All these jobs would be filled by immigrants from the global South, especially but not exclusively from Mexico and Central America. Generally, they have undergirded an expanding economy; in some cases, immigrant workers were recruited by subcontractors after employers destroyed unionized jobs, such as in construction and janitorial work.[17] Meanwhile, the growing computer, pharmaceuticals, and health care industries drew professional and technical workers from Asia. Asians and Mexicans developed chains of migration—legal and undocumented—based on the changing U.S. labor market and the rigid structural availability of green cards (or lack thereof).

Anti-immigration politics in the late twentieth century thus grew in the context of sectoral shifts and economic expansion. As in previous surges of nativism, the aggrieved are often from older industries, such as manufacturing, where domestic jobs were lost to automation and offshore production. The middle class also has suffered from increased property tax burdens resulting from tax breaks for the wealthy and shrinking federal and state budgets. A cult of celebrity surrounding successful individual entrepreneurs such as Jeff Bezos, Elon Musk, and, yes, Donald Trump fuels a toxic mix of envy and resentment.[18]

Immigrants are responsible for none of this. Yet once again, nativism harnesses grievance via a theory of difference, which in turn is weaponized by politicians. In our time, racism against immigrant communities of color, especially Latinx communities, is the fundamental core of nativism. It is bred not only from economic precarity but also from white Americans' fears of demographic change and loss of social and political power. But open racism became impolitic in the post-civil-rights era. It became cleverly dressed as a complaint against "illegal aliens." Of course, it is nothing new to associate immigrants with crime, but in the late twentieth century nativism went further, making "illegality"—that is, crossing the border without a visa—a kind of racial condition. Popular opinion assumes that most if not all Latinx people are undocumented and that illegal aliens constitute a large share of the workforce. In fact, nearly 80 percent of Latinx people living in the country are U.S. citizens. Undocumented workers account for 5 percent of the U.S. workforce.[19]

Nevertheless, focusing on "illegal immigration" and not openly or directly on race enabled conservative think tanks and policy organizations to promote a nativist agenda with a semblance of intellectual legitimacy. The website of the Federation for American Immigration Reform (FAIR), the most prominent anti-immigration group in the United States, states that its aims are to "defend our borders, national self-determination and the American quality of life ensured by responsible immigration limits." But it also offers provocative links: "Check Out President Trump's Immigration Accomplishments," "How Much Are You Paying for Illegal Immigration?" and "Stolen Lives: Victims of Illegal Alien Crime."[20] FAIR's connections to white supremacist organizations are not exactly hidden either. According to the Southern Poverty Law Center, FAIR has received funding from the Pioneer Fund, which underwrites studies on the alleged links between race and intelligence, and FAIR's executive director, Dan Stein, has "warned that certain immigrant groups are engaged in competitive breeding aimed at diminishing white power."[21]

The focus on illegal immigration appealed to moderates and liberals, who do not consider themselves racist but profess concern with "fairness" and "rule of law," values allegedly rejected by the undocumented because they cut in line and enter without authorization. It appealed even to more established Latinx and Asian immigrants, especially in the 1980s and 1990s, who were anxious about the low wages of the newest immigrants undermining their own often-modest but hard-won gains.

Trump's presidency, with its unapologetic racism and manifestly inhumane policies, obviated the need for any color-blind pretense. It excited his base of support among white supremacists. But the hard edge of contemporary nativism also pushed many people in the other direction, to reject the shrill anti-immigration rhetoric and agenda of the far right. Even before Trump's election, the campaign of the Dreamers—undocumented youth raised and educated in the United States—during the 2000s and 2010s shifted public opinion toward support for legalizing the undocumented. Harsh treatment of the undocumented and asylum seekers and hateful rhetoric against all immigrants have also diminished Republican hopes that they could generate statistically meaningful support among erstwhile conservative Latinx and Asian American voters.[22]

The coronavirus pandemic further laid bare how the claims of nativism have so little bearing on the truth of immigrants' lives and on the work that they do. The pandemic revealed that immigrants are the nation's essential workers—the ones laboring and dying in the fields and meat factories; the urban food-delivery workers serving those privileged to work from home; the doctors, nurses, and hospital workers in the emergency rooms and ICUs. Both immigrants and African Americans, who also work in low-wage "essential" jobs and lack access to decent health care, have suffered disproportionately from coronavirus infections and deaths. At Donald Trump's urging, the pandemic deepened nativism among some Americans—but that side of the political divide is arguably becoming smaller. Immigration politics may be at a turning point.

A critical analysis that analyzes the historical contingencies that enable nativist politics to be produced and mobilized is important for the contemporary immigrant rights movement. Such an approach avoids the pitfall of viewing racism or nativism as something in the nation's DNA, or a simplistic view that nativism is always present as inclusion's underside or evil twin—views that flatten history and render uncertain whether change is even possible. But we must view politics as always contingent and look for the conditions that create the possibility of alternatives. Otherwise we cannot account for the immigrant rights movement of the late twentieth century, which resulted in the legalization of nearly 3 million undocumented immigrants in 1986, the successes in immigrant union organizing, or the growing importance of the Latinx vote in state and national elections.

Here, we might discern another pattern: the counter-force to nativism, immigrants themselves and the second generation with birthright citizenship and access to the franchise. The Hart-Celler Act of 1965 passed with a broad coalition of urban liberals, industrial unions, religious organizations, and numerous ethnic groups. European Americans whose parents and grandparents had arrived at Ellis Island at the turn of the century stood at the center of that coalition. Their desire for inclusion and recognition both propelled and limited reform. The Hart-Celler Act of 1965 replaced hard-core nativism with a liberal nationalism that promoted "inclusion," but at the same time defined the terms of inclusion in problematic ways and with pernicious effects. It normalized a system of global restriction with low quotas disconnected from both the global and domestic labor markets, creating new streams of undocumented migrations.[23]

In our own time, Latinx, Asian American, and other immigrant communities of color provide the vision and the power for immigration reform and social change. They have stronger connections to the wider world than the European American ethnics of the mid-twentieth century and are more keenly attuned to the unequal relations of power between the global North and the global South, as well as within the global North.

The coronavirus pandemic has taught us the need for international cooperation and solidarity against the new deadly disease, which threatens humankind generally but also has much graver consequences in the poor regions of both global and domestic space. The same inequalities drive international migration. Immigrants and communities of color, ravaged by both nativism and the coronavirus, may point the way forward for us all.

Notes

1. Trump launched his bid for the Republican presidential nomination in 2015 with the claim that Barack Obama was not born in the United States. He revived "birtherism," a discredited theory cooked up by the right wing when Obama ran for the U.S. Senate in 2004. See Davis Richardson, "Former Trump Advisor Admits to 'Peddling Birtherism' About Obama," *The Observer*, Aug. 3, 2018.

2. Executive Order on Border Security and Immigration Enforcement Improvements, Jan. 25, 2017; Executive Order: Enhancing Public Safety in the Interior of the United States, Jan. 25, 2017; Executive Order Protecting the Nation from Foreign Terrorist Entry into the United States, Jan. 27, 2017.

3. Higham defined nativism as an "intense opposition to an internal minority on the ground of its foreign (i.e., 'un-American') connections"; it translates "broader cultural antipathies and ethnocentric judgments . . . into a zeal to destroy the enemies of a distinctively American way of life." Higham, *Strangers in the Land: Patterns of American Nativism, 1860–1925* (New Brunswick, NJ: Rutgers University Press, 2002 [1955]), 4.

4. Ibid., 5–11.

5. Mae Ngai, "Chinese Gold Miners and the Chinese Question in California and Victoria," *Journal of American History* 101, no. 4 (Mar. 2015): 1082–1105.

6. Henry George, "The Chinese in California," *New York Tribune*, May 1, 1869.

7. Mae Ngai, *The Chinese Question: The Gold Rushes and Global Politics* (New York: W.W. Norton, 2021). See also Alexander Saxton, *The Indispensable Enemy: Labor and the Anti-Chinese Movement in California* (Berkeley: University of California Press, 1971) and Stacey L. Smith, *Freedom's Frontier: California and the Struggle over Unfree Labor, Emancipation, and Reconstruction* (Chapel Hill: University of North Carolina Press, 2013).

8. Resolution, Nov. 18, 1881, of the Federation of Trades and Labor Unions, quoted in Andrew Gyory, *Closing the Gate: Race, Politics, and the Chinese Exclusion Act* (Chapel Hill: University of North Carolina Press, 1998), 219–20. (The organization renamed itself the American Federation of Labor in 1886.)

9. Dorothee Schneider, *Trade Unions and Community: The German Working Class in New York City, 1870–1900* (Urbana: University of Illinois Press, 1994),

64–65; Higham, *Strangers in the Land*, 71; U.S. Citizenship and Immigration Services, "Commissioners and Directors," www.uscis.gov/history-and-genealogy/our-history/commissioners-and-directors/terence-v-powderly.

10. Gwendolyn Mink, *Old Labor and New Immigrants in American Political Development* (Ithaca, NY: Cornell University Press, 1986), 71; Samuel Gompers and Herman Gutstadt, "Meat vs. Rice: American Manhood Against Asiatic Coolieism: Which Shall Survive?," American Federation of Labor, published as U.S. Senate Document 137, 1902.

11. Two classic studies of industrialization in the late nineteenth century are David Montgomery, *The Fall of the House of Labor: The Workplace, the State, and Labor Activism, 1865–1925* (New York: Cambridge University Press, 1987) and James R. Barrett, *Work and Community in the Jungle: Chicago's Packinghouse Workers 1894–1922* (Urbana: University of Illinois Press, 1987).

12. Francis A. Walker, "Restriction of Immigration," *The Atlantic*, June 1896.

13. Higham, *Strangers in the Land*, 131–57; Jane Addams, "Americanization," *American Sociological Society Publications* 14 (1919): 206–14; Franz Boas, "This Nordic Nonsense," *Forum* 74 (1925): 502–11; Randolph Bourne, "Trans-National America," *Atlantic Monthly*, July 1916; Horace Kallen, "Democracy Versus the Melting Pot," *The Nation*, Feb. 25, 1915. See also Katherine Benton-Cohen, *Inventing the Immigration Problem: The Dillingham Commission and Its Legacy* (Cambridge, MA: Harvard University Press, 2018).

14. Higham, *Strangers in the Land*, 300–330; on national origin quotas, see Mai Ngai, *Impossible Subjects: Illegal Aliens and the Making of Modern America* (Princeton, NJ: Princeton University Press, 2004), 15–55.

15. Ngai, *Impossible Subjects*, 227–64; Jane Hong, *Opening the Gates to Asia: A Transpacific History of How America Repealed Asian Exclusion* (Chapel Hill: University of North Carolina Press, 2019); Daniel Tichenor, *Dividing Lines: The Politics of Immigration Control in America* (Princeton, NJ: Princeton University Press, 2002).

16. Ngai, *Impossible Subjects*, 50–55.

17. Ruth Milkman, *L.A. Story: Immigrant Workers and the Future of the U.S. Labor Movement* (New York: Russell Sage Foundation, 2006); Ruth Milkman and Ed Ott, eds., *New Labor in New York: Precarious Workers and the Future of the Labor Movement* (Ithaca, NY: Cornell University Press, 2014).

18. David Koistinen, *Confronting Decline: The Political Economy of Deindustrialization in Twentieth-Century New England* (Gainesville: University of Florida Press, 2013); Lionel Fontagné and Ann Harrison, eds., *The Factory-Free Economy: Outsourcing, Servitization, and the Future of Industry* (New York: Oxford University Press, 2017); Robert Self, *American Babylon: Race and the Struggle for Postwar Oakland* (Princeton, NJ: Princeton University Press, 2003); Cary McClelland, *Silicon City: San Francisco in the Long Shadow of the Valley* (New York: W.W. Norton, 2019); "The Cult of the Founder and Silicon Valley's Lack of Moral Authority," *Equity* (podcast), episode 154, Sept. 20, 2019, techcrunch.com/2019/09/20/the-cult-of-the-founder-and-silicon-valleys-lack-of-moral-authority.

19. According to the Pew Research Center, in 2019, 79 percent of Latinx people

in the United States were citizens. See Luis Noe-Bustamante, "Key Facts About U.S. Hispanics and Their Diverse Heritage," Pew Research Center, Fact Tank, Sept. 16, 2019, www.pewresearch.org/fact-tank/2019/09/16/key-facts-about-u-s-hispanics. On undocumented workers, Jeffrey S. Passel and D'Vera Cohn, "Size of US Unauthorized Immigrant Workforce Stable After the Great Recession," Pew Research Center, Hispanic Trends, Nov. 3, 2016, www.pewresearch.org/hispanic/2016/11/03/size-of-u-s-unauthorized-immigrant-workforce-stable-after-the-great-recession.

20. www.fairus.org/?gclid=EAIaIQobChMI0LGT1_XZ6QIVw8D ACh33Eg8zEAAYASAAEgLZ0_D_BwE.

21. Southern Poverty Law Center, "Anti-Immigration Groups," Mar. 21, 2001, www.splcenter.org/fighting-hate/intelligence-report/2001/anti-immigration-groups.

22. Michael A. Olivas, *Perchance to DREAM: A Legal and Political History of the DREAM Act and DACA* (New York: New York University Press, 2020); Stephen Nuñoz-Pérez and Suzanne Gamboa, "Poll Shows Trump, Republicans Have Not Gained Latino Support," NBC News, June 25, 2019; Li Zhou, "Trump Could Be Turning Asian Americans into Reliable Democratic Voters," Vox, May 23, 2019.

23. Ngai, *Impossible Subjects*, 265–70.

History Shows That the Immigrant Threat Narrative Is Wrong

Ruth Milkman

Advocates of immigration restriction have elaborated a powerful narrative according to which low-wage immigrants, especially those who entered the United States illegally, have caused economic harm to Americans and contributed to the nation's decline. More specifically, in this view, U.S.-born workers have suffered because of "immigrants' use of welfare, health and educational services, their propensity to turn to crime, and their tendency to displace native citizens from jobs."[1] This immigrant threat narrative has been promoted for decades by media outlets such as Fox News and conservative talk radio, and recently Donald Trump has become its most prominent proponent. If immigration were summarily curtailed, border security established, and the estimated 11 million "illegal aliens" currently living in the United States removed, this rhetoric suggests, the American Dream and the living standards it once delivered to working people would be restored.

Is immigration really a key driver of the reversal of fortune U.S.-born workers have experienced since the 1970s, as Trump and other promoters of the threat narrative claim? The timing seems to suggest as much: soon after the passage of the 1965 law that ended four decades of highly restricted immigration, the economic status of non-college-educated workers began to spiral downward, and inequality in income and wealth grew dramatically.

Correlation is not causation, but there *is* extensive evidence that the deteriorating situation of the U.S. working class and the growth of low-wage immigration are tightly interconnected. However, the line of causality runs in the opposite direction from that implied by the threat narrative: immigration was not the *cause* of the massive shifts that began in the 1970s, such as the growth of economic inequality and labor degradation; rather, the influx of low-wage immigrants was a *consequence* of those developments.

The primary driver of labor migration, past and present, is economic demand. While "push" factors in sending countries can spur emigration, it materializes on a large scale only in response to employers' search for new sources of labor.[2] The 2008 financial crisis illustrates this vividly: as the U.S. economy imploded, and jobs in sectors such as construction and low-wage service industries evaporated, unauthorized immigrants abruptly stopped crossing the border. But from the 1970s up to the Great Recession, immigration grew in direct response to rising demand for cheap and pliable labor.[3]

In manufacturing industries that once offered high-wage blue-collar employment to non-college-educated American workers, millions of jobs have vanished over the past half century. Some of those jobs were outsourced to other parts of the world; others were rendered obsolete by new technology. No one suggests that immigrants are to blame for those developments. But in many other sectors, jobs did not disappear but instead were degraded by neoliberal business strategies such as expanded subcontracting, deregulation, and efforts to weaken or eliminate labor unions. As those developments unfolded starting in the 1970s, many U.S.-born workers abandoned the newly undesirable jobs, and then employers recruited immigrants to fill the resulting vacancies. In contexts where migrants did not arrive on their own in sufficient numbers, employers sent recruiters to Mexico and other parts of the global South to find them—often with blatant disregard for immigration laws and regulations, which until recently were notoriously poorly enforced. In this way both authorized and unauthorized immigrants entered the bottom tier of the labor market to take "jobs Americans won't do."

Demand for immigrant labor expanded not only in jobs degraded by the economic restructuring that began in the 1970s but also in paid domestic labor and other personal service fields. Here the key driver was not job degradation but instead rising income inequality: The increasingly prosperous professional and managerial classes devoted a growing part of their disposable income to purchasing services from housecleaners, nannies, and home care and elder care providers. In this period, affluent households often included two adults with long working hours, while changing expectations of parenting and the aging of the population stimulated growing demand for paid care work. Yet the traditional labor supply for domestic work was evaporating, as the civil rights movement opened up lower-level clerical and service jobs and other new opportunities to African American and Mexican American women. Thus U.S.-born women of color began to shun paid domestic work just as demand for it began to soar, which led households to hire immigrants instead.

These dynamics have remained largely invisible to the public, as the threat narrative has distracted attention from the actual causes of declining working-class living standards, and from the forces driving migration itself. Non-college-educated U.S.-born workers have every reason to be enraged by the degradation of previously desirable types of employment, rising inequality, and declining living standards, but their anger has been profoundly misdirected. It was not the influx of immigrants that generated these shifts, but rather employers' deliberate efforts to degrade formerly well-paid blue-collar jobs and public policies that widened inequality.

Employer Attacks on Unionism and the Immigrant Influx: The Case of Meatpacking

One example of an industry in which managerial opposition to unionism was the key driver of change is meatpacking. In that industry, the low wages and poor working conditions infamously depicted in Upton Sinclair's 1906 novel *The Jungle* have reemerged since the 1970s, reversing the process through which they were eliminated in the 1930s and 1940s, when unionization utterly transformed the industry. By the late 1960s, 95 percent of meatpacking workers outside the South were union members, and wages had risen to 115 percent of the national manufacturing average. At that time, the vast majority of the industry's workers were U.S.-born whites and African Americans. Collective bargaining agreements provided them with health insurance, pensions, and grievance procedures, while shop stewards enforced strict limits on managerial control over line speeds and other working conditions.[4]

That began to change, however, when a group of "new breed" meatpacking firms led by Iowa Beef Packers (IBP) introduced a series of cost-cutting measures that later became standard practice across the industry. First was the shift to "boxed beef" in the 1960s, which automated boning and cutting operations previously performed by skilled butchers. IBP also pioneered relocating slaughterhouses from urban centers closer to the sources of livestock, aiming to reduce transportation costs and take advantage of the low wages and weak union presence in rural areas.

Organized labor was anathema for IBP from the outset, although initially the union managed to follow the work as it moved to grain belt states such as Iowa and Nebraska. Yet even in IBP plants where the union gained a foothold, the company extracted wage cuts and productivity increases that involved dramatic speed-ups in the pace of work. "Management truly ran the plants," one IBP official boasted.[5] Like its other innovations, the company's hostility to unionism rapidly spread across the industry. As economist Charles Craypo noted, "Old and new [meat]packers alike had to imitate IBP's anti-union model once its competitive efficiency was evident."[6] From 1979 to 1990, real wages in meatpacking fell 30 percent; by 1990 they were 20 percent below the U.S. manufacturing average.[7]

Led by IBP, meatpacking employers devoted considerable energies to cost-cutting and union-busting, but initially they did not envision shifting from a U.S.-born workforce to a foreign-born one. They began recruiting immigrant labor only as labor shortages developed in the rural communities where packinghouses were relocated. Management did not anticipate that once the union had been defanged and pay and conditions thereby degraded, U.S.-born workers would increasingly abandon the industry. That abandonment was the impetus for hiring immigrants, as Faranak Miraftab noted in her ethnographic study of a packinghouse in rural Illinois: "It was the lowering of wages and the increasing harshness of working conditions that turned the industry to ethnic and minority labor, rather than the other way around."[8]

Some groups, such as African Americans in Chicago, historically a major meatpacking center, may have been displaced as production moved away from urban areas, but more often U.S.-born workers voluntarily exited, or declined to enter, the industry. In any case, the most dramatic upheavals took place not in cities but in the rural areas to which the industry increasingly migrated in the 1970s and 1980s. The typical dynamic is illustrated by a unionized pork-packing plant in Storm Lake, Iowa, that closed down in 1981 and then reopened as a non-union IBP operation the following year; fifteen years later it had grown into the world's second-largest pork-processing plant. Initially, IBP hired U.S.-born workers in the Storm Lake area, but a labor shortage developed as turnover spiked upward to as much as 100 percent annually. Under the previous owner, this plant had a stable workforce, but after IBP cut wages and sped up production, workers voted with their feet. Only then did the company begin to recruit Latinx immigrants, along with Asian and African refugees.[9]

Similarly, a packinghouse that IBP built in Lexington, Iowa, focused its initial hiring efforts on the region immediately surrounding the plant. Management had projected that local women, "mostly single mothers or farm wives," would be 60 percent of the processing workers, an IBP official told researchers, and the company even built an on-site day care center with this in mind. But after the plant began operating, turnover soared, and soon "the local supply of willing workers" proved inadequate. Only then did IBP begin to recruit workers from farther afield. "The majority of jobs in the meatpacking industry are unattractive to native-born workers," the researchers concluded.[10] Although the timing of the transition from U.S.-born to immigrant labor varied from plant to plant, the overall pattern was consistently driven by de-unionization. As Jackie Gabriel concluded, "Workers' bargaining power, as well as wages and working conditions, in the meatpacking industry declined *prior to* the rapid incorporation of Latino immigrants."[11]

By the early twenty-first century, immigrants, many of them undocumented, had become the dominant workforce in meatpacking. It is impossible to determine precisely the extent of unauthorized employment in the industry, but estimates range from 20 to 50 percent.[12] Indeed, slaughterhouses became a key target of Immigration and Customs Enforcement (ICE) raids in the 2000s. The largest workplace immigration raid in U.S. history was Operation Wagon Train, on December 12, 2006, when ICE agents simultaneously entered six Swift meatpacking plants, detaining more than 1,300 workers for immigration violations, most of whom were deported.[13] Other industries employed as many unauthorized immigrants, but meatpacking was a favorite target for raids because workers were so conveniently concentrated in large plants—unlike far-flung residential construction sites or office buildings cleaned by immigrant janitors.

As I have documented elsewhere, similar processes took place in other industries in which U.S.-born workers had historically dominated the workforce. In residential construction and janitorial work, just as in meatpacking, employers' deliberate efforts to weaken or eliminate unions led to falling wages, the elimination of health and pension benefits, and deterioration in working conditions. In response, U.S.-born workers abandoned the jobs affected, and employers then recruited immigrants to fill the resulting vacancies.[14]

Deregulation and Subcontracting: The Case of Trucking

In other settings, labor degradation was not the direct result of an employer anti-union offensive but instead was driven by deregulation, which indirectly spurred union decline. One revealing example is the radical transformation of the trucking industry after the Motor Carrier Act of 1980 eliminated price regulation and rules governing entry to the industry that had been in place since the New Deal era. Soon after the law took effect, unionization plummeted, from 60 percent in 1980 to only 25 percent twenty years later.[15] Drivers' wages went into free fall, and those no longer covered by union contracts lost health insurance and pension coverage, sick pay, and paid vacations. As working conditions deteriorated, the industry devolved into what Michael Belzer aptly calls "sweatshops on wheels." U.S. truck drivers' real earnings fell 21 percent between 1973 and 1995, nearly twice the average decline for blue-collar workers in that period.[16]

Deregulation led to a shift away from standard forms of employment and greater use of owner-operators and "independent contractors." Drivers (U.S.- and foreign-born alike) were often genuinely attracted by the idea of "being my own boss," and many therefore embraced the status of independent contractor. But as they soon discovered, the downside was that they were forced to absorb all the costs of owning and maintaining their trucks, and were vulnerable to unpredictable fluctuations in fuel prices, fines for overweight loads, traffic bottlenecks, and other factors beyond their control. Moreover, as independent contractors, they were no longer covered by minimum wage or overtime laws or other basic employment protections.

These changes affected the entire industry, but short-haul trucking from the nation's ports experienced the most dramatic upheaval, whereas in long-distance trucking the union maintained a precarious foothold. At the ports, despite their independent contractor status, drivers typically work for only one firm, which dispatches them to pick up specific containers. Paid by the load, not by the hour (as they were prior to deregulation), they receive no compensation while waiting to receive their cargo at the ports—waits that can consume many hours. Many earn less than the legal minimum wage, and in some cases their expenses actually exceed their revenues.[17]

As deregulation transformed port trucking from a well-paid, unionized occupation into a poorly paid, highly precarious one, many U.S.-born drivers abandoned that segment of the industry; some shifted into long-haul trucking and others into new lines of work. As a logistics trade publication reported in 2005, "As long as [port] trucking paid as well as flipping burgers, the 'chrome and cowboy' aspects of the job were reason to be driving. However, today fast-food jobs look increasingly attractive. . . . Qualified drivers are migrating to better-paying jobs in truckload, construction and other sectors."[18]

In the Los Angeles metropolitan area, home to both the nation's largest ports and a vast immigrant population, the foreign-born proportion of the trucking workforce was only 8 percent in 1970, but that changed dramatically with deregulation.[19] A 2004 survey found that only 11 percent of port truckers in Los Angeles and Long Beach surveyed were U.S.-born. But in contrast to most industries that rely heavily on foreign-born workers, unauthorized immigrants are few among port truckers, who must obtain commercial driver's licenses and who may be subject to federal security checks. Indeed, the 2004 survey found that 57 percent of port truckers were U.S. citizens.[20]

Rising Inequality and Immigrant Employment in Paid Domestic Labor

In contrast to industries such as meatpacking and trucking, paid domestic service was never extensively unionized or regulated; indeed, the jobs in this poorly paid, low-status, female-dominated sector have long been at the bottom of the labor market. But it too shifted from a U.S.-born to an immigrant workforce starting in the 1970s, as African Americans and other U.S.-born women of color abandoned the field once the civil rights movement opened up better employment opportunities to them. In the same period, demand for paid domestic workers began to expand, as the growing polarization of income and wealth made in-home services increasingly affordable for the affluent. As the relative cost of domestic help fell, Daniel Schneider and Orestes P. Hastings show, highly educated, higher-income women began to perform less housework and outsource more household services than less privileged women; over time this class gradient increased in tandem with growing income inequality.[21] Elizabeth Currid-Halkett calculated that in 2014 the top 1 percent in the U.S. income distribution spent about 20 times more on child care than the middle class (defined as the 60th to 90th percentile) and the top 10 percent spent about five times more. Spending on other types of domestic work was similarly top-heavy, especially in urban settings. "The top income groups have the option to have someone else mop their floors, mow their lawns, and water their plants, while the data suggest that lower income groups do these chores themselves," Currid-Halkett concludes.[22]

Domestic labor had been a declining occupation during the first half of the twentieth century, and especially after New Deal policies led to a sharp reduction in income inequality. But in earlier historical eras, domestic service was by far the largest female occupation in the United States, and one in which European immigrants were often employed. In the late nineteenth century, the field was dominated in northern cities by Irish and German immigrants, although in smaller towns outside the South, the majority of servants were U.S.-born well into the twentieth century. Foreign- and native-born white women alike gradually abandoned domestic service as they gained access to factory jobs and later to sales and clerical work, however. "Sometimes women were willing to accept lower wages [in other types of work] simply to avoid service," historian David Katzman notes, for domestic work had "the lowest status of any widespread occupation in American society."[23]

In the first half of the twentieth century the field became increasingly dominated by African American women, whose labor force participation rates were higher than those of white women and who were excluded from most other types of work, even in the northern and midwestern cities to which so many descendants of former slaves had migrated. By 1950, the proportion of African American women workers who were domestic servants was ten times that of white women.[24] At that time job opportunities for African Americans and other women of color remained highly restricted, and domestic service was often their only option.

That finally changed with the passage of the 1964 Civil Rights Act and the wider effects of the civil rights movement, which opened the doors for women of color to clerical and sales jobs and to other occupations from which they previously were excluded. Antidiscrimination efforts were particularly effective in the public sector, in which an upsurge of unionization also improved pay and working conditions in this period.[25] By 1980 only 5 percent of all employed African American women were in domestic work, down from 39 percent in 1960.[26] In that twenty-year period, occupational segregation between black and white women declined precipitously, with a dramatic effect on earnings: in 1960, African American women's average hourly earnings were about 65 percent of white women's, but by 1980 that figure was 99 percent. Yet job segregation by gender remained largely intact, so even as racial barriers fell, most African American women remained confined to traditionally female occupations.[27] Nevertheless, from 1960 to 1980, African American women with twenty or more years of work experience "had the largest increases in relative earnings of any gender-experience group over the period," economists Francine Blau and Andrea Beller found, noting that "their large gains were tied to a reduction in their concentration in private household employment."[28]

Just as the labor supply of African Americans in domestic service was being depleted, however, demand for labor in the occupation began to rebound, reflecting growing maternal labor force participation and the aging of the population. In 2012, "in-home workers," including agency-based direct-care aides, nannies, and house cleaners, 90 percent of them female, accounted for 3 percent of the nation's employed women—double the 1980 level.[29] By that time domestic work had become a major source of employment for female immigrants: in 2012, 7 percent of all foreign-born women, and 11 percent of those with a high school degree or less, were in-home workers. That year, 62 percent of all U.S. "maids and housekeeping cleaners" were foreign-born.[30] The immigrant share is even higher in large cities. For example, 81 percent of New York City's house cleaners, nannies, and home care aides were foreign-born in 2016.[31]

The abandonment of domestic service by U.S.-born women of color was not driven by de-unionization or deregulation, in contrast to the meatpacking and trucking industries, but the end result was the same: immigrant workers moved into jobs that "Americans" shunned. Yet that reality was obscured by the immigrant threat narrative described earlier in this chapter.

Beyond the Threat Narrative

The threat narrative that blames immigrants for the declining fortunes of U.S.-born workers is more than a set of ideas. It has facilitated draconian policy initiatives with vast ramifications for the nation's foreign-born population, and for American politics more broadly. On this basis, indeed, the Trump administration promulgated a Muslim travel ban, limited admissions of refugees and asylum-seekers, separated families at the border, and ramped up deportations.

Superficially, there is continuity in regard to the last of these: not for nothing was Obama tagged "deporter-in-chief." Yet most deportations in the Obama years involved newly arrived immigrants apprehended at the border and those with serious criminal records. The Trump administration, in contrast, prioritized "internal removals," regularly sweeping up immigrants with no criminal records and others who had resided in the United States for long periods of time. Under Trump, ICE agents arrested undocumented immigrants in courthouses and outside schools, locations previous administrations avoided. The administration has also revived workplace raids, which were rare in the Obama years, and sought to curb *legal* immigration—for example, by seeking to end the diversity visa lottery and to limit or end "chain migration" facilitated by the priority given to family members of citizens and legal residents under current immigration law.[32]

As detentions and deportations became increasingly arbitrary and unpredictable, fear and anxiety in immigrant communities spiked to levels not seen for half a century. At the same time, the immigrant rights movement was thrown on the defensive—not only by Trump's policies but also by his success in galvanizing white working-class political support by demonizing immigrants. Advocates challenged Trump's policies in the courts, with some success, but immigration reform virtually disappeared from the national conversation during his four-year term.

Against this backdrop, some prominent liberals came to believe that the only effective way to counter Trump is for his opponents to embrace restrictive policies themselves. Shortly after the 2018 midterm elections, for example, Hillary Clinton—who had supported liberal immigration reform policies during her presidential campaign two years earlier—declared, "If we don't deal with the migration issue, it will continue to roil the body politic." David Frum echoed that warning in more hyperbolic language in an article entitled "If Liberals Won't Enforce Borders, Fascists Will."[33]

Other commentators have ventured still further down this treacherous path. For example, in his 2018 book, liberal political analyst John Judis confessed his personal sympathy for Trump's nationalist agenda and explicitly invoked the immigrant threat narrative:

"Enormous numbers of unskilled immigrants have competed for jobs with Americans who also lack higher education and have led to the downgrading of occupations that were once middle class," he wrote, adding, "Without control of borders and immigration, it is very hard to imagine the United States becoming a more egalitarian society."[34] Similarly, left-wing sociologist Wolfgang Streeck, responding to the growing momentum of right-wing populists in Europe, lamented what he sees as left-wing "anti-statism dressed up as anti-nationalism" in Germany. "By fighting for deregulation of national borders to allow for open and open-ended immigration," he declared, "the Left abandons a central element of its historical pro-regulation agenda, which importantly involved restricting the supply of labor."[35]

On this side of the Atlantic, Angela Nagle has promoted this position as well, harkening back nostalgically to the days when U.S. trade unions embraced restrictive immigration policies while noting (accurately) that the primary supporters of open borders are free-market ideologues like the Koch brothers, along with employers reliant on cheap labor. Historically, she notes, U.S. unions took the opposite view:

> They [unions] saw the deliberate importation of illegal, low-wage workers as weakening labor's bargaining power and as a form of exploitation. There is no getting around the fact that the power of unions relies by definition on their ability to restrict and withdraw the supply of labor, which becomes impossible if an entire workforce can be easily and cheaply replaced. Open borders and mass immigration are a victory for the bosses.[36]

Although this perspective remains alive and well in some sectors of the U.S. labor movement, the AFL-CIO renounced it explicitly in passing a historic 2000 resolution supporting comprehensive immigration reform and a pathway to citizenship for the undocumented.[37] In any case, relatively few U.S. progressives actually advocate "open borders."[38] Instead, most recognize that there are compelling economic reasons to support generous immigration policies: while immigration does expand the labor supply, as commentators such as Nagle and Judis emphasize, it also creates additional economic demand and thus generates more jobs. In addition, the relatively youthful immigrant workforce contributes to the sustainability of Social Security and Medicare, an increasingly urgent issue as the population ages. Indeed, the expert consensus is that immigration has minuscule negative impacts on U.S.-born workers, and that those are more than outweighed by its economic benefits.[39]

Ultimately, however, liberals who support restrictive immigration policies focus less on economics than on politics, and specifically on the susceptibility of U.S.-born workers to right-wing populist appeals. If Democrats want to regain support from the white working-class swing voters who helped fuel Trump's 2016 electoral victory, in this view, they must adopt a kinder and gentler version of immigration restriction, renouncing the most draconian and cruel elements of the Trump administration's policies while retaining the goal of severely limiting immigration.

But progressives can instead craft a new approach that explicitly challenges the immigrant threat narrative. By highlighting the history of employers' strategies to systematically reduce wages and undermine the labor movement, and the history of the elite-sponsored public policies that have led to expanded inequality, we can make a compelling case that U.S.-born workers and immigrants share common interests. This left-wing populist counternarrative can help expose the fallacies of xenophobic narratives while simultaneously acknowledging the moral bankruptcy and corruption of the existing political system.[40] By challenging the power and legitimacy of the corporate elites who control that system, progressives may persuade substantial numbers of white working-class voters that immigrants are not their enemy. As Ian Haney López puts it, "The best response to divide-and-conquer is unite-and-build."[41] This approach dovetails with Steve Phillips's efforts to focus resources on voter registration and electoral turnout efforts in Latinx and African American communities, whose numbers greatly exceed those of the white working-class swing voters whose defections are so often lamented.[42]

Progressive attempts to regain support from white working-class voters and campaigns to register and promote turnout among people of color are not mutually exclusive, as the 2020 election showed. Insofar as this double-pronged approach involves efforts to win over white swing voters, however, it is crucial to explicitly counter the immigrant threat narrative by articulating the common interests of all working people in rejecting racism and xenophobia, in rebuilding the labor movement, in pressuring employers to upgrade jobs, and in demanding public policies to reduce inequality. The historical perspective sketched in this chapter is a necessary, albeit insufficient, tool for carrying out that project.

Notes

This chapter is adapted from Ruth Milkman, *Immigrant Labor and the New Precariat* (New York: Polity, 2020), with the permission of the publisher.

1. Marisa Abrajano and Zoltan L. Hajnal, *White Backlash: Immigration, Race and American Politics* (Princeton, NJ: Princeton University Press, 2015), 5.

2. See Michael Piore, *Birds of Passage: Migrant Labor and Industrial Societies* (New York: Cambridge University Press, 1979).

3. Refugee flows driven by natural disasters and other life-threatening developments in sending countries, which have grown worldwide in recent years, are another matter, beyond the scope of this chapter, but see Saket Soni's chapter in this volume.

4. Charles Craypo, "Meatpacking: Industry Restructuring and Union Decline," in *Contemporary Collective Bargaining in the Private Sector,* ed. Paula B. Voos (Madison, WI: Industrial Relations Research Association, 1994).

5. Jon K. Lauck, "Competition in the Grain Belt Meatpacking Sector After World War II," *Annals of Iowa* 57 (1988): 135–59.

6. Craypo, "Meatpacking," 88.

7. Roger Horowitz, "The Decline of Unionism in America's Meatpacking Industry," *Social Policy*, Spring 2002, 35; Kathleen Stanley, "Immigrant and Refugee Workers in the Midwestern Meatpacking Industry: Industrial Restructuring and the Transformation of Rural Labor Markets," *Policy Studies Review* 11 (1992): 109.

8. Faranak Miraftab, *Global Heartland: Displaced Labor, Transnational Lives and Local Place-Making* (Bloomington: Indiana University Press, 2016), 53.

9. Mark A. Grey, "Patronage, Kinship and Recruitment of Lao and Mennonite Labor to Storm Lake, Iowa," *Culture and Agriculture* 18 (1996): 14–18.

10. Lourdes Gouveia and Donald D. Stull, "Latino Immigrants, Meatpacking and Rural Communities: A Case Study of Lexington, Nebraska," Julian Samora Research Institute, Michigan State University, East Lansing, 1997.

11. Jackie Gabriel, "Organizing *The Jungle:* Industrial Restructuring and Immigrant Unionization in the American Meatpacking Industry," *Working USA: The Journal of Labor and Society* 9 (2006): 338.

12. Dell Champlin and Eric Hake, "Immigration as Industrial Strategy in American Meatpacking," *Review of Political Economy* 18 (2006): 63.

13. Julia Preston, "U.S. Raids 6 Meat Plants in ID Case," *New York Times*, Dec. 13, 2006; Julia Preston, "Immigrants' Families Figuring Out What to Do After Federal Raids," *New York Times*, Dec. 16, 2006.

14. See Ruth Milkman, *Immigrant Labor and the New Precariat* (Cambridge: Polity, 2020); Ruth Milkman, *L.A. Story: Immigrant Workers and the Future of the U.S. Labor Movement* (New York: Russell Sage Foundation, 2006).

15. Nancy L. Rose, "Labor Rent Sharing and Regulation: Evidence from the Trucking Industry." *Journal of Political Economy* 95 (1987): 1162; C.R. Perry, *Deregulation and the Decline of the Unionized Trucking Industry* (Philadelphia: Industrial Relations Unit, Wharton School, 1986), 110.

16. Michael Belzer, *Sweatshops on Wheels* (New York: Oxford University Press, 2000); Dale Belman and Kristen A. Monaco, "The Effects of Deregulation, De-unionization, Technology and Human Capital on the Work and Work Lives of Truck Drivers," *Industrial and Labor Relations Review* 54 (2001): 502.

17. Brett Murphy, "Rigged: Forced into Debt. Worked Past Exhaustion. Left with Nothing," *USA Today,* June 16, 2017.

18. Ted Prince, "Endangered Species," *Journal of Commerce*, May 9, 2005, 13–14.

19. Milkman, *L.A. Story*, 108.

20. Edna Bonacich and Jake Wilson, *Getting the Goods: Ports, Labor and the Logistics Revolution* (Ithaca, NY: Cornell University Press, 2008), 215.

21. Daniel Schneider and Orestes P. Hastings, "Income Inequality and Household Labor," *Social Forces* 96 (2017): 481–505.

22. Elizabeth Currid-Halkett, *The Sum of Small Things: A Theory of the Aspirational Class* (Princeton, NJ: Princeton University Press, 2017), 53–66, 168.

23. David Katzman, *Seven Days a Week: Women and Domestic Service in Industrializing America* (New York: Oxford University Press, 1978), 241–42.

24. Ibid.; Enobong H. Branch, *Opportunity Denied: Limiting Black Women to Devalued Work* (New Brunswick, NJ: Rutgers University Press, 2011), 59.

25. See Faye J. Crosby, *Affirmative Action is Dead, Long Live Affirmative Action* (New Haven, CT: Yale University Press, 2004); Alexis N. Walker, *Divided Unions: The Wagner Act, Federalism, and Organized Labor* (Philadelphia: University of Pennsylvania Press, 2020), chapter 4.

26. Branch, *Opportunity Denied*, 132–34.

27. Mary C. King, "Occupational Segregation by Race and Sex, 1940–88," *Monthly Labor Review* 115 (1992): 33; Branch, *Opportunity Denied*, 134.

28. Blau and Beller, "Black-White Earnings Over the 1970s and 1980s: Gender Differences in Trends," *Review of Economics and Statistics* 74 (1992): 285.

29. This figure does not include house cleaners and others employed by companies such as Merry Maids and dispatched to work in private homes, or workers hired through platforms such as Care.com, for which no reliable data are available; it does include child care workers who work in their own homes.

30. Heidi Shierholz, "Low Wages and Scant Benefits Leave Many In-Home Workers Unable to Make Ends Meet," Briefing Paper 369, Economic Policy Institute, Washington, DC, 2013.

31. Ruth Milkman, "Making Paid Care Work Visible," New York City Department of Consumer Affairs, Office of Labor Policy and Standards, 2018.

32. See Julie Hirschfeld Davis and Michael D. Shear, *Border Wars: Inside Trump's Assault on Immigration* (New York: Simon and Schuster, 2019).

33. David Frum, "If Liberals Won't Enforce Borders, Fascists Will," *The Atlantic*, Apr. 2019, 64–74.

34. John Judis, *The Nationalist Revival* (New York: Columbia Global Reports, 2018), 77, 146.

35. Streeck, "Between Charity and Justice: Remarks on the Social Construction of Immigration Policy in Rich Democracies," *Culture, Practice and Europeanization* 3, no. 2 (2018): 6–7.

36. Angela Nagle, "The Left Case Against Open Borders," *American Affairs* 2, no. 4 (2018).

37. David Bacon, "Labor Fights for Immigrants," *The Nation*, May 21, 2001, 15–22.

38. Thoughtful exceptions include Suzy Lee, "The Case for Open Borders," *Catalyst* 2, no. 4 (2019); Farhad Manjoo, "There's Nothing Wrong with Open Borders," *New York Times*, Jan. 16, 2019.

39. For an authoritative review of this literature, see Francine D. Blau and Christopher Mackie, eds., *The Economic and Fiscal Consequences of Immigration* (Washington, DC: National Academies of Sciences Press, 2017).

40. See Chantal Mouffe, *For a Left Populism* (New York: Verso, 2018).

41. Ian Haney López, *Merge Left: Fusing Race and Class, Winning Elections, and Saving America* (New York: The New Press, 2019), xxiii.

42. Steve Phillips, *Brown Is the New White* (New York: The New Press, 2016).

Stronger Together

Immigrant Workers and the Labor Movement

An Interview with Eliseo Medina

Eliseo Medina emigrated from Mexico to the United States with his parents at age 10 and became a United Farm Workers (UFW) activist as a teenager. His long career in the labor movement began with a decade-long stint working for the UFW. After that he joined the staff of the American Federation of State, County, and Municipal Workers, moving a few years later to the Service Employees International Union (SEIU), where he stayed from 1986 to 2012. There Medina began working on the legendary Justice for Janitors (JFJ) campaign, and also helped to spearhead labor's immigrant political mobilization efforts in southern California. He later emerged on the national stage as a leading labor movement champion of immigrant rights. After retiring from SEIU as its secretary-treasurer, the union's second-highest office, he led a twenty-two-day fast on Capitol Hill in 2013 to bring more public attention to the need for comprehensive immigration reform. In this interview with Deepak Bhargava and Ruth Milkman, Medina reflects on his long career in organized labor and in the immigrant rights movement.[1]

DB: *How did you get involved in organizing?*

EM: In 1956, my family sold our little farm in Mexico, and we came to look for the American dream that everybody kept talking about. I thought the U.S. was a place where money was on the streets—all you needed was a broom and a dust mop to pick it up! But then I went to work in the fields. That was a lot of work, and a lot of bad treatment.

At first I thought there was nothing you could do about it, that this was the life of an immigrant in the United States, to be treated like an agricultural implement that can be discarded at any moment.

But when I was nineteen, the Delano farmworkers' strike began. All of a sudden, all these people were marching in the streets, and they were all Mexicans just like me. I thought, "These guys are all going to get arrested, they're all going to be deported." But then I went to a meeting, which was when I first met César Chavez. He spoke about how we were poor but we had dignity. He said that we were supposed to be treated with respect, but the only way we would win that was if we stood up for ourselves. The next day I went and joined the union!

DB: *What did you learn from your experience in the UFW?*

EM: The first thing I learned, from being engaged in the grape boycott and the strikes and organizing around the country, was that the growers were not as powerful as we thought they were, and that the workers were not as weak as we thought. I got assigned to work on the boycott in Chicago, and we started talking to the consumers, to the unions, to the students, to the church parishioners. Once they rallied to our side, by not buying grapes and by joining demonstrations at the supermarkets, their consumer power was brought to bear, and the growers just collapsed. Then they swallowed their pride, negotiated a contract that increased our wages and provided benefits that we never, even in our wildest dreams, would have thought possible. Rest periods! Health care! Toilets! Before that you had to go hide under a grapevine if you wanted to go to the bathroom. But now, all of these things were possible, and we got treated with respect.

That taught me how much power we had when we came together. Without us, the growers were nothing. We were the key to producing their wealth and their power. When we refused to go along with what they wanted, and we stuck together, we could make change. That stuck with me for the rest of my life.

I did some organizing in Oxnard, where we knew lots of the

farmworkers were undocumented. We signed them up anyway, but sure enough, just before the union election the Border Patrol showed up and started arresting people. I remember them whispering to me as they were being taken away, "Don't worry about it, we'll be back tomorrow!" And forty-eight hours later, they were back. That inspired us to develop a new strategy toward the Border Patrol. We said, "Look, we're all going to be working here, but in case the Border Patrol shows up, how many of you have papers?" About half of them said, "We do." So we said, "Here's what we'll do. The minute *la migra* shows up, those of you with papers, swarm them to ask what's going on. Those of you that have no papers, disappear, go hide!" A couple of days later that happened, and the Border Patrol men were so busy talking to all the workers that had papers that they didn't have time to deal with all the others who had disappeared. The lesson was not only that people could avoid getting arrested. It also showed them not to be afraid of the Border Patrol, that you could actually come up with a strategy to fool them and deal with them. All of a sudden, the Border Patrol, this big boogeyman, became a bumbling policeman that couldn't figure out what was going on. It got people to see that they had more power than they thought.

RM: Tell us about your involvement in immigrant organizing after you left the UFW.

EM: From 1981 to 1986 I was in Texas organizing state workers, and after that I started working for SEIU in San Diego. One of my first campaigns was reorganizing the downtown janitors, as part of the Justice for Janitors campaign, which SEIU started in 1985, with organizing drives along the West Coast, from the border all the way up to Washington State. The janitors were all immigrants, and the vast majority were undocumented, especially in L.A., which was the capital of the Latino community in the United States. L.A. was the center of the JFJ campaign, with constant demonstrations in the streets, constant movement.

It was like an urban farmworkers' movement. The janitors, like farmworkers, were people that worked hard, didn't get paid very well, got no benefits, got mistreated. And like farmworkers years before, the janitors were standing up and saying, "We deserve better. We deserve respect!" And a lot of the tactics that we used came straight out of the UFW. Actually Stephen Lerner, who dreamed up the JFJ campaign, had been a boycott organizer with the farmworkers.

But unlike the farmworkers, SEIU is an institution of power, with 2 million members scattered all over the United States and Canada. In most places they are the largest organization in their community. They have a lot of money. They have political relationships. But an institution of power doesn't necessarily have to be shackled by its power and its size. It can be nimble. It can make decisions that lead to momentous change. In the 1990s, we built a consensus in SEIU that organizing was our salvation. Organizing was the way we could build power to deliver for our members. We presented the members with a proposal to increase dues by $5 a month, money that would only be used for organizing. Now, most people would think of that as suicide. It's like in government, you don't talk about raising taxes, because it's the kiss of death politically. Well, in unions, you don't go and raise dues, because that can also be the kiss of death. But we had faith that it would work if we actually had a conversation with our members and said, "This is why it matters: if you do this, this is what the money will be used for." When our members approved it, that gave us $300 million to go out and organize at a scale that hadn't happened since the 1930s. That allowed us to expand JFJ into a nationwide campaign, among other things.

DB: *How did SEIU become committed to supporting the immigrant rights movement?*

EM: Because of the janitors, SEIU already had a lot of experience organizing immigrant workers, and it wasn't a big deal to convince them to take the next step, to put staff and money into defending our members and fighting for immigration reform. Soon that became one of the union's top priorities—not only because it was the right thing to do, but because it impacted the people that we dealt with every day. By then it was clear that if we wanted to organize and bring more members into the union, we needed immigrants.

But we also knew—with all due respect to SEIU and the labor movement—that we were not strong enough by ourselves to win a change in national immigration policy. If we were going to succeed, we would have to build a broad coalition of all of the people that cared about this issue. For example, take the Catholic Church. The same people that we saw working during the week, the churches saw on Sunday, because they were the parishioners. Community organizations knew immigrants too, from their social service work, so they had an integral interest in trying to fix the situation. And businesses needed immigrants, both as employees and as consumers. They wanted to be seen as pro-immigrant to build brand loyalty to their products, so they also had an interest in trying to fix this broken system—if not because of the righteousness of the cause, but because they needed to have workers and to sell their products. Then there was the Latino and ethnic media. Their viewers were immigrants—that's who gave them their Nielsen points. They wanted to have as many people watching as possible so they could sell commercials to the companies, to say, "If you want to reach this community, you advertise with us." It turned out that a lot of the reporters and the announcers were immigrants themselves, since they had to look like the people they were trying to reach. So the ethnic media had a deep interest in this. And finally, the immigrant-sending countries. People come to the U.S. to work, and send money back home to support their relatives, so those countries have an interest in maintaining stability for their nationals in this country. Understanding all that allowed us to build a broad coalition, and to create a drumbeat throughout the community about how immigration reform was critically important. If you went to church on Sunday, the priest would be preaching about immigration reform. If you went to your union meeting, there was a discussion about immigration reform and why it mattered to labor. If you went to your community organization, people would be talking to you about it. If you watched the news, or listened to the radio, there was something about immigration reform.

RM: *In 1994 California voters passed Prop 187, which—if it hadn't been struck down in the courts—would have denied the undocumented access to all public services, from health care to public schooling. How did that affect the budding immigrant rights movement?*

EM: Pete Wilson was the governor at the time, and he was up for reelection in 1994, so he got behind 187, which had been introduced by some Republican activists. He ran on an anti-immigrant platform, much like Trump in 2016. I still remember the TV commercials. They had a grainy picture showing people running across the highway, with a voice-over saying, "They keep coming!" It gave the image of an invasion, of foreigners coming in to take advantage of what was available to them in this country. Prop 187 really galvanized the anti-immigrant sentiment that had been bubbling up. And at the time, immigrants were not particularly well organized. They had some community organizations that were very small and weak. The unions were not as focused on the issue, and in fact the AFL-CIO still had an anti-immigrant platform.

Prop 187 passed overwhelmingly, and Pete Wilson got reelected. But that really energized the immigrant rights movement. That was the first time that the community came together in massive numbers. It was a huge fight-back—not just undocumented workers but the whole Latino community, with students walking out too. And SEIU Local 399, the L.A. janitors local, became super-engaged, because our members were immigrants. So that began to cement the relationship between labor and the community.

In 1995, right after the 187 fight, the AFL-CIO had a major change in leadership. Lane Kirkland was retiring, and John Sweeney, who up until then was the president of SEIU, decided that he would run to replace Kirkland at the top of the AFL-CIO. John had a progressive slate of candidates with a progressive campaign focused on how to organize in the future.

After Sweeney became the AFL-CIO president, we had our own internal battle within SEIU about who would succeed him. It was the progressive forces in the West against the more conservative elements in New York, Chicago, and other places. We had a battle internally, not just about who would head SEIU but where the union was heading. The slate headed by Andy Stern won, and he became SEIU president in 1996. I then became a vice president and moved to Los Angeles.

At that time there was also a contest for the head of the L.A. County Federation of Labor. I knew the County Fed's political director, Miguel Contreras, from back when he was a farmworker organizer. He was running for secretary-treasurer, on an organizing agenda. I met with all our locals and they all agreed to support him, and he was elected.

After that, a bunch of us got together in Los Angeles to figure out a plan to mobilize the Latino community. Ben Monterroso, who had been one of the key leaders of the anti-187 protests, was on the SEIU Western Region staff by then, and Maria Elena Durazo headed up Local 11 of the Hotel Employees and Restaurant Employees union (HERE), whose base was Latino hotel and restaurant workers. They were a lot like SEIU, where our base was the Latino janitors.

The road map, for us and for Miguel as well, came from our experiences with the farmworkers. During the grape boycott we had created coalitions of labor, church, community, students, and everybody else. And in L.A., the head of the Catholic archdiocese, Cardinal Mahoney, had also been involved with the farmworkers. So there were all these people that had this common background, and a lot of our ideas came from that. We were going to tackle immigration reform the way we had tackled the grape boycott. One difference, though, was that the Latino media played a much greater role. By the 1990s they had a huge megaphone into the community. But otherwise we were all operating off of the playbook we had gotten from the UFW. I look at the immigrant rights movement as the child of the farmworkers movement.

RM: *The L.A. labor movement became known in the late 1990s for its success in Latino political mobilization. How did that come about?*

EM: After Miguel became the leader of the County Fed, we decided to form an organization to focus on Latino civic participation, funded mainly by SEIU but also supported by HERE. We called it the Organization of Los Angeles Workers, which would later become Mi Familia Vota nationally. But at that time, it was strictly an L.A. operation. Ben became the full-time director, I was the president, and Maria Elena was the secretary-treasurer. We worked closely with Miguel. We started civic engagement programs, voter registration, voter education, voter mobilization. At the time a bunch of progressive Latinos were running for office, like Fabian Núñez, who got elected to the state assembly, and Antonio Villaraigosa, who was elected Speaker and who would later become the mayor of L.A. We were not partisan, we were not supporting Fabian or Antonio, but they were the beneficiaries of our success in turning out Latinos to vote.

We wanted to create a culture of participation. Our approach was that this was a fight for our whole community, and everybody had a role to play. And this was repeated on television, on the radio, in the churches—wherever we went. We said, "If you're a citizen and you're not registered to vote, you have to register. And if you register, you need to vote, because if you don't, you are doing a disservice to your community, to your family, and to yourself. If you're a permanent resident and you're eligible for citizenship, you need to apply for citizenship, and we will help you do that." We held immigration workshops to counsel people on how to fill out their paperwork. Thousands of people would come. And we said, "The minute you get your citizenship, you register to vote." And to the undocumented, we said, "Okay, so you can't become citizens, and you can't vote, but you can help. You can knock on doors, you can make phone calls, you can make signs. Everybody has a role to play in this movement."

One of our more successful tactics was asking Univision and Telemundo anchors and reporters to walk precincts with us, with their cameras. They came and then they would report from the field, and that created a kind of echo chamber with the same message. People loved it, because the anchors were like celebrities. When they showed up at the door, they'd say, "Oh my God, you're so-and-so!" People were tremendously excited. It became a blending of the media and the community.

We put up quite a bit of money and put together a nonpartisan campaign that went out to knock on doors. We had about a thousand people, mostly from HERE and SEIU, but also from churches and the immigrant rights groups. We asked them all to send volunteers, and we paid them a stipend. We went to Cardinal Mahoney and asked if we could get the local churches involved. I spoke at a whole bunch of masses about the importance of coming out and voting—with the full support of the cardinal. We were all working together, doing the canvassing. Later we quantified the impact that it had, and found that in every precinct where we canvassed, we increased turnout by over 20 percent. It was huge!

One thing that I often tell people is that what you see in California today, you're going to see in the U.S. tomorrow. Because some of the same forces that transformed California are in play throughout the country. First, you had an enemy that was intent on demonizing immigrants and using the politics of division to create and maintain power. But never underestimate the power of your enemies to overplay their hand, which is what they did with Prop 187. They thought immigrants were an easy target: "They're weak, they have no power, and we can use them to continue our control." And if you look back, before 187, the Republicans were in control of both houses of the California legislature, but today the Democrats have supermajorities in both houses. Every statewide elected official is a Democrat, and three or four of them are Latinos. Even down to the smallest cities in California now you see Latinos in power or African Americans or Asian Americans. We just recently had the state bar swear in an undocumented worker to practice law. In terms of acceptance and support of immigrants, the transformation of California has been incredible, and that shows what is possible. What created that momentum was 187 and changes within the labor movement that allowed us to take advantage of the moment that they presented to us. And I think you're going to see the same thing sooner or later in the rest of the country.

RM: How did your work in California in the 1990s impact the national labor movement?

EM: After Sweeney got elected as head of the AFL-CIO, SEIU along with the farmworkers, HERE, and UFCW [United Food and Commercial Workers International Union], all of whom were organizing immigrant workers, put a resolution on the floor of the 1999 AFL-CIO convention calling for support of immigration reform. I remember when Ben Monterroso came to see me about it, and at first I was doubtful. I said to Ben, "There's too many old white guys there that don't care about this issue." But he kept insisting, so finally I said, "Okay, let's take a look at it." Then we reached out to HERE and the farmworkers, and both of them were interested. John [Sweeney] was going to be chairing the AFL-CIO convention for the first time, and he and his slate were in full support. So we put it on the agenda and organized for it on the convention floor. We had speakers talking about immigrant workers' rights, and we made the point that if this labor movement is going to succeed, it needs to organize immigrant workers. Immigrants are key workers in transportation, in agriculture, in hospitality, in factories, and without them, there's no way we can succeed. By then, people had seen the janitors campaign and some other immigrant union drives win, so there was this air of change. And this was a total reversal of the AFL-CIO's immigration policy.

It was way more successful than I would have expected. Not one person at the convention stood up to speak out against us; it seemed like there was overwhelming support. But John wisely said, "Well, we're not going to call for a vote yet. We're going to hold it in abeyance and go out and talk to everybody to make sure that they are all on board." He appointed a committee that went around the country to meet with all of the key unions. I was on that committee, along with John Wilhelm, the president of HERE, Arturo Rodriguez from the UFW, and Joe Hansen from UFCW. We met with union leaders all over the country and created a consensus, so that when it came back to the AFL-CIO Executive Council in March 2000, it was adopted unanimously. From that point forward, the labor movement was four-square in support of immigration reform. Of course, it didn't mean that the building trades were in agreement, but they were quiet now instead of actively opposed, and that made a big difference. The fact that we got a majority of people to say yes, and the others were just quiet, allowed us to move forward.

Once we adopted the resolution, we had news conferences to announce that the labor movement was now on the side of immigrant workers. The Latino media covered it extensively. And then the AFL-CIO set out to do a series of hearings around the country on immigration reform. They were designed to have about three hundred participants each. But in L.A. we wanted to have a much bigger event. We had a long argument with the AFL-CIO, who had a model they wanted us to follow. We said, "Look, we don't want to do three hundred. Don't count on us to do that. We need something big!" Finally they agreed, provided we followed the agenda they wanted. A boring agenda, but we agreed to that to keep all of us working together.

In the end we got about twenty thousand people to come to the event, which was held in the L.A. Sports Arena, and there were another five thousand that couldn't get in. It just blew everyone away.

We got every immigrant rights group and every union in L.A. to send delegations. Every partner that signed on was asked to contribute, even though SEIU had put up the money for it. We wanted everyone to own it, to put in whatever money they could. Some put up $500, others $2,000. But everybody was expected to turn people out, so it belonged to all of us. We had bands that came and played for free. We invited Cardinal Mahoney to come and speak, which he did.

Andy Stern and a lot of people from the national AFL-CIO came, and when they saw this huge crowd, their eyes were as big as saucers. So that was another big turning point in terms of building the movement. Miguel was very supportive; he loved the fact that we were doing this kind of stuff. It really resonated in the community, it built on the campaign about 187 and the L.A. political organizing, and it reinforced all our relationships with the different sectors that were tied to the Latino community.

A little later, SEIU started a TV program in L.A., with Univision as our partner. The very first subject that we picked was immigration reform. We asked all the community groups and legal aid folks to send volunteers, and we had fifty people on the phones. Univision then said, "We are here live from SEIU, if you have a question about your rights as an immigrant, call this number." We had over three hundred thousand phone calls over a period of thirty minutes—the response was so huge that the system crashed. But that showed us the hunger within the community, and Univision provided us a forum for reaching millions of people in the metro area.

The more things that we did like that, things that were very public and very big, the more people wanted to join in. That sports arena deal was a huge success because it had never been done, and it involved everybody. The civic engagement program we did in L.A. had never been done, and it became a community-wide effort. Every time we did something like that, it helped to solidify our belief that the way to win was to include the most people because we were not strong enough by ourselves to do the job. It needed to belong to everybody.

Honestly, we weren't just thinking about winning immigration reform. From my perspective, and for all of us that were working on it, the long-range goal was making sure that immigrants' contributions were recognized and that they were allowed to become full participants in the life of this country. And in order to be full participants, you have to be citizens, you have to have your political voice heard, you have to be able to have a job that allows you to earn a decent living so that your kids can go to school and have more opportunities. It was about becoming integrated into society with all the responsibilities and benefits of that. That's what we were interested in. We didn't think it would take this long! I honestly believe we would have won immigration reform then, had it not been for 9/11. We were on track to get that done, and then 9/11 came along, and it set us back, many years behind.

DB: *Tell us more about that, and how the movement recovered from it.*

EM: In 2001, we were having good conversations with Teddy Kennedy and other people in the Senate. It looked like we were really going to make progress. George Bush was in the White House and he was supportive of immigration reform. So we had a president that was ready to do something, we had a Senate with some powerful allies. Even though the House was not so good, I really thought that we were going to get it done; it seemed like the time was right. And then 9/11 happened and everything changed. The president's attention, Congress's attention, the public's attention—all turned inward. There was a rise in fear of immigrants, as personified by the people that were involved in the hijacking of the airplanes.

So that totally derailed us. But soon we started talking about how we could come back. Because as a movement we have to be able to deal with setbacks. Then in 2003, HERE decided they wanted to do the Immigrant Workers Freedom Ride, with people taking a bus trip around the country. HERE took the lead on organizing and funding it and we in SEIU jumped in to support them. Wherever the bus caravan went, the Freedom Ride got a tremendous amount of coverage and support. So that helped to refocus us on the work that we needed to do.

The next big turning point was in 2005, when Jim Sensenbrenner, a Republican from Wisconsin, introduced a Proposition 187–type bill in Congress, which tried to criminalize immigrant workers. That led to the 2006 mass immigrant rights marches. Those were much bigger than what we had been able to do in California ten years before with 187, and it took the movement national, as marches started happening organically in just about every nook and cranny of this country. In California, we had a million people marching. In Houston, where I was at the time, we had about seventy thousand people marching. In Dallas, Texas, a hundred thousand people marching. Garden City, Kansas, ten thousand people marching. Garden City is just a little baby town in Kansas. All over. At the peak we had 120 cities with over 5 million people marching. There were immigrants from Africa, from Asia, from Ireland, Poland, from Mexico, from Central America; men and women, young and old. And it wasn't just immigrants, it was everybody. It was America speaking up and saying, "This is wrong. We need to do something about it!"

One of our slogans was "Today we march, tomorrow we vote!" And after the marches, civic engagement became one of the national movement's key strategies, because we wanted to make sure that opponents of immigration reform knew that there would be a price to pay at the ballot box. That immigrants couldn't be picked on with impunity. That they would be held accountable.

RM: Let's turn to 2008, when Obama was elected, and when there was a lot of hope for immigration reform.

EM: We had a huge debate within SEIU in 2007 and 2008 about who we should support for president. People were all over the map. The people from Chicago were steadfast in their belief that this new guy, Barack Obama, was a wonderful candidate that we should all be supporting. But I was one of many who said, "Barack Obama? Who the hell is that? Some guy who just got elected senator and is now running for president? Nobody ever heard of him! What are you guys talking about?" But I remember when I first met Obama directly, myself and somebody else from labor, and I left that meeting thinking, "This guy gets it. Maybe it's his history of being a community organizer, but he gets what we're trying to do and why. This is the guy that we should support." And of course, in the end we got behind him.

One of the things that we learned off of that election is the limits of presidential power. Because we had elected a president, not a king of the United States. And unlike kings, he couldn't just decree that this thing would happen and it would happen. It also depended on Congress. I remember when he first got elected and Mitch McConnell said they were going to focus on making sure that he was going to be a one-term president. It was all about obstructing.

I became part of a group that regularly met with the president to talk about immigration reform, and there was always a tension about how do I move this with the Congress and how do I move it with the public to make sure I have enough support, and there's a limit as to what I can do. I can't do it by myself. Obama wanted to get immigration reform done, but he figured he needed to be able to show the public how he was a hardass on enforcement of immigration law, as a trade-off. His belief was that they also needed to be enforcing the law in order to convince the public to support doing something about legalizing the 11 million. It became a very difficult situation for those of us pushing for immigrant rights. The Republicans wouldn't let reform happen anyway, and now we're stuck with the bad part of it, without the good parts.

We continued organizing to try to move the president to start doing things with his executive power. Eventually he got to the point that he knew that something needed to be done, and the decision was made that they would do something for the Dreamers, who had become a very sympathetic cause for the American people. They saw all these young kids who looked like their sons and daughters, who were working hard, who were studying hard and getting good grades, and all they wanted was the opportunity to stay in this country that had been their home forever. So the president came up with this idea of DACA, and of course we welcomed it even though we were concerned that that might become the end of it, and we wouldn't get anything for everybody else. Nevertheless, it showed that it wasn't impossible to do immigration reform, and the world wasn't going to end because that was done—that it was a good public policy that helped and didn't hurt anybody. And so that was a tremendous thing that President Obama did, especially considering the limits on his power. Then we tried to get the president to start thinking about the parents and others, about expanding the executive order. We never did get there, and less and less attention was being paid to solving the bigger problem.

DB: After you left the SEIU, early in Obama's second term, you led a hunger strike at the Capitol. What was the thinking behind that?

EM: By 2013, we had lost our original focus on immigrant workers and why it mattered that they were in this country. By then the Republicans had been very successful in demonizing us. I personally felt that it was important to try and remind this country of why immigrants matter, and why their hopes and their dreams were no different than the hopes of everybody else. So we decided that we would do a fast right near the Capitol in Washington, DC. We wanted to be right in front of the policymakers that could put an end to the misery that immigrants were going through. We purposely didn't call it a hunger strike, because first of all, a hunger strike is something that you do *against* something, and we wanted to have a fast *for* something. As we said when we announced it, we wanted to reach out and touch the heart of America. We wanted to remind them about our values as a nation, and that it wasn't right that over three hundred people died every single year trying to come here, looking for the American dream. All they wanted was to be able to support their families and to be able to build a better future for them, and our broken immigration system was preventing that. It was also about the billions of dollars that we were spending on the border—money that we needed for health care, money that we needed to provide for our people in this nation, that was just being wasted.

So we set up at the Mall, and then we invited other people to come in, because even though I had committed to do the fast, I didn't want to do it by myself, because then it would be about the person rather than the issue. And we purposely asked for families, because the focus was on the families that were suffering. When it started there were nine of us that began the fast, and we said it would be for an indefinite period of time. We knew that our bodies would get weaker, but our spirits would grow stronger as we went through this whole process. And that's what happened. We fasted in front of the Capitol, and every day we invited people to come and visit with us. Politicians, public figures, civil rights leaders, church leaders, union leaders. Everybody that came to visit with us, we would tell them our story, and every day more people decided to join us. Some people would come and fast for a day, some came for four days, some for a week. One came and stayed for the whole time, thirty days. We had over three hundred people come and visit, including the president and the First Lady. We had people from all over the world, because now with the internet, nothing's secret. It's broadcast everywhere. We had an order of nuns that had ten thousand members all decide that they were going to join and fast. We had members of Congress deciding that they would fast. And they invited us to a meeting of the House of Representatives, and they introduced us, and everybody stood up and applauded. It was very successful. We did not get immigration reform, but I think we refocused the debate on the right things.

DB: What's your take on comprehensive reform of the kind that we were promoting in the Obama years? How do you view that framework now?

EM: We still need a holistic model now. It may not be feasible given the partisan divide that we have in this country, but I do think we need to be able to have it once again be comprehensive. But I am opposed to a system that relies on a fence, or mass troops at the border to keep future people out. That's not true to our values about the dignity of human beings. And besides, it would be totally ineffective. It would be a waste of resources. We would be lying to the American people if we said that's going to fix the problem. Because as long as there's poverty, as long as there's repression in some countries, people will immigrate. If their children are suffering, if they're hungry, no fence and no troops are going to stop people from pursuing their dream of a better future for their families. So I don't think that's a solution.

But we do need a comprehensive solution that deals with both the undocumented today and the workers of tomorrow, the future flow. That divides into two parts. There are some people that just want to come, earn some money, and go home and live their lives. Make it possible for them to do that. Create a flexible system that allows for that to happen. And while they're here, they should have full human and labor rights and protections, but later they can go home. As for those that want to make their life in this country, they can earn it. They can come with some kind of visa and then be able to petition to stay here. I think we can figure that out. It's not brain surgery. It just takes political will. It happens in Canada and it happens in other countries. Why can't it happen here?

We need to create a system which gives people a legal, orderly way to get here, that is responsive to the needs of the economy, so that you don't have all of this buildup at the border, all of these people that get arrested and detained, and all of that other crap that goes along with it. I think it can be done. It will be tough, but it's not impossible. But we need to have a serious conversation rather than a political conversation, which is what we've been having all this time with the Republicans.

I think that the vast majority, not 100 percent, but the vast majority of the American people, believe that everyone deserves to be treated fairly and with dignity. And we make a mistake if we write them off as potential allies. You're never going to get the white power reactionaries to agree with you, absolutely not, but not everybody is like that. Trump has been an obstacle, but he's also given us an opportunity, because like Pete Wilson, he's forced people to choose sides. And when you pursue a policy that is more about personal interest rather than the community or the society, you wind up with a very, very small slice of society being with you. Trump has sown the seeds for the destruction of the politics of division.

As organizers, we are not saviors. Our role is to set people's hearts and minds on fire, and then direct the heat where it can do the most good. We have to be creative, using strategies that invite rather than repel people from being a part of our movement and listening to our message. I've been an organizer since I was nineteen years old. Between the farmworkers movement and the immigrant rights movement, I've had many opportunities to see the goodness of the American people. So I don't feel pessimistic about the future.

Note

1. This interview took place on April 10, 2020. It has been edited for length and clarity. The text also includes excerpts from Medina's remarks as a guest speaker in a class at the CUNY School of Labor and Urban Studies on March 31, 2020.

From the Ground Up

The Growth of the U.S. Immigrant Rights Movement

An Interview with Angelica Salas

Angelica Salas, a lifelong leader in the immigrant rights movement, has been executive director of the Coalition for Humane Immigrant Rights (CHIRLA) since 1999. She also serves as president of the CHIRLA Action Fund, the organization's political arm. She emigrated from Mexico to the United States as a child. She was undocumented and was able to adjust her status in the 1980s and eventually naturalize. She began volunteering for CHIRLA in 1995, just after the fight over Proposition 187. Under her leadership, CHIRLA pioneered strategies to organize day laborers and domestic workers, mobilized recently naturalized citizens to vote, invested in leadership development among immigrant youth, and advanced other policies that helped make Los Angeles in particular and California more generally a central node of the immigrant rights movement. Nationally, Salas was a key instigator and architect of the push for mass legalization of undocumented immigrants that began in the late 1990s. In this interview with Deepak Bhargava and Ruth Milkman, Salas reflects on the history of the immigrant rights movement, lessons learned, and the challenges that lie ahead.[1]

RM: *Could you tell us about your own immigration story and how that spurred your work in the movement?*

AS: My father and his brothers came to the United States in the early 1970s, hoping to make money so we wouldn't lose our land back in Mexico. He thought it was only going to be for a short stint, but then there was a moment when my mom realized it was going to be longer, so she joined him. My brother was born here in 1974. But my sister and I stayed in Mexico with my grandmother and my aunt. Later, when my mom and dad were able to put together enough money, they sent for us, and we made the trek across the border. I was only four years old. We came with my aunt, who was fourteen, and my uncle, who was sixteen, and then my older aunt, who was about twenty years old. I remember that it was scary. We were picked up by immigration, and I still remember the very bright fluorescent lights of the detention center. We were sent back, and later my sister and I came again with one of my uncles who was already a U.S. citizen.

Pasadena, California, has been our home ever since. My mom was a garment worker and my father did construction; he spent forty years as a roofer before he passed away. Nobody had any documents. In the late seventies, my mom got picked up by *la migra* along with some of my uncles and aunts and they were deported back to Mexico. It was very scary; I thought I'd never see my mom again. But later we got help from an organization, the International Institute of Los Angeles. Because my brother had been born in the United States, we were able to legalize our status.

RM: *Was that before the Immigration Reform and Control Act [IRCA] of 1986?*

AS: No, we were part of a lawsuit, the *Silva* case, that led to allowing children under twenty-one to petition for us, so we were allowed to apply through my brother, who at that time was just a little kid. And so we legalized our status.

I was fifteen years old in 1986 when IRCA passed—we called it "amnesty" at the time. That allowed some of my uncles and aunts to legalize their status. I was the one who knew English, I knew how to type. I would finish my homework, and then my uncles and my aunts and cousins would come over and I would sit there and type their IRCA applications. I remember when they started getting green cards, it was wonderful. Their lives changed so much. They became homeowners. I remember the joy, the relief.

So I know what it is to be undocumented, and I also know what it means to get legal status. To this day, half of my relatives are naturalized citizens, or were born here, but a lot of others are still undocumented. For IRCA, you had to be here before 1982, but some of them arrived later.

I still live in our old home. In those days, it was the first place that many of my aunts and uncles or cousins would stay right after they had crossed into the United States. I would get so upset whenever somebody else arrived, because I had to give up my bed. They would sometimes stay for a week, or stay for months. I had one cousin who stayed for about two years! I also remember their harrowing stories of crossing. Once my mom and my dad had to go rescue one of my cousins in Tijuana who had been kidnapped by a *coyote*. I know that all this had an impact on me and what I do.

My parents always wanted me to have an education. I went to Occidental College, where I became a history major. That was when I first realized this was not just about my family but about systems, and that there were many other people in the same situation.

I graduated in 1993, and then was admitted to Yale for a master's in international relations. But I was almost penniless, so I decided to defer and try to make some money. I got a job in New Jersey with the Mercer County Hispanic Association. It was a social service agency. I was finding housing for people, I also ran the food pantry. I started there just when a big group of immigrants from southern Mexico and Guatemala began arriving in the area. This was something new; up until then the organization had mostly dealt with *dominicanos* and *puertorriqueños*. In fact, I was shocked to see *puertorriqueños* who were U.S. citizens but were still poor and homeless—I had always thought citizenship was the key to everything! But when folks from Mexico or Guatemala would come in, my boss would say, "Go talk to her. She'll help you." They would say, "Yeah, we're going to go see that *mexicana*," because I was the only Mexican there.

I had asked Yale for a deferment of two years, and I came back to California in April of 1995, toward the tail end of the fight against Proposition 187. That September I was planning to go back to school. But then I started volunteering for CHIRLA that April. It was after Prop 187, and I started running the hotline. They offered me a job, and I told them I could only do one more year, but I ended up staying.

RM: I know you weren't there at the very start, but could you tell us the history of how CHIRLA was formed?

AS: It started in 1986, when a bunch of organizations came together to form CHIRLA. They needed a group that was not all Mexican, or all Central American, or all Asian, a space where all immigrants could unite and strategize together. The first director was a priest, Father Luis Olivares, from Our Lady Queen of Angels church, which was a sanctuary for Central Americans at the time. When IRCA passed, CHIRLA got a big grant from the Ford Foundation to do outreach and education in the community and to help them apply for the amnesty program.

The other piece of IRCA was employer sanctions, and CHIRLA also tried to educate people about what this meant and to educate immigrants about workers' rights. The organization has always been involved with worker rights, from the very beginning. And it would also participate in coalition-building—that's why the word coalition is in its name. It was the place, and continues to be the place, where people and organizations gather to develop strategy on these issues.

RM: Which organizations were part of that coalition in the beginning?

AS: It was a mix of new organizations and very old ones. It included CARECEN [the Central American Resource Center], the Asian Pacific Legal Center, La Hermandad Mexicana, and the International Institute, the group that helped my family get legal status. Also they had El Rescate, a lot of activist legal groups, and Our Lady Queen of

Angels. The Catholic Church was very involved from the start.

DB: *Tell us about the growth of worker centers and other immigrant rights organizations in the 1980s and 1990s, the story of that surge of activity.*

AS: In California things really took off with Prop 187 in 1994. But there was a lot of work before that, starting in the late eighties, around day laborers and domestic workers. In 1989, the Harbor City Day Labor Center opened, and a little one opened up in North Hollywood. Then in 1991, our domestic worker committee was formed. CHIRLA advocated for day labor centers with the city of Los Angeles, and in 1997 we started running the day labor centers with city funding, which allowed us to hire more staff. We were also having a fight with L.A. County about the rights of day laborers to look for work on street corners. In 2000, we won a precedent-setting case that established that right. Organizers came from all over to visit CHIRLA to understand what we had done, and that led to the creation of even more worker centers around the country and eventually to the formation of the National Day Laborer Organizing Network (NDLON).

So workers' rights was always a central component of our work. As a result of subcontracting and employer sanctions, we began to see more and more wage theft and other abuses in the garment industry, restaurants, the ethnic grocery stores, and so on, not just day labor and domestic work. For example, we helped form the Garment Worker Center in L.A. to help protect their rights. At first we didn't have much to do with the unions, some of whom were suspicious of immigrants, but as the leadership slowly changed, there was more synergy, and we built those connections.

Around this time, we also got a big grant from the Open Society Foundation to work on citizenship drives, which we thought of as the way to build power so we would never have a repeat of Prop 187. Many progressives and labor leaders who were pro-immigrant began to run for office. We knew that immigrants needed to build electoral power, so we began to work with Mi Familia Vota, a one hundred percent union-led effort.

The other big fight CHIRLA was involved in was around driver's licenses, because in 1994, the state passed a law requiring a residency card to renew your license. By the late nineties, people's licenses were expiring and they needed to drive to work. So that was the beginning of the driver's license campaign. We also started working on in-state tuition for undocumented students, to help young people who wanted to go to college. So by the turn of the century, we were engaged in many campaigns, continuing our fight for workers' rights but also working on access to higher ed, and access to driver's licenses. Our first big victory was in 2001, when we won in-state tuition for undocumented students in California.

DB: Can you describe the origins of the national push for mass legalization in the 1990s?

AS: We gradually became more involved in national organizing, especially after the 1996 Illegal Immigration Reform and Immigrant Responsibility Act (IIRIRA). Deepak, I will always remember the day that we met in Washington, DC. By then I was the executive director at CHIRLA, and for a while we had been meeting quarterly in DC with five other state-based immigrant rights coalitions to share information and learn from each other. You came to tell us about the National Campaign for Jobs and Income Support, a grassroots coalition sponsored by Community Change to fight for economic justice, which three of us decided to join. That was transformational for the immigrant rights movement, because it connected us to multi-racial anti-poverty groups organizing around housing, transportation, and access to the safety net. The relationship between immigrant rights and multi-racial community organizations that emerged in that space was crucial. Immigrant rights groups learned the difference between the policy advocacy that we had been doing before and true grassroots organizing, and at the same time we challenged the economic justice groups to see immigration as integral to poverty reduction.

Part of the National Campaign was a subcommittee for legalization. It was the first national formation that dared to advance a demand for amnesty at the national level. That led to the formation of the Fair Immigration Reform Movement (FIRM), a national coalition of grassroots immigrant rights groups and coalitions, which soon became the backbone of the national movement for immigration reform. FIRM connected all the local work we were doing—with day laborers, with immigrant students, and with domestic workers—to something bigger. Before that, our local work didn't fit as well into the policy and advocacy of our colleagues in DC. But afterward it felt like our leaders and organizers finally had a national home.

This was significant because immigrant communities had to contend with so many attacks at the same time, and we needed a national vehicle to respond. With Prop 187, and then welfare reform and IIRIRA, people were losing their rights. U.S.-citizen and mixed-status families started seeing their loved ones who had committed minor crimes in the past suddenly be picked up by immigration authorities. There was more and more evidence that lacking status meant having things taken away from you. Suddenly access to going to the hospital and getting care was being taken away. Suddenly your husband or wife could be deported because of a drug offense they had as a teenager. We organized a group at CHIRLA called Citizens and Immigrants for Equal Justice, made up of U.S. citizens who had had their family members deported because of IIRIRA.

There was a big push from community-based organizations to say, "Wait, this is unacceptable." People just wanted to be formally recognized and to live without fear. That led us to focus more and more on winning a path to legalization. If we have papers, we will regain access to driver's licenses, our kids will go to college. And labor exploitation will be curtailed because employers won't be able to use legal status to get power over workers.

The demand from our community was for a new amnesty as the solution. There were a few key labor leaders—Maria Elena Durazo, Eliseo Medina, Arturo Rodriguez—who had this vision that nothing moves without immigrant labor. They were kindred spirits. But it's important to remember that the demand for a new amnesty as a solution emerged from the community and immigrant rights organizations. The community pushed labor, because at the time a lot of unions were hostile to immigrants. So when the AFL-CIO embraced amnesty in 2000, it felt like the culmination of a lot of work—all the external pressure from community groups and the internal organizing by progressive labor leaders paid off.

I remember that some of our national partners felt like the demand for legalization was not realistic. I was told, "You're creating false expectations." But through the National Campaign for Jobs and Income Support and then FIRM, we forced the conversation about federal immigration reform. With the leadership of Community Change, a new immigrant rights coalition took shape, with a circle of other like-minded groups. It's staggering to see how many immigrant rights coalitions exist now. This did not happen by accident. It was a strategic decision by the existing immigrant rights coalitions in FIRM and Community Change to create and nurture new organizations in states like Tennessee, Wisconsin, Florida, Arizona, and Colorado, where there had been huge growth in the numbers of immigrants but very little organizational infrastructure. We knew we needed a footprint across the country to be able to pass national legislation.

DB: I think the audacity of immigrant leaders was crucial. Skeptics were saying, "These people think that they can pass a bill through Congress to legalize millions of people? Them and what army? How's that going to happen?" It just changed the whole conversation.

AS: Citizenship matters. It matters so damn much. You can't live persecuted and afraid. And yet that's how we live. I always say to our immigrant leaders, "Look, you guys, you have already demonstrated courage. You're here. You decided to leave your country, leave your family, your roots, your ancestors, everything, to have a better life. I don't see what better demonstration of courage there is! So we have to continue to have courage, to fight for our rights, and for our rightful place in this country, which we've earned."

DB: Can you talk about the emergence of the immigrant youth movement and its relationship to the broader movement?

AS: Around that time, CHIRLA went through a strategic planning process in which we decided to do more to include youth in the immigrant rights movement. We realized that no movement has ever won without young people. So we formed Wise Up, which focused on immigrant youth organizing starting in high school, and later we helped lead the California Dream Network. Nationally, through FIRM, we created a network called Youth Changing a Nation that brought together youth leaders from around the country. Many of them would later become nationally known leaders in the Dreamers movement. We launched the first national campaign to save a Dreamer, Marie Gonzalez, from deportation, along with her parents, under the banner "We Are Marie." Marie won a reprieve but her parents were deported to Costa Rica.

The dynamic between older and younger leaders has sometimes involved differences about strategy and tactics. There was a moment when we believed that these young people—because they translate for their parents in day-to-day life, they speak English, they are culturally American—maybe they can also be translators of the movement to Congress and the public? But the DREAM Act enabled some legislators to see young people as victims of bad decisions by their parents, which almost created a separation of the fight for young people from the fight for their families. Many of my adult leaders who have been in the fight for over twenty years, and who have always supported the DREAM Act, say, "Yes, but we need legal status too. I'm too old and

I'm still without papers. Maybe I need to return to my home country, where I can die with dignity." These are the kinds of hard conversations we have.

There is a reward in America for being "closer to whiteness," and because many of the youth leaders speak perfect English, they have gotten more attention than older immigrant leaders who are incredibly eloquent in their own languages but when they are translated they have not been listened to in the same way. Some of the movement's most difficult moments have come when we've faced choices about pursuing the DREAM Act instead of legislation that would legalize everyone, raising the age-old division between "deserving" and "undeserving" immigrants. More recently many young leaders have put forward a vision that is much more aggressive about including the whole community in legalization, which is a very positive development. I believe the power is with all of us, with the whole family fighting together.

RM: Let's turn to the huge 2006 immigrant rights marches. That was a national phenomenon, but with L.A. playing a key role. How did the momentum develop?

AS: The first big march in L.A. was on May 1, 2000, and they continued every May Day for years after that. Even in 2002, when we were still reeling from 9/11, we had a huge turnout for our May 1 march, with over 15,000 people marching in L.A. demanding legalization. But the anti-immigration push of the years after 9/11 was extreme.

In 2006, the fight was in response to the Sensenbrenner bill, H.R. 4437, which had been passed in the U.S. House of Representatives in late 2005. It would have made it a felony to be present in the country without papers, or to provide any help to undocumented immigrants. If they were in your car, you would be guilty of a felony for harboring and transporting them. That level of criminalization was just too much. It was a moment in which we all felt, "Enough is enough!" Across the country millions of people marched in over four hundred cities on May 1, 2006, including the largest march of half a million in Los Angeles.

It was a very important moment for the movement, to know what can happen when communities are activated with support from so many different forces. The churches actively called out the injustice of the act. The unions did the same thing. Latino elected leaders as well. And the ethnic press—everyone knows about the importance of the radio stations. But also it was other parts of the ethnic press. Everybody was on the same page: "This is wrong, we have to stand up, we have to demand what is right." It was the one time that I have seen everybody acting together, and those marches were so powerful. It didn't matter where you were. You were there. I knew something special was happening when my father was marching and I didn't even know he was going to be on the streets. He was like, "Of course I would be here!" And I was like, "No you wouldn't, you would be working!"

The next year, May 1, 2007, we got beaten up by the L.A. police. It was one of the scariest moments in my life. And that was no coincidence: in 2006 we march in the millions and in 2007 we get beat up by the LAPD. It was horrible. All of a sudden May 1 was tied to brutality and violence, and that repression created fear that depressed turnout at future marches.

DB: Can you speak about electoral strategies in the movement and what role they've played, in California and more broadly?

AS: One of the slogans of the 2006 marches was "Today we march, tomorrow we vote." We formed the We Are America alliance to spark a broad-based national movement for civic engagement across the country to build power. In fact, many of the people marching in 2006 were U.S. citizens, who were eligible to vote. But to connect the work of those mobilizations to participation in elections, we launched massive citizenship drives, helping people who were legal permanent residents to become naturalized citizens. One of the most important effects of the 2006 marches was the realization that mobilization at the polls has to be as important as mobilization in the streets, and vice versa. And it's not just getting our people into the voting booth, but also electing people who actually support a pro-immigrant agenda. We created political arms in states throughout the country like the CHIRLA Action Fund, 501(c)4 organizations, because we knew we needed to be able to tell voters who is on their side. We also learned through our campaign to pass national legislation that we needed 218 votes in the House and 60 votes in the Senate, which meant we had to expand beyond the big cities into small towns and rural areas, which also deepened the movement's reach. California is such a testament to the power of this strategy. In 2019, when the U.S. House of Representatives passed H.R. 6, the American Dream and Promise Act, many California House members wore green CHIRLA sashes we had given them. These members represented districts that had previously been represented by Republicans, and now they were supporting the DREAM and Promise Act. That moment was one of my biggest joys. It signaled a momentous power shift. Just look at how much California has changed!

DB: Let's talk about the Obama years and executive action. What are the lessons from that period that the movement needs to take to the next phase of the struggle?

AS: We did not realize how much opposition we had inside the Democratic Party when President Obama was elected. He came in with a promise of action on immigration reform. The economic downturn made it hard, of course, which is something we're also facing now. But we had focused on the president without doing enough to understand the Democratic political infrastructure. We thought they were on our side, but we misread that badly. Some of them saw us as a liability and opposed taking action on immigration. For them, health care was the winning issue. Rahm Emanuel and the moderate wing of the Democratic Party were in control, and we didn't understand that at the time. So there we were trying to convince the president, and yet there was a whole apparatus against us, and in the middle of an economic crisis.

As we move forward, we have to think about that. Next time we can't just think about the president. We need to look at the decision-making process more broadly. With that said, I also believe that President Obama did not exercise the full power that he had—not just on immigration but on many other things. What we did accomplish on his watch was due to the courage of our movement to really confront him and move him. We put a mirror to his face, forcing him to face what he was doing, including multiple tough meetings with him in the Roosevelt Room at the White House that I and other grassroots leaders were a part of, and waves of civil disobedience targeting the White House. He was continuing rather than challenging a legacy of punitive deportations which were terrorizing our communities.

Deepak, you did a great job of preparing us to go into those meetings with Obama, reminding us not to get star-struck, that if we did we would lose our way. This was the first time I'd ever been in the White House, and I decided that I had to tell him the truth about the pain in our communities and how he was putting our families in danger, even if it meant I would never be invited back. I believe to this day that he absolutely believed that immigration reform was something that needed to move forward. But he prioritized other issues and waited for Congress to take action, and that wait was incredibly harmful. The end result was that we got no legislation, and even worse, we got increased deportations.

One of the hardest moments was soon after a tough meeting with Obama, when I returned to California and learned that in Orange County there had been a huge raid. The disconnect between Obama's eloquence and rhetoric and the reality on the ground just pissed everybody off. I don't think anyone will ever forgive him or the Democratic Party for having had the House, the Senate, and still not doing immigration reform.

DB: *Looking ahead, what is your hope for the immigration rights movement in the post-Trump era?*

AS: We have to work to align the next administration and the Democratic Party, and force them to take real action on legalization and everything else we've been fighting for. Legalization of *all* the people who are undocumented has to be our primary demand. We need a legalization program that is actually accessible to people. I don't want to create a system that gets status for only a third of the undocumented—which is what happened with IRCA.

That's going to take time, but there are things that can happen right away. We need to release the children held in detention on day one. We need to hold people accountable for the caging of families and children, for those gross violations of human rights. And then there's the low-hanging fruit. We already have H.R. 6 for the Dreamers and TPS [Temporary Protected Status], finalizing legal status for them. That's an easy one. The same thing with farmworkers. We need legalization right away.

We also have to radically reconfigure enforcement and push for a moratorium on deportations while we're trying to fix the system. Otherwise we're going to be in the same boat we were in with Obama. Stopping deportations allows people to breathe while we struggle for permanent changes in the immigration system, changes that won't just lead to more undocumented people and more worker exploitation.

We can't lose sight of the fact that what we have now is a corrupt and racist immigration system, set up for the benefit of employers and against workers, against people of color. So if we want to dismantle it, what do we create in its place? I'm hopeful because I see so many more progressives in the Democratic Party. It's a real moment of opportunity. But we do have to strike while the iron is hot.

Note

1. This interview took place on July 9, 2020. It has been edited for length and clarity.

Part II

LESSONS OF ORGANIZING CAMPAIGNS

The Immigrant Youth Movement

Here to Dream and Here to Fight

Cristina Jiménez Moreta

My family and I migrated from Ecuador to New York in 1998. Like many immigrants, we were fleeing poverty and made the courageous decision to seek a better life in the United States. As undocumented immigrants, my family and I have experienced some of the worst this country has to offer: workplace exploitation, wage theft, racial profiling, fear of deportation, and police violence. But as part of the immigrant youth movement and United We Dream, I have also experienced the power of people coming together, taking action, and winning change. In this chapter, I share my history in that movement over the past two decades, highlighting its strategic victories and visions.

In 2001, I was a junior in high school preparing for the college application process. I had big dreams, but they were shattered when my school's college advisor told me that I could not go to college because I was undocumented. At first I felt hopeless and ready to give up. But my parents' sacrifices and their dreams of their children having not only food and shelter but also access to education in this country fueled my determination to defy my advisor. I searched for help and found teachers who helped me apply to the City University of New York (CUNY) and to join the fight for policy change at the state level that would allow students like me to go to college. Organizations like CUNY's union, the Professional Staff Congress; Jobs with Justice; Make the Road New York; the New York Immigration Coalition; and many others were leading a campaign to reinstate in-state tuition for undocumented students, which CUNY had eliminated in a spasm of nativism after 9/11. I was amazed to read in the local newspapers that undocumented students were fasting to pressure state legislators and the governor to pass a law changing this policy. These efforts proved successful and in 2002, a few weeks before my first semester in college, New York's governor, George Pataki, signed a new law guaranteeing in-state tuition for undocumented students across the state.

I and many of the other co-founders of the United We Dream Network had joined state-based immigrant rights organizations around the country as young students. We had dreams of a college education, but we also organized out of survival: to protect ourselves and our families from deportation. In the early 2000s, about 65,000 undocumented students were graduating from high school each year.[1] All of us lived with the fear of deportation and family separation, while facing barriers to college education, exploitation at work, and a future filled with uncertainty. But young undocumented immigrants were fighting back against these injustices in places like California, Texas, New York, Florida, Colorado, Illinois, and Massachusetts. In New York, California, and Massachusetts, we were engaged in tuition equity campaigns anchored in state-based immigrant rights organizations. California's and New York's undocumented youth organizing also had support from statewide immigrant advocacy coalitions and networks of campus-based organizations. These groups provided a space for us to develop organizing and advocacy skills, but young people had limited autonomy and were not yet in leadership roles. The parent organizations controlled the campaign strategies.

Tuition equity advocacy efforts resulted in many states passing in-state tuition laws like the one in New York that benefited me. That allowed undocumented students to go to college and pay the lower in-state resident tuition rates, but undocumented students still had no access to financial aid. And these laws offered no protection from deportation for young immigrants or their families, nor did they provide pathways to adjust their immigration status or gain U.S. citizenship. Since immigration law is a federal matter, only the U.S. Congress could deliver such protection. In 2001, the Development, Relief, and Education for Alien Minors Act, which soon became known as the DREAM Act, was introduced by Senators Durbin (D-IL) and Hatch (R-UT). If enacted, that proposed law would protect people like me from deportation and also provide many undocumented youth with a pathway to citizenship.

Although immigrant youth continued leading local tuition equity campaigns, as well as efforts to give undocumented students access to financial aid, the need for a permanent solution at the federal level led us to focus increasingly on the DREAM Act. Along with other immigrant rights and civil rights advocates, we started to come together nationally to work toward that goal, with the acknowledgment that the DREAM Act would be one of the possible legislative solutions for undocumented families. The New York State Youth Leadership Council; the Student Immigrant Movement in Massachusetts; the University Leadership Initiative in Austin, Texas; Students Working for Equal Rights in Florida; and the California Dream Network were among the early groups building momentum for immigrant youth organizing.

The effort was set back by the terrorist attacks of September 11, 2001, which conflated immigration and national security in new and troubling ways. Suddenly all immigrants were suspected of being terrorists. In 2002, President Bush created the Department of Homeland Security (DHS), within which immigration and immigrants were considered matters of national security, even as Muslims and immigrants of color were increasingly targeted by racial profiling, often leading to detention and/or deportation. Two young undocumented immigrants threatened with deportation—Kamal Essaheb in New York and Marie Gonzalez in Missouri—were among the thousands impacted by the post-9/11 enforcement regime. Their cases spurred a campaign demanding that they be allowed to remain in the United States.

Together with activists and organizers from across the country, I poured myself into the work to stop Kamal's and Marie's deportations. We mobilized people to write letters and to telephone elected officials demanding that the government allow them to stay in the United States, winning extensive media attention. Although Marie's parents were deported, our organizing efforts stopped the deportation of Marie and Kamal. This was a bittersweet moment, but it taught me that people closest to the pain are also closest to the solutions that our communities need. At the time it was unheard of for undocumented immigrants to publicly fight to remain in the United States and stop deportations. Yet undocumented youth and their families, in defiance of conventional wisdom, launched campaigns to share their stories, pressure those with decision-making power, and win deportation relief. These were the first national campaigns that I joined, and that led me to commit to the work of ending detention and deportations and to building a youth-led movement for immigrant justice.

Participation in these campaigns forged deeper relationships among immigrant-youth-led state groups, and by 2005 we were regularly working together to stop deportations and to advocate for the passage of the DREAM Act at the federal level. National organizations like the National Immigration Law Center, Community Change, and the National Council of La Raza provided legislative analysis and trainings, as well as resources for conference calls and convenings, enabling the various undocumented-student-led groups around the country to develop a joint campaign strategy. With their support, undocumented youth not only shared their stories with members of Congress and in the mainstream media but also developed tactics like mock "Dream graduations," staged in Washington, DC, to pressure Congress to pass the DREAM Act.

Over time, however, many undocumented youth began to question and challenge the conventional wisdom of some of the established immigrant rights organizations, as well as advocates and academics, in regard to narrative and strategy. We began to reject the narrative about undocumented youth that depicted us as "exceptional immigrants," honor roll students and valedictorians, as well as the notion that we were brought to this country "through no fault of our own," which the parent organizations believed would be most effective in persuading the public and policymakers to support the DREAM Act. We came to believe that this narrative further criminalized immigrants by positioning "deserving" young immigrants in contrast to their "undeserving" parents, many of whom had risked their own lives to come to the United States to give their children a better life.[2]

The conventional wisdom among immigrant rights advocates was that the movement's legislative strategy needed to turn down the volume on the DREAM Act and focus squarely on a comprehensive immigration reform (CIR) bill. That package of policies, including the DREAM Act, would marry increased enforcement and border security with a pathway to citizenship for the undocumented and the ability to bring in future workers needed by the U.S. labor market.

Immigrant youth leaders increasingly disagreed with that strategy and began to long for an autonomous space. As undocumented youth directly impacted by the injustices of systemic racism and the immigration system, we wanted to disrupt and reshape the politics, policy, and discourse on immigration, and to build a movement of young people to fight for immigrant justice.

By 2007, both CIR and the DREAM Act had repeatedly failed to win over Congress, undercutting the theory that the only way for legislation to move forward was as a comprehensive package. Against that backdrop, undocumented youth and their allies decided to create an autonomous national organization, leading in 2008 to the creation of the United We Dream (UWD) Network by youth-led organizations from New York, Massachusetts, Florida, California, Colorado, and Texas. As co-founders, we envisioned building an organization that would transcend the CIR framework and a narrow focus on legislation, and instead build a sustainable movement led by young undocumented immigrants. By then we had developed substantial organizing skills, which we wanted to use to defend our communities from deportation and to ensure that all immigrants, regardless of immigration status, could live without fear, accomplish their dreams, and thrive.

UWD's leadership, majority female and queer, set out to build a national campaign to pass the DREAM Act and to expand our network by recruiting and training immigrant youth. Today it is the largest immigrant-youth-led organization in the United States, with over eight hundred thousand members across twenty-eight states.

UWD played the roles of convener, catalyst, and mass recruiter and trainer for the immigrant youth movement. National convenings brought hundreds of undocumented youth and allies together to strategize and learn organizing and campaigning skills. That resulted in a relentless campaign to win passage of the DREAM Act by Congress in 2010. Inspired by the civil rights and LGBTQ movements, we led "coming out" actions, sit-ins at congressional offices, fasts, a walk from Florida to Washington, DC, and mass mobilizations at the U.S. Capitol.[3] The campaign went against the conventional wisdom among advocates of CIR, but it successfully forced members of Congress to vote on the bill. The DREAM Act passed that year in the House of Representatives but failed in the Senate by five votes.

That failure to win passage of the DREAM Act, although disappointing, ultimately made the movement stronger as all of us deepened our commitment to the fight. Young immigrants and their families were still living with the threat of deportation, even as the number of immigrants facing deportations kept increasing. The urgency of stopping deportations, and the development of a power analysis suggesting that congressional action was unlikely, led immigrant youth leaders to rethink our strategies and consider alternatives to legislative action.

Part of that process involved learning from grassroots movement organizations fighting deportations, such as Families for Freedom in New York, as well as working with movement lawyers to explore alternative tactics to stop deportations. We soon realized that, in the absence of congressional action, President Obama had the power to administratively stop deportations of young immigrants. Obama had publicly committed to passing immigration reform, and he was preparing to run for reelection in 2012. At UWD's 2011 national congress, attended by more than two hundred undocumented youth and allies, we launched a national Education, Not Deportation effort along with the Right to Dream campaign, to intensify the pressure on President Obama to stop the deportations of young people.

Immigrant youth leaders from UWD and other immigrant-youth-led organizations coordinated efforts to increase the pressure on the president to act. Contrary to the arguments used by the White House, we knew, and we let the public know, that Obama in fact had the power and legal authority to issue an administrative order to stop the deportations of immigrant youth. After almost two years of campaigning, sharing stories, exposing the human impact of the enforcement regime, fighting deportations publicly, and leading direct action and civil disobedience, our movement succeeded in June 2012, when President Obama issued an executive order creating the Deferred Action for Childhood Arrivals (DACA) program, which protected close to eight hundred thousand young people from deportation. Our movement successfully created the conditions that led members of Congress to pressure President Obama to take action and led him to do so. DACA was the most significant policy breakthrough and victory on immigration in almost three decades.

The DACA victory also created an unprecedented organizing and power-building opportunity, as UWD offered support to undocumented immigrant youth who wanted to apply for DACA. That led us to recruit thousands of new people to the movement. Deportations, however, did not stop. Neither DACA nor administrative deportation priorities issued by the Obama administration protected the broader undocumented community from deportation. Immigration and

Customs Enforcement (ICE) and Customs and Border Patrol (CBP), the two agencies primarily responsible for immigration enforcement, both of which include agents with explicitly racist and white supremacist ideologies, continued to target immigrants for detention and deportation, with little oversight or accountability. Moreover, the Obama administration aggressively expanded enforcement programs and collaboration between ICE and local police, causing immigrants to be detained and deported for traffic stops and other minor violations. Under the political calculation that ramping up enforcement would bring Republicans to the negotiating table, the Obama administration deported a record number of immigrants. More than 3 million people and families were deported and/or separated from their loved ones during the eight years he was president, which led our movement to label Obama the "deporter in chief."[4] His administration failed to pass legislative immigration reforms that would provide a pathway to citizenship, while the enforcement regime steadily grew in resources and power. This exposed the false logic that victories for immigrants are possible only if our movement publicly accepts increases in enforcement.[5]

While a path to citizenship for undocumented people has still not been realized, the CIR policy framework that more enforcement is a necessary precondition for it has normalized the growth of increasingly brutal deportation actions. Year after year, failure at the immigration policy negotiation table was followed by near-silent acceptance of annual budget increases and increases in authority for ICE and CBP. Those two agencies together employ over eighty thousand people, with a massive budget of $25.3 billion in 2020 ($8.4 billion for ICE and $16.9 billion for CBP), more than all other federal law enforcement agencies combined.[6] Their charge is massive as well, ranging from inspections of container ships to detaining and deporting immigrants. The deportation force of ICE and CBP, built by administrations led by both political parties, was completely unleashed under the Trump administration, as ICE and CBP agents put children in cages; targeted immigrants in workplaces, schools, places of worship, hospitals, and their homes; and broke down doors and abducted parents from their children, among other abuses. The Trump administration also was responsible for the deaths of twenty-four immigrants, including children, in detention camps.[7]

In the four years following Trump's election as president, immigrant communities experienced increasing deportations, ongoing threats to dismantle DACA, and a drastic reduction in refugee programs. In 2020 these injuries were compounded as immigrants suffered disproportionately from the impact of COVID-19. At the peak of the pandemic, for example, immigrants in meatpacking (a third of the industry's hourly workers are foreign-born) were forced to continue working shoulder to shoulder on the slaughterhouse line without proper protection. Twenty-five percent of the largest COVID-19 outbreaks in the country happened at meatpacking plants, with ten thousand cases tied to the industry.[8]

Yet undocumented workers and their families were excluded from federal pandemic relief. Immigrants are often the first responders to the human needs of America, but *their* human needs are continually ignored. Without jobs, with no unemployment support, and without access to health care and other safety net programs, undocumented immigrants were devastated by the pandemic, which compounded the damage inflicted by expanded policing and immigration enforcement in recent years.

Despite these painful realities, our movement persists and continues to grow, led by directly impacted young immigrants. We have achieved significant victories like DACA, which changed the narrative and politics of immigration and even survived the initial attacks of the Trump administration when it won support in the Supreme Court. But our goal is for all people in this country, regardless of immigration status, to live freely, with full dignity, and have the ability to thrive. In order to get there, we must be part of the larger struggle against white supremacy and racism, rooted in interlocking systems of policing, mass incarceration, and immigration enforcement that by design target immigrants and communities of color. We must also face the reality that past strategies have failed, leading to more criminalization, detention, and deportations, creating more harm and pain in our communities.

At United We Dream, most of our staff, leaders, and members are immigrant youth and families who are undocumented and have personally experienced the pain and trauma of a political system that has increasingly normalized immigration enforcement. UWD alone has fought against more than a thousand deportation cases in the last decade, and on a weekly basis we receive hundreds of calls to Migra Watch, our free call-in hotline, which offers immigrants help when facing detention and deportation.[9] Our key demands are to end deportation and detention, abolish ICE, and win citizenship for all. They reflect our practical assessment of the CIR legislative framework and strategy, which has repeatedly failed.

Organizations of Muslim and black immigrants have been calling for abolishing ICE since its inception post-9/11, long before this demand gained greater traction in the movement. Organizations such as Families for Freedom and Desis Rising Up and Moving (DRUM) in New York City have been at the forefront of this movement, although until recently their demands to abolish the system were often considered unrealistic, non-strategic, and "fringe" by the broader immigrant rights movement. Under the Trump administration, however, after the implementation in 2018 of the zero-tolerance policy that separated more than three thousand migrant children from their parents and put them in cages, the demand to abolish ICE moved into the mainstream, winning support from large segments of the immigrant rights movement as well as the broader progressive and social justice movements.[10]

Although we did not always have a sophisticated abolitionist analysis and framework, over the last decade UWD leaders have made the demand for abolition central to our vision, work, and movement strategy. Because of our lived experience, we know that ICE and local police work together to racially profile immigrants. For many in our communities, a traffic stop or any other contact with local police is the first entry point to the deportation pipeline. ICE can request that local jails, without court approval, detain undocumented immigrants for an additional forty-eight hours so that they can be taken into custody and deported, even in the absence of criminal charges. UWD unequivocally stands with the demand by the Movement for Black Lives to defund the police, because we know that the police, ICE, and CBP work together to disproportionally target Black immigrants. We also know that the same people who profit from the mass incarceration of U.S.-born Black and Brown people also profit from immigrant detention and deportation.

Many organizations have ramped up calls to dismantle the deportation machine and have also joined the demands of Black organizers and communities to defund the police and end systematic racism. One way in which UWD and partners such as the Detention Watch Network are advancing this work is through a national campaign to defund the deportation force, #DefundHate, whose demands include abolishing ICE, ending detention, defunding the deportation force, and protecting people from detention and deportation permanently without hurting the immigrant community.

Public opinion has become increasingly supportive of immigrants. A 2019 Gallup Poll found that 81 percent of the American people believe that undocumented people should be permitted to become U.S. citizens.[11] Another survey that year conducted by the Pew Research Center found that 62 percent of respondents believe that immigrants strengthen the country.[12] And in 2020, Gallup reported that the share of Americans who favor expanded immigration exceeds the share who want less, for the first time since they began asking the question in 1965.[13] In addition, ICE has become one of the least popular federal agencies—with 45 percent of people surveyed by Pew in March 2020 viewing it negatively.[14]

For those who disagree with our demands and point to a lack of majority support for abolishing ICE or defunding deportation, it is useful to remember that in the early 1960s, polls showed that a majority of Americans did not support civil rights protests either.[15] It often takes time to win public acceptance. But the cultural and political shifts necessary to provide relief to our people are underway. For example, negotiations with the Defund Hate Coalition, which includes Indivisible, MoveOn, and many other progressive organizations, helped to stop over $7 billion from going to the deportation force.[16] And our efforts have led the number of House members committed to rejecting more funds for ICE and CBP (through votes on DHS appropriation bills) to grow from nineteen in February 2019 to seventy-five in December 2019—about one-third of the Democratic caucus.[17] Our demands also gained traction among Democratic presidential candidates, with Senators Warren and Sanders committing to the dismantling of the deportation machine during the presidential primaries of 2019.[18] The movement to defund the police, led by the Movement for Black Lives, is also gaining traction.

The Deferred Action for Childhood Arrivals program has brought concrete benefits for nearly eight hundred thousand immigrant young people without enforcement trade-offs. Far from a permanent victory, DACA was a stepping-stone, though it brought crucial safety for those who benefited from it. We must push for much larger and more permanent administrative and legislative changes under the new Democratic administration, including an immediate moratorium on deportations, the expansion of deportation relief programs like DACA, halting all detention of children and families, and ending collaboration between ICE and local police. We also must push to defund the deportation force, to repeal the 1996 immigration laws that criminalize immigrants, and to win a pathway to citizenship for all undocumented people.

We should not rely on the same analysis in 2050 as we do in 2020, and by the same token, our analysis in 2020 should be different today than when I started organizing in 2002. We are engaged in a lifelong journey toward racial, gender, and economic justice. With each victory, our sense of what is possible should grow and our understanding of the vulnerabilities of our adversaries should deepen. A world where our communities do not have to live with the fear of deportation and detention is possible. A world in which ICE does not exist and where the safety, health care, education, and well-being of our communities is a priority is possible. I have witnessed and participated in a movement of undocumented people who have transformed the politics and policy of immigration with a bold vision of freedom and dignity for all people, regardless of immigration status. That movement has shown that a new world is possible, if we follow the leadership and vision of those closest to the pain and injustice.

Notes

1. See Jeffrey S. Passel, "Further Demographic Information Relating to the DREAM Act," Urban Institute, Oct. 21, 2003, www.nilc.org/wpcontent/uploads/2015/11/dream_demographics.pdf.

2. See Walter Nicholls, *The DREAMers: How the Undocumented Youth Movement Transformed the Immigrant Rights Debate* (Palo Alto, CA: Stanford University Press, 2013).

3. On the phenomenon of female and queer leadership in the larger immigrant youth movement, see Veronica Terriquez, "Intersectional Mobilization, Social Movement Spillover, and Queer Youth Leadership in the Immigrant Rights Movement," *Social Problems* 62, no. 3 (2015): 343–62.

4. See Muzaffar Chishti, Sarah Pierce, and Jessica Bolter, "The Obama Record on Deportations: Deporter in Chief or Not?," Migration Policy Institute, Jan. 26, 2017, www.migrationpolicy.org/article/obama-record-deportations-deporter-chief-or-not.

5. The failure to pass any CIR bills is not limited to the Obama years. Since 2005, four major CIR bills have failed to pass Congress: The Border Protection, Antiterrorism, and Illegal Immigration Control Act of 2005 (H.R. 4437, as passed by the House in the 109th Congress), the Comprehensive Immigration Reform Act of 2006 (S. 2611, as passed by the Senate in the 109th Congress), the Comprehensive Immigration Reform (S. 1639, as considered by the Senate in the 110th Congress), and the Border Security, Economic Opportunity, and Immigration Modernization Act (S. 744, as passed by the Senate in the 113th Congress).

6. American Immigration Council, "The Cost of Immigration Enforcement

and Border Security," Sept. 23, 2013, www.americanimmigrationcouncil.org /research/the-cost-of-immigration-enforcement-and-border-security.

7. NBC News, "24 Immigrants Have Died in ICE Custody Under the Trump Administration," June 9, 2019.

8. Alexander Stephens and William D. Lopez, "Governments and Corporations Have Deemed Immigrant Workers Expendable During the Pandemic," *Jacobin,* May 11, 2020.

9. United We Dream, "The Truth About ICE and CBP: A Comprehensive Analysis of the Devastating Impact of the Deportation Force by Immigrant Youth and Families Who Know It Best," Feb. 2019, unitedwedream.org/wp-content /uploads/2019/02/TheTruthICECBP-02052019-v3.pdf.

10. "How Abolish ICE Helped Bring Abolitionist Ideas into the Mainstream," *Vox,* July 9, 2020.

11. Gallup, "Immigration, Public Opinion and Congress," Feb. 12, 2019, news.gallup.com/opinion/polling-matters/246665/immigration-public-opinion -congress.aspx.

12. Pew Research Center, "Majority of Americans Continue to Say Immigrants Strengthen the U.S.," Jan. 31, 2019, www.pewresearch.org/fact-tank/2019/01/31 /majority-of-americans-continue-to-say-immigrants-strengthen-the-u-s.

13. Gallup, "Americans Want More, Not Less, Immigration for First Time," July 1, 2020, news.gallup.com/poll/313106/americans-not-less-immigration-first -time.aspx.

14. This poll found the public almost evenly divided in their favorable/unfavorable view of the agency (46 to 45 percent). Pew Research Center, "Public Holds Broadly Favorable Views of Many Federal Agencies, Including CDC and HHS," Apr. 9, 2020, www.pewresearch.org/politics/2020/04/09/public-holds-broadly -favorable-views-of-many-federal-agencies-including-cdc-and-hhs.

15. Gallup, "Protests Seen as Harming Civil Rights Movement in the '60s," Jan. 21, 2019, news.gallup.com/vault/246167/protests-seen-harming-civil-rights -movement-60s.aspx.

16. Personal observation.

17. Roll Call 87, H. J. Res. 31, United States House of Representatives, Feb. 19, 2019, clerk.house.gov/Votes/201987; Roll Call 690, H. R 1158, United States House of Representatives, Dec. 17, 2019, clerk.house.gov/Votes/2019690?Page=2.

18. Simon Lewis, "Democrat Sanders Vows to Halt Immigration Raids, Deportations if Elected President," Reuters, Nov. 7, 2019; Gregory Krieg and Leyla Santiago, "Elizabeth Warren Says She's Open to Moratorium on Deportations as Part of Immigration Negotiations," CNN, Nov. 8, 2019.

The Nevada Turnaround

Immigrant Workers Build Political Power

An Interview with D. Taylor

D. Taylor is the international president of UNITE HERE, a union whose three hundred thousand members work across the United States in the hospitality industry as well as a variety of other sectors. As staff director starting in 1990 and then as secretary-treasurer from 2002 to 2012, Taylor played a critical role in building one of UNITE HERE's most dynamic and powerful locals, Culinary Workers Local 226 ("the Culinary") in Las Vegas, Nevada, which represents casino and hotel workers up and down the Vegas Strip. A majority of Culinary members are women and people of color, and many are immigrants, coming from over 170 countries and speaking forty languages. After a bruising strike and membership losses in the 1980s, Taylor helped to rebuild and restructure the Culinary as a rank-and-file union whose diverse and growing membership increasingly took the lead in its organizing and political work. Today, immigrant rights are at the center of the union's political action. Through its Citizenship Project, the union has helped more than eighteen thousand Nevadans become U.S. citizens, and Culinary members have registered tens of thousands of voters and knocked on hundreds of thousands of doors to support pro-immigrant, pro-worker politicians and policy. The Culinary has been the driving force behind Nevada's march from "red to blue," decisively supporting Hillary Clinton in 2016 and making Nevada the only state to flip a Senate seat to the Democrats in 2018. In this interview with Ruth Milkman and Deepak Bhargava, Taylor discusses his union's strategic and transformative commitment to immigrant rights, its success in developing immigrant leaders and leaders of color, and how its multi-racial, robust rank-and-file model might be useful to other unions' struggles for immigrant rights and progressive political change.[1]

RM: *Let's start with the history of your union and the role of immigrants in it.*

DT: Our union was founded in 1891. The hotel and restaurant industries have always been gateways for recent arrivals to the United States, and so the history of our union has been an immigrant tale. Today about half of our members are foreign-born. In the early days, the workers were mostly Irish, Italian, and East European Jewish. By the second and third generations, they were no longer considered immigrants. But then in the 1960s and 1970s, a new wave of immigrants came into the union from Asia, Latin America, and sometimes Africa. In the nineties, we also had lots of refugees from places like Bosnia and Serbia. We also have had a lot of African American members for most of our history.

My own experience with the union began in restaurants in Williamsburg, Virginia, where I'm from. There the workforce was largely broken down by race. You had a lot of white folks in the front of the house, and the back of the house was largely African American. An exception was the waiters from the old railroad unions, where almost all the servers had been African American. When the dining cars went away, those waiters came into restaurants. We had a lot of African American waiters who had come from the rail cars in the restaurant where I first became a shop steward.

But depending on what part of the country you are in, it varies. In the San Francisco Bay Area, you still had the Irish, second or third generation, and Italians, front of the house. In the back you had mostly Asians and some Latinos. Not too many African Americans. When I first came to Las Vegas in 1984, it was predominantly white and African American, and the only Latino population was Cuban—people who left after Castro shut down the casino industry. For them, Vegas was the largest relocation destination outside of Miami. And I remember when I was doing a campaign in New York in 1985. That was the first time I had run into Latinos from a lot of different places. Before I had worked with Mexicans and Cubans, but then when I hit the East Coast, there were a lot more from the D.R. [Dominican Republic] and also Puerto Rican folks. Same thing in Atlantic City. In Boston, there are a lot more people from the West Indies, and the same thing in Toronto. So it depends on where you are.

No matter where they are from, people who have immigrated here mostly have come here with nothing, and they are tougher than nails. They've had to go through more crap than 90 percent of the people born in this country. Not only have they had to deal with poverty, they've had to deal with language, they've had to deal with culture, they've had to deal with status, all those things. They've had to deal with family issues and separation. So they're a lot tougher than all of us.

RM: *Today you have a lot of immigrant leaders in the union. How did that come about?*

DT: If you look at the history of the labor movement, its foundation and early growth was with immigrant workers, and many of them became leaders too. But later, the labor movement became pretty reactionary, because we viewed immigration as something that was undercutting labor. I credit [former UNITE HERE president] John Wilhelm for helping to turn that around. John was assigned to the West, and he looked around at who the workers were and who the potential workers were.

Some unions had immigrants in their membership, but the leadership was not reflective of that. But it was different out west. Local 2 in San Francisco was always a very, very progressive union. And L.A. and Las Vegas were transformed in the 1990s in some of the big fights we had. The Frontier strike in Las Vegas—when we were out for six years, four months, and ten days—was led by Latinas. Not solely, but they were the backbone. And when people are leading in a big fight, a lot of misconceptions go away. And out of that you get leaders. I think that helped people see that this was our future. And John really was the driver of that.

What really turned the switch for us was after 9/11, and the backlash against quote-unquote foreigners. Against immigrants. Soon after that Maria Elena Durazo, who was the head of our local in Los Angeles, came up with the idea of the Immigrant Worker Freedom Ride. The idea came from the 1960s civil rights freedom rides. I was very familiar with that, being from the South originally myself. We had all these buses converging on the Statue of Liberty in New York. The point of what we did there was to declare that we were not going to be afraid. Immigrants are what makes this country work. And we took that challenge head-on.

But in those years, we still had a real lack not just of immigrant leaders but of African American leaders too. I kept hearing this had to do with problems in the "pipeline." And I said, "Screw the pipeline. That's a BS excuse to have somebody not get moved up." I think it had a lot to do with some of our folks who are good progressive white college kids. If you didn't speak a certain way or have all the skills, you were not recognized as leadership material. So we needed a systematic way to give people training in English, and in other skills.

A lot of immigrant workers are natural leaders, but they are held back by their English, and often feel like they can't deal with management. To address this we started an educational program in the union a few years ago, both for folks whose first language is not English and for staff members and leaders who have not had the opportunity to have a good education in America. It's been largely Latinos and African Americans, and some Asians, who have participated. We ease them into leadership roles. If a member says, "Well, we have to negotiate a contract," we say, "No, just do a grievance first. That's really negotiations." Once they are comfortable with that, we build up from there. Are we where we need to be? No. But we've seen real improvement.

RM: How have you dealt with tensions between different groups of workers—immigrants, African Americans, and other U.S.-born workers?

DT: What we have found is that you have to unify people around their own economic self-interest. I'm not naive enough to think that's always easy. But I remember one time I was in negotiations, and we were talking about health care costs going up. This white bartender stands up, he was like in his fifties. And he goes, "You know, the problem with our health care costs, it's all these kids." He was looking at the large immigrant female Latino workforce in housekeeping. I go, "Nah, kids aren't expensive. You're expensive! You cost a lot more than kids. If you have heart problems or cancer, that's usually people in their fifties, not five- or six-year-olds." It was really funny.

The other way we worked to unify folks is to point out that we can't win alone, we can only win together. I know it sounds simple. I've seen many cases where different groups start talking about each other. That goes on, let's not be naive. And what you find when you break it down is that the boss has been pretty good at playing one group off another. So, as the union, you get folks talking and working together. "Listen, both groups are getting screwed, so why fight each other?" That kind of talk is important, but if you actually have to work on something together, that's when it really changes. For example, when we have negotiations, we have big negotiating committees. When you're in the trenches and they're shooting at you, you don't say, "What color are you?" You join forces and try to win.

You have to prove yourself trustworthy. I'm from the South, so I'm very familiar with the African American and white dynamic. What a lot of white folks don't understand is that the minute you come around to an African American, they're going to be suspicious. That's just how it is, so you have to prove yourself. It's also true in places like Atlantic City with white working-class folks, who might be pro-union and conservative about other things.

DB: I remember hearing about the union's efforts to deal with discrimination against African Americans in hiring, when employers had developed a preference for immigrant workers over African Americans and UNITE HERE made an effort to try to counter that. What was the process?

DT: First, we did surveys of our membership to show that the industries had systematically not hired African Americans. Then we negotiated changes using those statistics. I remember negotiating in '07, and we did a thorough survey of the gourmet food service on the Las Vegas Strip. There are a lot of gourmet rooms, but we had less than ten African American gourmet food servers. So I said to the management that we had to have a career ladder and a very specific target of training African Americans to get into that part of the industry. We also took away the excuse "Well, they're not trained." We've made particular efforts to recruit and train workers from the African American community and get them into our training centers. The training center in Vegas is run by an African American, and it's located in a heavily African American neighborhood, which also helps.

RM: Let's turn to Culinary Workers Local 226 in Las Vegas, which is unusual in so many ways. Nevada is a right-to-work state, and yet it's become this extraordinarily powerful and vibrant labor organization.

DT: Originally the local was built by a guy named Al Bramlet, in the 1950s and 1960s. He was a genius. He would leave Las Vegas for several months of the year and recruit labor. Poor African Americans in Louisiana, Arkansas, and Texas, and then high-skill front-of-the-house people from the Midwest and back East. They've died out now, but there used to be a Fordyce, Arkansas club and a Monroe, Louisiana club. When I worked there, I knew so many people from Monroe or Fordyce. When Bramlet started in 1954 there were a thousand members, and by '67 there were sixteen thousand, so that's a pretty good trajectory.

When I first came to Nevada, in the eighties, it was called the "Mississippi of the West." It was a cowboy town in every way possible. It was completely controlled by a few families, and I'm not talking about the Mafia. Wall Street had already taken over. The workforce was changing, with many more Latinos joining the African Americans and whites, but the whites still controlled the union.

We started building rank-and-file committees, and we tried to set up situations where people who didn't speak perfect English had the chance to be leaders and speak. We decided that we were going to fight for all workers, whether they were black, brown, yellow, white, or purple. And we had these epic fights. The Horseshoe was a nine-and-a-half-month strike in 1990, which we thought was a long strike until we had the Frontier strike, from 1991 to 1998. These struggles built the union and created a whole new generation of leaders.

But the biggest change came in 2002. Geoconda Argüello-Kline had become president of the Culinary. I was secretary-treasurer. And we made the contract fight all about housekeeping workers, who by that time were predominantly Latino, with a fair number of Bosnians and Serbians too.

We almost had a city-wide strike, because after 9/11, the companies had taken advantage of us, and people wanted blood! The leaders were Latinas. Our chant was "The housekeepers will take us to victory!" There was real empowerment in that. When people have ownership of something, they fight for more, they care about it more, it's theirs. If they don't have ownership, not so much.

DB: *What are the ingredients in the culture of the Culinary? What's the secret sauce?*

DT: Whatever we have done, it has been done by a lot of people. You only do good stuff with real teams, and we have a really good team. And for one thing, we're really tough on accountability. Every week, we have a chart. If you're a shop steward, your name is up here. All of the shop stewards sign members up; the staff do much less of that. The stewards say, "Okay, here's your list." They also collect tip cards for political action contributions. Vegas has by far the highest percentage of members who make the PAC contributions. You have to put your membership and your PAC numbers up in front of everybody every week: "From this hotel, here's how many members, here's how many tip cards I got this week." So people are accounted for.

Two, there's a lot of attention to detail. If you don't take care of grievances and problems in the workplace, you'll never get to doing the external work on the outside because you'll always have chaos on the inside. The boss is always trying to violate the contract. We've got a pretty strong shop steward system, and they're systematic about that. We've set up a separate grievance and arbitration department to focus on enforcement.

Another thing in that sauce is no PR or fake wars. You have to have real battles. When I hear people say, "We have to build a movement," I say, "Well, if you're talking about it, then you're missing the point. You have to confront the bosses, and you have to take risks." And you never know if you're going to win. You're always on the edge. It's not like we look for that, but that's just what the industry is. At the end of the day, you've got to walk the walk and not just talk the talk.

If you tell the workers all the information, almost all of them do the right thing. They might not agree with you at first. Some of the very best people I've ever organized were the people most resistant at first. Because they're tough, and they have a lot of pride. Folks sometimes are afraid of strong personalities, but I think the labor movement only gets built by bringing those strong personalities in.

Never underestimate how smart workers are. I don't care where they're from. They disprove Voltaire, who said that common sense is not so common. Workers have a lot of common sense. They're very practical. Sometimes we enter this with an ideological bent, and that's a big mistake. Workers are practical, because guess what: they have to survive! They don't give a hoot what you say, it's what you do.

Also, you need to have veterans as well as new blood. It's like in sports. You have an old veteran team, and if you never change it, after a while it doesn't work. The future is with the next generation, and we have to incorporate that energy along with a little wisdom. No movement has ever been built by old people!

So if you have faith in workers, you have an organizational structure, you hold people accountable, you expect a lot from folks, you work hard, and you figure out a strategy, not just a bunch of tactics, you can win.

DB: You've built a political powerhouse in Nevada. What was the path to do that, and how did it intersect with the labor organizing?

DT: If we do politics separate from the union organizing, it's a dead loser. We always make it about the union, because our members are no different than anybody else. They're pretty cynical about politicians. So we've never done it about a politician per se.

That's why we ran our own members. Our first member run was Maggie Carlton. She was a waitress at the Treasure Isle. In 1998 she won a seat in the state senate, and she's now over in the assembly side, chairing Ways and Means.

Our first really big race was in 1996, against a woman named Senator Sue Lowden, who owned the Santa Fe casino, where we had won an election. She was fighting the union. So we went for it: "So long, Sue!" She was the only incumbent that lost that year, and she was being groomed to be the next governor of Nevada.

We also made a difference in the '98 election, when Harry Reid ran against John Ensign and won. It was really about Sheldon [Adelson, the ultra-conservative political donor and casino magnate], who tried to recall two or three county commissioners who had voted with us.

DB: *Reid went from being not so good on immigration to being a champion of reform—how did that come about?*

DT: Well, after the 1994 Contract with America, we had a meeting with him, and I said, "Senator, we've got to make a little bit of change here." I remember telling him, "Senator, the future is not with those who voted for you in the past. The future is with who's going to vote for you in the future. And they're looking for somebody to be their champion." Now, I'm not sure what that did or did not do, but around that time we put this Latino woman in as the head of the Democratic Party in Nevada.

We do these big ground games, we always invite the politicians to come, and they look at the crowd, which is largely Latino. And we were getting voters who normally wouldn't register, or normally wouldn't vote, registered and to the polls. We were doing that not only in Las Vegas but also in Reno. Starting in '08, we started running operations in Reno too, because Washoe County [where Reno is] could be in Oklahoma. . . . We knew we had to win big in Clark County [where Las Vegas is], and break even in Washoe, because we were going to get killed in the rural areas.

In 2011, we also started working in Arizona, when we decided we were sick and tired of Sheriff Arpaio. Now, Arizona is a crazy-ass state. I thought Nevada was crazy, but it's nothing like Arizona. Arpaio was a symbol that we felt we had to take down. Arizona reminded me a lot of when I lived in California in the early eighties, where there was a huge disconnect between the voting population and who actually worked and lived there. And we wanted to change that. So we made Arpaio into our Pete Wilson. And we organized, we registered 35,000 people to vote in Phoenix, mainly very young Latinos. Our volunteers often were thirteen- or fourteen-year-olds who were documented in this country and their parents weren't, and they wanted to make a fundamental change. Even though we lost the Arpaio campaign, in fact we won.

Over the years we've continued to do diligent work in Nevada, which has become a completely blue state. We were the first union in the country to endorse Obama. I remember that was very tough, because there was a big divide between our African American members and our white members, and our immigrant workers. But in the end, we brought them together. We accelerated that even more in '16. We were the only swing state that went blue for Clinton. That year we also elected the first Latina to the U.S. Senate, Catherine Cortez Masto, and we changed the state legislature to all blue. In '18, we elected another woman, Jacky Rosen, who beat a Republican who had never lost any election in his lifetime, and we elected a governor.

This had a huge payoff. For the first time, we got collective bargaining rights for some state employees. So we have won real reforms in Nevada, which you would not expect in what was known as the "Mississippi of the West" only a few years ago.

The immigrant vote was crucial in all this. We realized that there was no central place for people to become naturalized citizens, so we set up a citizenship project. The union funded it at first. But then we figured out we could generate royalties from designated license plates, the Aztec Suns, and now that helps pay for the citizenship project. We also worked with the Boyd School of Law at UNLV to get free legal advice. Our citizenship project was the largest mover of folks into citizenship in the entire state. And it wasn't just Latinos; we had Afghanis, Iraqis, Chinese. Yvanna Cancela, the state senator, who used to be the Culinary's political director, now directs that citizenship project. It's been systematized over a long period of time, and it's an ongoing institution.

So now we have one-stop shopping. We have the training academy, the citizenship project, and the housing fund all in one place. Now people don't have to go to three or four different offices, and the union pays for the day-to-day operations.

DB: *What should we be doing in terms of the immigrant struggle in the next period?*

DT: We need to find a systematic way to lift up the immigrant story. I don't think "Well, your grandparents were immigrants too" works. If it did, we wouldn't have had the problems we have faced in the Trump era. We have an opportunity right now, in this pandemic, when a large number if not the majority of essential workers are made visible as immigrant workers or people of color. We've got to make them heroes. If you look at the number of nurses who are foreign-born, it's a huge number. And that's just one piece of it. We should focus on these workers and lift up not just who they are but also the work that they do. And because the government does not give a shit about them, we also need to make it clear that unionization is their only real protection. We have to unionize these folks, and we have to fight.

After 9/11, firefighters were the greatest people in the world, but that went away pretty quickly when the Republicans started going after public sector pensions. The same thing will happen here if we don't seize on this opportunity. Let's keep on reminding people exactly who helped save America. Then we can have a different conversation about immigration!

Note

1. This interview took place on May 13, 2020. It has been edited for length and clarity. The text also includes excerpts from Taylor's remarks at the CUNY School of Labor and Urban Studies webcast, "Rethinking Immigration," May 1, 2020.

Taking on Corporate Complicity in the Trump Era

The "Corporate Backers of Hate" Campaign

Javier H. Valdés, Deborah Axt, Daniel Altschuler, and Angeles Solis

For many years, the primary focus of analysis in U.S. immigration politics has been inside the Beltway. Will federal immigration reform pass? If so, what constituencies will come together and what could a final bill look like? Some important analysis has also focused on state and local campaigns, by immigrant rights and anti-immigrant forces alike, and their implications for the national conversation. Much less attention, however, has been paid to efforts to hold corporations accountable for their role in the immigration system—and immigration enforcement in particular. In this chapter, we tell the story of one such effort, a campaign focused on private immigrant detention and the technology that helps the deportation machine run, which we believe has wider implications for both policy and the strategic orientation of the immigrant rights movement going forward.

When Donald Trump won the 2016 election, members and staff at Make the Road New York (MRNY), where we work, were crestfallen. As immigrants and working-class people of color who've lived in this country for years, they had long been aware of the presence of white supremacy in this country. But, even for those who'd been on the receiving end of xenophobic and racist attacks, the ascent of an unabashed racist to the White House was beyond the pale. The next four years would mean the fight of our lives.

A great deal of that fight involved resisting the worst excesses of the Trump administration's policies. From the Muslim ban to the zero-tolerance border policies and increasingly militarized ICE raids that target our communities, and more, our members have had to stand up time and again to denounce the terrifying decisions being made in Washington. We have also dedicated ourselves to expanding protections and support for communities through state and municipal governments—for instance, new policies in Westchester and New York City that limit cooperation with federal immigration enforcement and the restoration of access to driver's licenses for all immigrants in New York.

But as we analyzed the landscape in 2016, we also identified another crucial dimension to the attacks on our community: corporate power. Even before Trump took office, it was clear that the profit motive was fueling the criminalization of immigrant communities, with corporate actors seeking enormous contracts and then advocating for the expansion of anti-immigrant policies and more detention. For instrumental as well as intrinsic reasons, removing the profit motive from the equation has become critical to achieving a progressive vision of immigration policy.

With a corporate tycoon in the White House, we knew that the corporate pressure to expand detention would only grow. Predictably, many of the United States' biggest corporations lined up to benefit from the new administration's policy agenda. Private prison and immigrant detention companies such as Geo Group and CoreCivic, which had suffered a major blow when the Obama administration announced they would cease federal contracting in 2016, donated heavily to Trump's campaign and inauguration. Oil companies and financial institutions including JPMorgan Chase and Chevron also gave huge sums to the inaugural fund. And major CEOs were all too happy to join Trump's Business Council and Manufacturing Council.

While in the recent past some advocates have focused on building alliances with business interests sympathetic to immigration reform, these potential "allies" are all too often exploiting our members in the workplace and in their communities, and are largely silent and absent from (or on the wrong side of) the policy fights that matter. Thus we decided to shine a bright light on their behavior as well as the ways that the Trump administration's politics were padding the pockets of corporate executives while hurting our communities. Applying direct pressure to these corporations and exposing their complicity would make it more difficult for policymakers to put corporate profits over communities *and* make it less comfortable for corporate executives, who often feel greater sensitivity to shame than the Trump administration, to support its policies.

We also knew that our approach had to be intersectional. The corporations to which we were going to stand up controlled vast portions of the American economy and exploited members of our community in manifold ways: private prison companies caged Black and Brown citizens *and* undocumented immigrants and subjected them to dangerous conditions, while exploiting their labor in slavery-like conditions. The situation was particularly dangerous for transgender, gender-non-conforming, intersex, and queer (TGNCIQ) community members, who faced even more violence and abuse. To take on such companies, we had to grasp the complexity of their operations and the multiple dimensions of their impact on our communities. By embracing intersectionality, we also believed we could be more powerful.

Focusing Our Efforts

Recognizing the need to challenge corporate power, we faced a question: on which sectors and corporations should we focus? Working with our partners at the Center for Popular Democracy, New York Communities for Change, and our sister Make the Road organizations in Connecticut, New Jersey, and Pennsylvania, we undertook a research project to assess dozens of corporations that had shown an early eagerness to work with the Trump administration. We looked at a dozen criteria, including direct links to the Trump administration, connections between policies beneficial to companies and the harm caused to communities, political contributions to Trump and his allies, whether companies had profitable government contracts, and more. We prioritized companies that were recognizable to the general public and which would be susceptible to public shaming.

In the end, nine corporations rose to the top: BlackRock, Blackstone, Boeing, Disney, Goldman Sachs, IBM, JPMorgan Chase, Uber, and Wells Fargo. These behemoths had long played an outsize role in our economy and our government and had positioned themselves to profit from administration policies. These were leading corporate entities financing private prison and immigrant detention companies set to mushroom under Trump and others that had positioned themselves to benefit from policies that undermined workers' rights, environmental protection, and more. All of them had clear ties to either Trump or his administration, with seven companies joining Trump's Business Council or Manufacturing Council (BlackRock, Blackstone, Boeing, Disney, IBM, JPMorgan Chase, and Uber), one of them maintaining a revolving door with the administration (Goldman Sachs), and one of them being a direct creditor of Trump's companies (Wells Fargo).

We produced detailed research memos on each of these corporations and the ways they had cozied up to the administration and positioned themselves to benefit from its policies, and we decided to call them "Corporate Backers of Hate." We launched our campaign just before May Day, 2017. On April 27, we launched the campaign website, which was featured in *Time* magazine and included detailed memos on each company, as well as a tool to submit letters directly to the companies' CEOs and board members. As *Time*'s Charlotte Alter wrote, "The idea is for activists to pressure the individuals making the decisions at these companies in the same way they would pressure the individuals making decisions in Congress."[1]

On May 1, we and our allies marched with more than five hundred community members through the streets of midtown Manhattan to the headquarters of JPMorgan Chase, demanding the company cease financing private prison and immigrant detention companies. Ten days later we returned to the Chase headquarters, this time with New York State Assembly members Francisco Moya and Nily Rozic and State Senator Gustavo Rivera standing with us and vowing to stop the private prison and immigrant detention industry in its tracks.

Exposing the Banks Financing Private Prisons and Immigrant Detention

While all of these companies (among others) met our campaign criteria, we knew from the outset that it was not possible to actively campaign against nine corporate behemoths at the same time, particularly given our ongoing policy campaigns at the municipal, state, and federal levels. With the ramp-up of immigration enforcement under Trump, we were hearing horror stories about detention conditions on a daily basis, while also seeing the ways that the private operators were making campaign contributions and quietly lobbying for policies to swell the ranks of the detained. And we knew this affected not only immigrants writ large, but also trans immigrants and Black and Brown people held in these same companies' private jails and prisons. Thus private detention became our primary focus.

The campaign was especially personal for our members, many of whom either had survived harrowing conditions in detention centers themselves or had loved ones face this trauma. Take Melissa Nuñez, a transgender Latina immigrant who was detained in a CoreCivic detention facility in Elizabeth, New Jersey, for 183 days in 2016 and early 2017 after defending herself from an attack based on her gender identity. Upon arrival at the facility, Melissa asked that she be identified and treated as a woman. Instead, she was mocked by guards, called by a male name, and forced to shower with and sleep in open areas with twenty men. She was sexually assaulted by another detainee, and her report of the assault to a guard was ignored. To protest the abusive conditions that she experienced in the facility, Melissa went on a three-day hunger strike, and she continued her activism after being released. She then joined our members to protest private detention and the banks that were financing the industry. "No one should suffer what I suffered in that CoreCivic facility," said Melissa, who spoke at our first public action outside of JPMorgan Chase (JPMC). "And no reputable bank should provide financing to companies operating such facilities."

We decided to focus on the leading financiers of Geo Group and CoreCivic, JPMC and Wells Fargo, rather than the detention companies themselves. We did this for various reasons. First, we knew that other progressive organizations, including Freedom to Thrive (then Enlace International), the National Prison Divestment Campaign, Dream Defenders, and the Detention Watch Network, were focused directly on Geo and CoreCivic and exposing their misdeeds. Second, we determined that those companies were unlikely to change their practices through shaming alone. In contrast, the financiers, who were far more image-conscious, would be much more susceptible to exposure.

Unlike Geo and CoreCivic, banks such as JPMC and Wells Fargo are engaged in myriad sectors, including retail banking, and care very deeply about their public image. Early in the Trump administration, JPMC CEO Jamie Dimon joined the president's Business Council. Even as his company continued to finance immigrant detention, Dimon repeatedly issued public statements claiming to support immigrants. Thus we centered our campaign focus on the companies that were bankrolling Geo and CoreCivic, demanding that they withdraw from the private prison and immigrant detention industry.

The strategy made particular sense because of Geo and CoreCivic's corporate structure. Both had incorporated as real estate investment trusts (REITs) for the tax benefits, and they relied heavily on debt financing. As we and our allies noted in a published report, "At the end of 2017, 9 of every 10 dollars CoreCivic had on hand were borrowed. For Geo Group, it was 19 of every 20 dollars." The same report found that JPMC held $168 million in the two companies' debt, while Wells Fargo held $28 million. Both companies had increased their stock holdings in Geo and Core Civic, with JPMC's number of shares increasing by 97 times (i.e., 9,700 percent) between September 30, 2016, and December 31, 2017. With the early increase in value during the Trump administration, the value of JPMC's shares increased 168 times (16,800 percent) during the same period.[2] The banks were helping keep this industry alive, and the public deserved to know about it.

Finally, there was a geographic dimension to our strategy. JPMC made sense as a prime corporate focus for MRNY because it was based in New York and had long been known as a centerpiece of the corporate landscape in the Empire State. It was thus more easily accessible for both direct action and in-state political efforts. After mapping the branch locations of JPMC and Wells Fargo, we confirmed that affiliates of our partners at the Center for Popular Democracy and the other Make the Road state organizations (which grew to include Nevada) had a physical presence in dozens of states where these banks operated branches and offices.

The Campaign Steams Ahead, and Wins

Over the next two years, our members—with leadership from immigrant TGNCIQ members who either had directly experienced harrowing detention or knew others who had done so—launched a steady stream of direct actions. We held press conferences outside of JPMC headquarters, using powerful symbols including shoes and silhouette cut-outs to highlight cases of immigrants who had died in detention. We and our allies also launched online petition efforts, delivering hundreds of thousands of petition signatures to our corporate targets. And in May 2017, hundreds of our members crashed the JPMC annual shareholder meeting, marching and protesting outside as others went inside to directly confront Jamie Dimon about the company's practices. The tactic worked: Dimon earned himself a series of negative headlines when he responded to our members' questions by saying he was a "patriot" for serving Trump.[3]

We scored an early campaign victory in August 2017 when, in the aftermath of the Charlottesville massacre, we and allies (most notably Color of Change) escalated pressure on companies to leave Trump's Business Council and distance themselves from the administration. Our members delivered hundreds of thousands of petition signatures to JPMC and Blackstone headquarters on August 16, 2017.[4] That very day the council dissolved, as the CEOs could no longer stomach the negative attention they were getting for their ties to the administration.

We kept on pushing to highlight JPMC's complicity with the private prison and detention industry, with regular direct actions, research reports, and first-person stories exposing the horrors of detention, among other tactics.[5] When the company refused to engage with our members and take our critiques seriously, we escalated the campaign. In the summer of 2018, our members marched to Dimon's house and protested outside, blasting the recently surfaced ProPublica audio recordings of immigrant children wailing from inside immigrant detention facilities.[6] Eight of our members and allies participated in a civil disobedience action blocking Park Avenue and were arrested that day.

Broadening our coalition proved critical to our success. That same season, we got a major boost when we connected with the Families Belong Together (FBT) corporate accountability committee. As people across the country became outraged by the zero-tolerance policies that resulted in children being separated from their parents, dozens of organizations that engaged in FBT's rapid-response mobilizing also decided to highlight corporate actors' complicity, adopting JPMC and Wells Fargo as key targets, and we joined forces. This coalition included organizations such as MomsRising and CREDO Action, digitally savvy groups with the capacity to launch online and distributed actions (where people take action simultaneously in different places) across the country.

Under the dual banners of #BackersofHate and #Families BelongTogether, our organizations unleashed letter deliveries to JPMC and Wells Fargo bank branches in multiple states, carried out actions at the Wells Fargo headquarters in California, and generated extensive negative publicity for these companies. The diversity of our expanded coalition proved powerful. Not only were our immigrant, Black, and Brown community members taking action, but they were now joined by white suburban mothers (whom companies tend not to want to alienate) in delivering letters to bank branches.

We also engaged political allies, which helped ensure that both the media and the corporations whose behavior we were calling out took the campaign seriously. From the outset, New York State legislators committed to introducing legislation focused on this issue. In 2017, we secured a historic commitment from New York City comptroller Scott Stringer to divest city pension funds from all Geo and Core-Civic holdings. At the state level, similarly, New York State comptroller Tom DiNapoli announced the divestment of state pension funds from the private prison companies in 2018. Both these announcements made headlines, communicating that this industry was truly toxic—not just to activists but also to major financial entities.

Then, in early 2019, Rep. Alexandria Ocasio-Cortez joined an MRNY forum and committed to congressional oversight hearings on the banks' role in boosting private prison and immigrant detention companies. Eventually the pressure became too much for the companies.[7] On March 5, 2019, just three weeks after more than one hundred of our members paid a Valentine's Day visit to Jamie Dimon's house with a mariachi group, demanding he "break up with" private prison companies, JPMC announced it would stop financing private prisons.[8]

Our members were elated by this historic victory, particularly since it led to an immediate decline in private prison companies' stock prices. We knew there was also potential for a domino effect influencing other banks who were financing the sector, since none of them wanted the same negative publicity that JPMC had been receiving. In less than a week, under questioning from Rep. Ocasio-Cortez following ongoing communication with our coalition, Wells Fargo's CEO said his company was stepping away from private prison companies as well.[9]

Building on this success, our coalition quickly turned the spotlight onto the other major banks that were financing the detention industry. In April 2019, the Center for Popular Democracy, the Public Accountability Initiative, and In the Public Interest published a data brief called "The Wall Street Banks Still Financing Private Prisons."[10] Our collective efforts that spring focused on those banks, especially Bank of America, BNP Paribas, SunTrust, Barclays, Fifth Third Bank, US Bank, and PNC, all of which ultimately announced they would cease financing private prison and immigrant detention companies. By the summer of 2019, after all these banks had distanced themselves from the private prison industry, Geo and CoreCivic faced a gap of nearly 90 percent of their previous financing.[11]

Through a combination of direct actions that centered the experiences of directly affected people, coalition building, strategic research and communications work, and effective political strategy, our coalition achieved what initially seemed improbable: we made the role of these banks in financing the private detention industry broadly visible around the country and shamed them into changing their practices. The result was that the industry was positioned to lose the bulk of its financing. By early 2020, the stock prices of Geo and CoreCivic had fallen as low as when the Obama administration announced the end of federal private prison contracts in 2016—a remarkable achievement given that the Trump administration had done so much to boost the business.

The Next Phase: Amazon

Having achieved our goals vis-à-vis the major financiers of private detention, we and our allies continued to monitor these banks' compliance with the commitments they had made, while also working to seek federal government action to end private incarceration and immigrant detention. But we also knew that other major corporate entities were playing a role in implementing and aiding Trump's immigrant detention and deportation agenda.

On June 21, 2019, a *New York Times* headline read, "'There Is a Stench': Soiled Clothes and No Baths for Migrant Children."[12] Related news reports included images of people tightly packed in holding cells and children sleeping on the floor. A wave of stories during the Trump era exposed ICE holding conditions, drastic cuts to aid for migrants, and rising profits for the private corporations involved.

As the spotlight continued to shine on the dangerous conditions in detention centers, especially those of children being held near the border, research and strategy discussions led us to a focus on Amazon, the wealthiest corporation in the world, which was deeply complicit as an enabler of the administration's policies.

Building on the strategies of the successful bank campaign, we turned to another dimension of the deportation machine—the technology that makes it run. Amazon rises to the top of the list for its role in the infrastructure Immigration and Customs Enforcement (ICE) uses for the surveillance, detention, and deportation of immigrants.

Amazon Web Services (AWS) provides ICE with the technology to execute mass deportations. In 2018, Mijente, the National Immigration Project, and the Immigrant Defense Project published a report, "Who's Behind ICE? The Tech and Data Companies Fueling Deportations," revealing that Amazon had more federal authorizations to process and sustain government data from government agencies than any other company.[13] Furthermore, Amazon had a multimillion-dollar contract with Palantir, the corporation that creates data profiles of immigrants on technical applications used by Customs and Border Patrol and ICE, hosted on AWS.

Our research on Amazon's involvement with the deportation machine was tied to another local campaign protesting the decision to bring the corporation's second headquarters (HQ2) to Queens. Behind closed doors, New York State governor Andrew Cuomo and NYC mayor Bill de Blasio had signed a deal with no community input and offering the company at least $3 billion in subsidies. In addition to its complicity with ICE, Amazon's HQ2 threatened the livelihoods, working conditions, and housing of the city's working people, including our members. This quickly led to another broad coalition campaign, as dozens of groups focusing on affordable housing, immigrant rights, and labor rights came together to protest the promised tax giveaways and likely mass displacement of our members in Queens, knocking on doors, targeting elected officials, and organizing powerful demonstrations. By February, Amazon was forced to withdraw from the HQ2 deal: the barrio beat the billionaire.

This effort energized our broader campaign exposing Amazon for its role as one of the corporate #BackersofHate. As in our campaigns against JPMC and Wells Fargo, we adopted an intersectional approach, exposing the harm they were doing to immigrants, people of color, workers, and neighborhoods alike.

The core focus was the company's complicity with ICE and Trump's deportation machine. In the summer of 2019, MRNY and allies organized one of the largest demonstrations thus far held against Amazon. More than six hundred community members marched and rallied in a line in front of the huge building hosting the annual AWS Summit in New York City. As thousands of corporate clients, Amazon employees, and tech workers entered the conference site, they saw and heard us exposing Amazon's role in the deportation machine, with shouts, cries, songs, and calls for #NoTechForICE. Community members inside the summit also disrupted a presentation by Amazon's chief technology officer by playing the ProPublica recording of the cries of detained immigrant children and speaking the names of children who had perished. Amazon's stock price dropped as the news spread across the country.

As with our efforts focused on the banks, the coalition focused on Amazon was remarkably diverse. At the same time that immigrant, Black, and Brown New Yorkers were organizing direct actions, allies at Jews for Racial and Economic Justice and the #NeverAgain movement organized marches, occupations, banner drops, and more in dozens of cities to protest against Amazon and other corporate enablers of ICE.

Meanwhile, we were also engaged in organizing Amazon warehouse workers and calling on elected officials to hold the corporation responsible for rolling back decades of hard-fought worker protections and putting workers at risk on the job. We contributed to research reports drawing on data collected in dozens of Amazon warehouses, exposing their inhumane labor standards and high injury rates. And, to illustrate the lessons of the HQ2 campaign, our coalition introduced a "Beyond Amazon" legislative platform—an economic development agenda to secure worker protections, accountability, and transparency in job growth and corporate subsidy programs.[14] This was a multi-dimensional fight that brought together immigrants, Black and Brown people, and workers more broadly. Rather than immigrants fighting for immigrant rights and workers fighting for workers' rights separately, this coalition effort linked the issues and broke down silos.

The campaign brought testimonies of Amazon's abuses to the home of Jeff Bezos himself. On July 15 (Amazon's "Prime Day"), Karen De Leon, a high school senior, spoke on the doorstep of the penthouse of the richest man in the world, protesting the technology that could break apart her immigrant family. Ibrahim Sangare, an Amazon warehouse worker and immigrant from the Ivory Coast, who had been fired in retaliation for speaking out against his employer, dropped off bottles symbolizing the measures his co-workers had to take when denied access to the bathroom.

The campaign also exposed Amazon's increased production of surveillance technology for sale to police precincts and federal agencies—most notably the Department of Homeland Security. Advocacy groups and community organizations raised critiques of Amazon's facial recognition software, Rekognition, given its high rate of error on women and people of color and its dangerous potential to further criminalize Black and Brown communities. (Following intense public pressure in the wake of the police murder of George Floyd, in June 2020 Amazon announced a one-year moratorium on making Rekognition available to law enforcement.)[15]

Given the size and power of our opponent, along with the Partnership for Working Families, New York Communities for Change, and additional allies, we founded a national coalition, Athena, which brings together local and national organizations organizing against Amazon around issues of labor, immigrant rights, racial justice, surveillance, tax accountability, and more. Recognizing Amazon's monopoly power, the coalition is also campaigning for meaningful antitrust legislation to force a breakup of the corporation. Amazon reported $87.4 billion in total revenue in 2019, fueled in large part by the massive profits earned through AWS, which is also the branch of the company providing services to ICE. The size and scope of this corporate behemoth's activities put our communities and democracy in peril; it must be broken up.

Conclusion

The "Corporate Backers of Hate" campaign has exposed multiple corporate abuses and mobilized intense community-led pressure against some of the biggest and most powerful companies in the world. Because many of these corporations exploit not only immigrants but also Black and Brown people, trans people, and workers more broadly, we have engaged in multi-dimensional campaigns.

This approach has extracted major commitments from financial institutions to stop bankrolling private prison and detention companies. In late 2019, reeling from the big banks' decisions to stop financing them, the private prison companies launched a new public relations effort to repair their tarnished image. But this will prove to be an uphill battle for companies who are now widely understood to be profiting from imprisoning immigrants, refugees, and Black and Brown people more broadly in conditions that systematically violate human rights.

This phenomenon expanded in the Trump years, but it dates back to the immediate aftermath of the attacks of September 11, 2001, when the privatization of immigration enforcement, detention, and deportation took off. Once the profit motive was introduced, corporate power became integral to this infrastructure—not only in the business of detention but also in surveillance and the collection of big data that accompanies it.

Advancing a progressive immigration vision—one that centers the humanity of immigrants and seeks to dismantle the enforcement gauntlet—requires naming and shaming these corporate actors and insisting on full de-privatization of everything related to immigration. This is crucial not only for reining in the immediate rights abuses perpetrated against immigrants but also for reducing the momentum of the ever-increasing enforcement machine—momentum driven by the quest of private companies for profits.

Notes

1. Charlotte Alter, "Activists Try to Turn Anti-Trump Protests Toward 9 Companies," *Time*, Apr. 27, 2017.

2. Center for Popular Democracy, Make the Road New York, Enlace International, New York Communities for Change, and the Strong Economy for All Coalition, "Bankrolling Oppression: How Wall Street Companies Finance the Private Prison and Immigrant Detention Industry," 2018, maketheroadny.org/wp-content/uploads/2018/04/Report-CBOH-Digital-1.pdf.

3. Dawn Giel, "JPMorgan CEO Jamie Dimon: 'I'm a Patriot' So I'll Help Trump," *CNBC*, May 16, 2017.

4. Julia Horowitz, "Blackstone and JPMorgan CEOs Still Under Pressure over Trump," *CNN Money*, Aug. 16, 2017.

5. For an example of the first-person narratives shared in the press and at direct actions, see Jonathan Cortes, "I Was Detained in a Hellish Private Prison—and Wall Street Corporations Are Behind It All," *Alternet*, May 3, 2018, www.alternet .org/2018/05/i-was-detained-hell-private-prison-funded-wall-street-corporations.

6. Jake Offenhartz, "Multiple Arrests During Immigration Protests Outside Jamie Dimon's UES Home," *Gothamist*, July 25, 2018, gothamist.com/news /multiple-arrests-during-immigration-protests-outside-jamie-dimons-ues-home.

7. Max Abelson, "Ocasio-Cortez Wants Hearing on Banks Funding Immigrant Prisons," *Bloomberg News*, Feb. 25, 2019.

8. David Henry and Imani Moise, "JPMorgan Backs Away from Private Prison Finance," Reuters, Mar. 5, 2019.

9. David Dayen, "The Private Prison Divestment Movement Just Had an Incredible Week," *In These Times*, Mar. 14, 2019.

10. In the Public Interest, Public Accountability Initiative, and the Center for Public Democracy, "Data Brief: The Wall Street Banks Still Financing Private Prisons," Apr. 2019, www.inthepublicinterest.org/data-brief-the-wall-street-banks-still -financing-private-prisons.

11. Gin Armstrong, "Private Prisons Face 87.4 Percent Financing Gap as Banks Continue to Flee," *Truthout*, Aug. 17, 2019, truthout.org/articles/private-prisons -face-87-4-percent-financing-gap-as-banks-continue-to-flee.

12. Caitlin Dickerson, "'There Is a Stench': Soiled Clothes and No Baths for Migrant Children at a Texas Center," *New York Times*, June 21, 2019.

13. Mijente, the National Immigration Project, and the Immigrant Defense Project, "Who's Behind ICE? The Tech and Data Companies Fueling Deportations," 2018, mijente.net/2018/10/whos-behind-ice-the-tech-companies-fueling -deportations.

14. Make the Road New York et al., "Beyond Amazon: Reshaping New York's Approach to Economic Development," May 2019, maketheroadny.org/beyond -amazon-reshaping-new-yorks-approach-to-economic-development.

15. Karen Weise and Natasha Singer, "Amazon Pauses Police Use of Its Facial Recognition Software," *New York Times*, June 10, 2020.

Part III

FUTURE IMMIGRATION
POLICY

Five Freedoms

A Twenty-First-Century Policy Vision for Immigrant Rights

Marielena Hincapié

Introduction

The global pandemic, the economic crisis, and continued racial violence and injustices have exposed preexisting fractures in our society, threatening our collective health, safety, well-being, and ability to not merely survive but thrive. Even before COVID-19, this country was experiencing a collective trauma and a sense of hopelessness and despair over the state of our democracy. For immigrants, it has felt like nothing short of a war waged by the Trump administration against them and their loved ones. While the Trump administration's rhetoric focused on undocumented immigrants, it also enacted radical restrictions to the legal immigration system in an attempt to slow down the demographic shift toward a majority-minority society, and to disenfranchise future citizens and voters of color.

Learning from Past Failures

As the country emerges from the most virulent anti-immigrant administration in recent times, we cannot pick up where we left off in 2016 and return to the failed strategy of comprehensive immigration reform (CIR). In recent decades, much of the focus has been on addressing the presence of the 11 million undocumented immigrants as a "problem" that requires a policy solution, rather than seeing them as valuable members of our communities and as part of the larger foreign-born population of 45 million, almost half of whom are naturalized citizens.

Aside from the failure of Congress to enact federal legislation that provides a path to citizenship for long-standing undocumented residents, the basic premise underlying CIR is deeply flawed. Republicans and Democrats alike—as well as many in the immigrant rights movement—have operated with an underlying assumption that legalization can only be won in exchange for more interior and border enforcement, more criminalization of migrants, and further restrictions on immigrants' access to health care and safety net programs. Yet instead we have had unfettered immigration enforcement, along with the militarization of Immigration and Customs Enforcement (ICE) and Customs and Border Protection (CBP). We have seen more restrictions on access to health care, so that immigrant youth with Deferred Action for Childhood Arrivals (DACA) protections are prohibited from accessing the Affordable Care Act, and lawfully present immigrants (including permanent residents with green cards) are excluded from Medicaid and the Children's Health Insurance Program for five years after arriving. All this has taken place *without* fulfilling the other half of the CIR vision—namely, adjusting the status of the 11 million undocumented immigrants now residing in the United States.

As COVID-19 has made evident, this failed legislative strategy also endangers our collective well-being: everyone's health is at risk when immigrants are afraid of being tested, seeking medical care, or utilizing services because they lack health insurance, fear being detained by ICE, or fear that they will be unable to gain or maintain legal status due to Trump's "public charge" rule.[1] Under the Trump administration, it became obvious—if it had not been before—that it is futile to continue the CIR approach. That strategy failed to win inclusion for the undocumented or to prevent attacks on lawfully present immigrants; instead it led to increased detentions, deportations, and family separations, inflicting enormous emotional trauma and damage to the basic humanity and dignity of all the nation's immigrants.

In place of CIR, we must have the moral imagination to develop a new vision of a just and equitable society. In 2020, amid the triple crises of the pandemic, the downward-spiraling economy, and historic uprisings calling for structural and systemic anti-racist reforms, we saw the seemingly politically impossible move from the margins to the mainstream of public debate. In a matter of weeks, Congress enacted sweeping stimulus bills that invested trillions in relief packages, and progressive ideas ranging from the Green New Deal to police reform moved closer to becoming reality. A similar shift in the boundaries of what is possible could change the public discourse about immigrants and help to win the immigration policies we need.

To make that happen, we need a bold new approach. We need a vision that meets this moment in history, one that is inspiring for movement leaders and robust enough to meet our communities' needs. We need a paradigm shift toward a people-centered approach that asks what it would take for everyone, including immigrants, to be able to fulfill their full human potential, support themselves and their loved ones, and contribute to building healthy and beloved communities.

A New Vision for the Immigrant Justice Movement

Amid the pain and suffering that immigrant communities experienced under Trump—as well as the courage and resilience they displayed—a group of us in the immigrant justice movement prioritized creating and developing a long-term vision and narrative, one that is not subject to today's political constraints. We met for more than eighteen months in 2019–20, during the height of the crises and chaos created by Trump. I had the honor of co-leading this immigrant movement visioning process with a group of fifty immigrant justice leaders. Although our initial goal was to develop a vision for immigrant justice, this process instead gave birth to a vision for transformational change for everyone in the United States. It is centered around five freedoms: freedom to stay, freedom to move, freedom to thrive, freedom to work, and freedom to transform.

The Freedom to Stay

The freedom to stay is premised on the notion that all human beings should be able to remain in their home countries. We must recognize that migration is a global phenomenon with strong, dynamic, and nonlinear currents that often pull and push people out of their home countries and away from their families, loved ones, culture, language, food, and everything that makes them whole and healthy human beings. The global North's foreign and economic policies, which enable transnational corporations' freedom to traverse borders, have compelled the migration of record numbers of people. Countries and corporate actors in the global North must take responsibility for their actions, some of which have forced people to migrate, such as the U.S. military intervention in Central America in the 1980s, as well as policies and practices that have accelerated climate change. We should require a migration impact analysis (similar to an environmental impact analysis) of all foreign policy initiatives and trade agreements to assess whether they would cause more migration, including the internal displacement of people that is a frequent precursor to transnational migration.

Such a global and regional approach would address the root causes of migration and enable people to thrive in their home countries instead of being forced to migrate. For example, in regard to migration from the Northern Triangle of Central America, we must invest in programs to counter the alarming levels of gender-based violence, human rights abuses, corruption, and political impunity, as well as climate disasters. The United States could take a transformational approach to migration in the Western Hemisphere by investing in strengthening civil society across the region, empowering women- and indigenous-led organizations working to address domestic and intra-familial violence through prevention and trauma-informed healing programs. We should partner with civic leaders to address human rights abuses, and with labor leaders in the United States and Central American countries to develop economic models that lead to sustainable jobs and decrease poverty. The U.S. government should invest foreign aid in educational and employment opportunities to empower local populations, while withholding foreign aid from governments that violate human rights. U.S. policy should also foster greater government transparency, accountability, and healthy democratic participation in the region. The main goal of these policies should be to strengthen the region's economic and political infrastructure so that no one is forced to migrate and so that people have the freedom to remain in their home countries.

The Freedom to Move

The freedom to move is predicated on the fact that migration is a natural and global phenomenon. Simply put, human beings have been moving throughout our history as a species and will continue to do so. We move across cities, states, nations, continents, and oceans. In the United States, however, immigration has been seen primarily as a domestic issue, and has been dangerously placed within a "national security" framework, rather than recognized as the global human reality it has always been. Policies enacted under the Trump administration, like the travel bans targeting Muslim and African migrants, as well as the public charge rule, further constrained legal immigration. Instead, we must ensure that migration is affordable and not restricted based on race, wealth, or faith. We must restore people's ability to seek freedom in a country where they feel safe, including the United States. An individual's right to seek international protection must be upheld, with full due process rights, including rights not to be detained indefinitely, not to be returned to danger, and to maintain family unity and not be separated from loved ones, especially so that children are not subjected to the psychological trauma of being separated from their parents.

We should create a new system of immigration laws and policies that facilitates circular migration, with full visa portability and labor and human rights, for guest workers and permanent immigrants alike. As part of its broader efforts to address climate change, the United States must partner with migrant and climate change leaders to create a comprehensive and holistic climate migration agenda to tackle one of the greatest drivers of migration.

Because we do not yet know how the pandemic will reshape migration across national borders, let alone across states and cities within the United States, the freedom to move also envisions guaranteeing individuals' ability to freely travel without fear of being racially profiled or placed into the deportation pipeline, including being able to access a driver's license regardless of immigration status.

The Freedom to Thrive

The freedom to thrive represents a paradigm shift away from a scarcity mentality and austerity measures to a mentality of abundance, recognizing that every human being has basic needs that must be met. All people, including immigrants, should be able to live safely in their communities without fear. Everyone should have the freedom to thrive at home, at the workplace, and in their communities. Advocates and policymakers organizing and advocating for progressive policy changes must recognize that the only way to truly improve the lives of everyone in a community is to meet the basic needs of immigrants for affordable and quality health care, nutrition, housing, and education (from early childhood education through debt-free college), along with universal safety net programs designed to ensure that everyone can thrive. This paradigm shift counters the notions of scarcity that underlie the narrative of immigrants "taking jobs" and living off welfare, notions that are at the core of so much white nationalist sentiment. It also recognizes immigrants as taxpayers, whether through payroll taxes on their wages, federal income tax, sales taxes, or other federal, state, and local taxes. Undocumented immigrants contribute an estimated $12 billion per year to the Social Security system, subsidizing programs to which many currently do not have access.[2]

Immigrant advocates must think about migration policies not only from the perspective of the rights of immigrants and their families but through an economic justice lens that assesses how policies contribute to the well-being of the whole community, how the admission of new migrants impacts the working conditions of local workers, and related concerns. Policymakers, in turn, must take a two-generation approach to affirmatively set up migrants for success, rather than simply allowing them entry into the United States and then letting them fend for themselves. One out every four children in the United States has at least one immigrant parent, and setting those children up for success depends not only on provisions for their own health and well-being but also on their parents having the freedom to thrive and to build vibrant local communities.[3]

The Freedom to Work

The freedom to work recognizes that most immigrants come to the United States in search of new economic opportunities and a better life for themselves and their families, like generations of new Americans before them. They take on essential roles in our communities and in our economy, helping to make our nation stronger for both present and future generations. All people deserve to work in a safe workplace, with a living wage and access to health care. Many people also migrate to fulfill their dreams of becoming an entrepreneur, as evidenced by the fact that immigrants make up about 25 percent of small business owners.[4]

Given the aging of the U.S. population and other demographic shifts, policymakers must understand the role immigrants will play in the future workforce and ensure their ability not only to survive but also to thrive and contribute to the United States' role as a global economic leader. The freedom to work requires an increase in the minimum wage and improved workplace benefits so that all workers, including immigrants, are not relegated to the working poor.

This necessitates robust enforcement of federal and state labor and employment laws, and a repeal of the employer sanctions enacted as part of the Immigration Reform and Control Act of 1986. For almost thirty-five years, employer sanctions have become de facto employee sanctions. Employers are almost never punished for knowingly hiring undocumented workers, but when their status comes to light, those workers often lose their jobs, at best, or are detained and placed into deportation proceedings, at worst. Instead, government resources should be focused on auditing employers' compliance with labor and employment law, and on removing any incentive to use knowledge of workers' undocumented status to gain greater control over them. Employers who recruit undocumented workers and retaliate against them when they seek to exercise their rights should be held liable, and workers who are victims of such retaliation should be invited to cooperate with federal law enforcement in exchange for legal status, through the creation of a new whistleblower visa category.

Finally, this freedom is grounded in the belief that migrant workers should be supported in efforts to join with U.S.-born workers to form unions and engage in collective bargaining. A robust, healthy, and inclusive labor movement is essential to making progress on all five freedoms, and especially this one.

The Freedom to Transform

The freedom to transform reflects the reality that all human beings make mistakes and that racism is deeply embedded in the U.S. penal system. This presents an opportunity for the immigrant justice and racial justice movements to work together, recognizing that white supremacy and economic greed have been operating through the private prison systems at the direct expense of Black and Brown people.

The long-overdue national conversation about divesting from the over-policing of communities of color that followed George Floyd's murder in 2020 has drawn attention to these expensive, inefficient, and inhumane systems. It is equally crucial to address the structural reforms needed within the U.S. Department of Homeland Security (DHS), a new federal agency created in the aftermath of the tragic events of 9/11 when fear was at its height. Since DHS was created in 2003, we have spent a combined $381 billion on the ICE and CBP agencies within it—more than on all other federal law enforcement combined, including the FBI, Drug Enforcement Administration, Secret Service, U.S. Marshals Service, and Bureau of Alcohol, Tobacco, Firearms, and Explosives.[5] In the summer of 2020, DHS agents were deployed to quell the historic protests calling for racial justice, threatening Americans' First Amendment rights in cities from Portland to Chicago, exposing the dangers inherent in such militarized agencies.

We are at an inflection point in U.S. history and have an opportunity to shift away from punitive immigration policies that inflict disproportionately harsh and cruel punishment on immigrants who have committed crimes, replacing those policies with a regime of restorative justice that provides individuals the freedom to transform, allowing their families and communities to also heal in the spirit of Dr. Martin Luther King Jr.'s "beloved community."

Priorities for a Post-Trump Administration

As COVID-19 taught us, we are all interdependent and rely on each other to preserve our health and well-being. COVID-19 has also exposed our dependence on the formerly invisible work of millions of immigrants who care for our children and loved ones, harvest our food, and deliver goods to our homes. Nearly 70 percent of the immigrant workforce—including undocumented workers and others with varying types of immigration status—are essential workers who again and again risked their lives while keeping the country afloat through the pandemic.[6]

Because immigration was Trump's defining issue, the next administration must confidently and unequivocally counter with a pro-immigrant vision for the United States. The floor for what should be done was captured by the Biden-Sanders Unity Task Force on Immigration, which I had the honor of co-chairing.[7] The task force proposed three key priorities: (1) ensuring a just and effective recovery for all from COVID-19, (2) undoing the harms of the Trump administration and righting the wrongs of the past, and (3) constructing a progressive twenty-first-century immigration system, based on the Five Freedoms framework. To build on the task force recommendations, the following policies should be pursued and implemented by the next administration.

Ensuring a Just and Effective Recovery from COVID-19

To ensure a just and effective recovery, the following steps are necessary:

- During any pandemic or public health crisis such as COVID-19, ensure that testing, treatment, medical services, rehabilitation, and vaccines as well as preventive medicine are available to everyone, regardless of immigration or economic status, so that we are all prepared for any future public health crisis.
- During a public health crisis, release as many civil immigration detainees as possible to protect their health and the health of staff at detention facilities and the surrounding communities, many of which are in rural areas that are underresourced medically.
- Provide states and localities with funds to be used for economic recovery for all their residents, without immigration status restrictions.
- Recognize that immigrants are taxpayers and should be

included in tax credits, including the Earned Income Tax Credit and Child Tax Credit, as well as any tax rebates and economic relief to help working people emerge more resilient from pandemics and economic crises. Remove Social Security number and immigration status requirements for tax credits for immigrant taxpayers.

- Address discrimination against immigrants based on national origin and/or language in access to health care, safety-net programs, employment, and housing.
- Ensure that immigrants have access to safe and affordable housing and that families can live together in the same public housing, regardless of family members' immigration status.
- Recognize the role of immigrants as essential to the recovery from COVID-19 and to reconstruction during climate disasters by fast-tracking essential and critical workers onto a path for citizenship.

Undoing the Harms of the Trump Administration and Righting the Wrongs of the Past

Decades of injustice in our immigration and legal systems grew exponentially worse under the Trump administration. We must restore dignity, civility, and equality by immediately taking steps to undo the harms of Trump's anti-immigrant measures, as well as by introducing long-overdue reforms to the dysfunctional immigration system. The next administration must rapidly rescind all of Trump's immigration-relation executive orders:

- Rescind the punitive and arbitrary Muslim, African, refugee, asylum, health care, and other immigration bans.
- Rescind the public charge regulation, which is an immigrant wealth test.

- Reestablish asylum procedures at the border, reversing the Trump policies that have effectively ended the U.S. asylum system.
- Restore the international definition of refugees, which has been decimated by hostile attorney general opinions, and end policies limiting access to asylum for those already in the country.
- Rescind the interior and border enforcement executive orders that made everyone a priority for deportation and further militarized the southern border, and reinstate updated protocols for prosecutorial discretion, including deferred action and other forms of targeted and humanitarian relief.
- End worksite and community raids and immigration enforcement at or near sensitive locations, including places of worship, schools, and hospitals, and expand the definition of sensitive locations to include courthouses, shelters, benefits offices, and DMV offices.
- End family detention, and immediately institute a moratorium on detention and deportations until Congress enacts a broad legalization program. This would balance the scales while the administration conducts a full-scale study to develop recommendations for transforming DHS.
- Conduct a case-by-case review of current practices in the immigration enforcement system, and implement reforms to ensure that individuals caught in the Trump deportation pipeline are assessed to determine whether they can instead be placed on a pathway to legal status. Provide all individuals with the right to legal counsel.
- Reform the Department of Justice, restoring the Civil Rights Division to ensure oversight of local, state, and federal police departments.

  o Restore independence in judicial proceedings and due process for people in deportation proceedings.

- o Rescind the memos issued by Attorney General Sessions and Attorney General Barr regarding the prosecution of immigrants.
- o De-prioritize prosecutions for unlawful entry, reentry, and immigration status violations.
- o End Operation Streamline, Operation Legend, and similar efforts that undermine due process and compromise the integrity of the legal system.

Building a Progressive Twenty-First-Century Immigration System Grounded in the Five Freedoms

We advocate a new immigration system grounded in the five freedoms.

- *Freedom to stay:* Support a budget that drastically reduces funding for detention and deportations in the interior and at the U.S.-Mexico border, and redirect these funds to address the root causes of migration, support humanitarian relief, and encourage sustainable development so that people have the freedom to stay.
- *Freedom to move:* Sign executive orders restoring and expanding DACA, restoring protections for the parents of U.S. citizen and lawful permanent resident children, and redesignating and expanding Temporary Protected Status (TPS) and Deferred Enforced Departure (DED), including protections for immediate family members. Increase funding to address visa backlogs and to promote legalization and naturalization, including streamlining the process under which individuals can apply for deferred action or parole in place. Transform legal channels for future migration, including visa portability and full labor and civil rights for any temporary workers, as well as paths to legalization and naturalization for those who wish to remain in the United States.

- *Freedom to thrive:* Divest taxpayer funds from DHS and invest them in legalization and naturalization services. Ensure universal legal representation for all immigrant detainees. Provide grants to state and local governments to support social cohesion, immigrant inclusion, English-language and adult education services, and other programs that recognize immigrants as a strength to our nation.
- *Freedom to work:* Shift funding from DHS to the U.S. Department of Labor, OSHA, the Equal Employment Opportunity Commission, and the National Labor Relations Board to strengthen labor and employment rights for all workers, and create robust workforce development programs to prepare for changes in the future of work.
- *Freedom to transform:* End collaboration between local law enforcement agencies and immigration agents. Terminate all contracts with private prisons and remove the profit motive for using state and local jails for immigrant detention. Repeal provisions making minor contacts with the criminal legal system or convictions for crimes committed more than a decade ago triggers for deportation. Restore discretion to immigration judges so that they can make decisions on a case-by-case basis. Ensure full access to judicial review.

Conclusion

This moment demands that we respond boldly and confidently with a vision that speaks to the needs of all Americans, including immigrants. The next administration has a historic opportunity to unite and heal the country by crafting reforms that put working people first and make real the fundamental American promise that no matter what you look like, where you were born, or how much money you make, you will have the same protections and opportunities to thrive as everyone else. We must be prepared to both address the myriad short-term priorities—most urgently, to ensure a recovery that works for all of us—and elaborate a long-term vision. We must understand the Trump administration's anti-immigrant agenda as an attack on our democracy and an attempt to redefine who is worthy of being an American. For far too long we have accepted an America that only keeps its promises to a wealthy, well-connected few. It is time for change. The five freedoms—the freedoms to stay, move, thrive, work, and transform—offer a blueprint for the transformational change we need.

Notes

1. In 1882, as part of the Chinese Exclusion Act, Congress established a rule allowing the U.S. government to deny admission to any immigrant who "is likely at any time to become a public charge," but without clearly defining the term. The Trump administration advanced an interpretation defining any non-citizen who has received one or more public benefits (such as Medicaid, food stamps, or Temporary Assistance to Needy Families) for more than twelve months within any thirty-six-month period as a "public charge." Although the U.S. Supreme Court gave the Trump administration a green light to begin implementing the public charge rule in Feb. 2020, the issue remains unresolved in the federal courts, leaving immigrant families in legal limbo.

2. Social Security Administration, Office of the Chief Actuary, "Effects of Unauthorized Immigration on the Actuarial Status of the Social Security Trust Funds," Actuarial Note No. 151, Apr. 2013, www.ssa.gov/oact/NOTES/pdf_notes /note151.pdf.

3. Migration Policy Institute, "Frequently Requested Statistics on Immigrants and Immigration in the United States," section on "Children of Immigrants," Feb. 14, 2020, www.migrationpolicy.org/article/frequently-requested-statistics -immigrants-and-immigration-united-states#Children%20of%20Immigrants.

4. Sari Pekkala Kerr and William R. Kerr, "Immigrants Play a Disproportionate Role in American Entrepreneurship," *Harvard Business Review,* Oct. 3, 2016.

5. American Immigration Council, "The Cost of Immigration Enforcement and Border Security," July 7, 2020, www.americanimmigrationcouncil.org /research/the-cost-of-immigration-enforcement-and-border-security.

6. Donald Kerwin, Mike Nicholson, Daniela Alulema, and Robert Warren, "US Foreign-Born Essential Workers by Status and State, and the Global Pandemic," Center for Migration Studies, May 2020, cmsny.org/wp-content/uploads/2020 /05/US-Essential-Workers-Printable.pdf.

7. See Biden-Sanders Unity Task Force Recommendations, joebiden.com/wp -content/uploads/2020/08/UNITY-TASK-FORCE-RECOMMENDATIONS .pdf.

When Democrats Are Not
the Party of Ideas

Justin Gest

In immigration policy, Democrats are not the party of ideas. Amid a Trump administration that was elected on an ambiguous plan to secure American borders, admit immigrants based on "merit," and protect American jobs from newcomers, Democrats' response often seemed to suggest that there was little wrong with the country's system for admitting new immigrants in the first place. The terms of comprehensive immigration reform that many congressional Democrats supported as recently as 2012 are no longer good enough for many of today's party leaders.[1] Aside from its concern with the status and treatment of the country's undocumented population, which I will address later, the Democratic Party has conditioned any immigration expansion or reform on the maintenance of a system of preferences for who gets admitted that has remained largely unchanged since the 1960s.

Meanwhile, today's Republican Party has plenty of ideas, most of which are ill-advised, inhumane, or driven by intolerance rather than the national interest. The Trump administration's signature policy moves—all of which were enacted by executive order—included a ban on entrants from several Muslim-majority countries, drastic cuts in refugee admissions, the stricter application of "public charge" rules to poorer immigrants, the slower processing of citizenship and visa applications, the use of emergency funding to extend a border wall, and the imprisonment of child asylum seekers and their separation from parents. The administration also used the COVID-19 pandemic to justify the suspension of various forms of visa processing and entry.

It is little wonder that many Americans are frustrated by the state of immigration policy when one side suggests that little reform is needed and the other side's priority is to target the most vulnerable newcomers. Neither platform is in line with the preferences of American majorities, who—according to polling data—believe the immigration system is "broken" but want to see it repaired in a manner that strategically addresses the national interest and does not indiscriminately open borders.[2] This chapter explores the dynamics that have produced intractability on the Democrats' left flank, contextualizes American policymaking in the context of peer countries worldwide, and then proposes a path toward a new consensus.

Retrenchment

There is no shortage of irony in Democrats' lack of imagination on immigration policy. Their Republican opponents have pursued a retrenchist politics of nostalgic nationalism that resists a globalized modernity. Donald Trump's platform evoked a yearning for earlier eras that predate global governance, multilateralism, and proactive government bureaucracies. But on immigration, in their desire to preserve policies that were put in place between 1965 and 1986, it is the Democrats who are presenting obstacles to progress.

Indeed, as far back as the beginning of the twentieth century, the United States was viewed by the world as an immigration policy trendsetter. Then a rising power that solidified its grip on a continent by settling immigrants from far and wide on disputed land, the United States established the world's first federalized admissions restrictions in 1882. Other immigrant magnets such as Canada and Australia would follow its precedents in governance—however morally questionable—for generations. In those days, merely regulating human movement at all was pioneering.

However, thanks to decades of partisan brinkmanship and polarizing identity politics, it has now been thirty-five years since Congress passed a major piece of legislation governing immigration—a matter of pivotal social and economic consequence. It has been even longer since the landmark 1965 Immigration and Nationality Act abolished quotas based on national origins and focused American policy thereafter on the admission of people with family ties—principles that still form the foundation of U.S. immigration policy today. Since then, other countries have put in place new regimes that admit and integrate immigrants as part of modern national strategies related to labor recruitment, business development, and demographic aging.

Ostriches

The U.S. military doesn't deploy 1980s weaponry. The Securities and Exchange Commission doesn't use 1980s financial software. Medicare doesn't finance 1980s medicine. But America has immigration regulations designed for an era that preceded the internet, free trade, and the end of the Cold War.

Modernizing the system, however, comes with trade-offs. Like the era before World War II, when governments crudely excluded ethnic groups in light of eugenicist ideologies about racial hierarchy, other countries' twenty-first-century policies that recruit immigrants based on new ideals of merit can neglect humanitarianism. The Gulf Arab *kafala* system devalues family togetherness; widespread reluctance to welcoming refugees ignores the potential for immigration to save lives and stimulate developing economies; and new temporary migration programs often treat immigrants as disposable labor. Preserving anachronistic policies hinders our competitiveness yet reflects the spirit of equality and humanity that infused the civil rights and immigration reforms of the late 1960s. Other countries have been debating these trade-offs for decades.

But Democrats in Washington, DC lack the internal consensus to take the lead in updating the system. The problem is that, on immigration, the party is fractured. The constituency most mobilized about immigration policy is the movement of immigrant rights groups who advocate for the maintenance and faster processing of the family reunification visas made possible by the original 1965 legislation—which historically (and unintentionally) made the U.S. system one of the world's most humane.[3] Separately, cosmopolitan liberals and foreign policy liberals advocate broadening the U.S. refugee and asylum program, which has historically rescued people being persecuted by their governments and victims of violent conflicts in which the United States had a hand. And then there are a variety of business-focused moderates who advocate for shifting admissions policies to expand the admission of unskilled laborers to fill undesirable jobs, professionals to address high-skill shortages, and people with extraordinary talent to spur innovation and economic growth. With these three constituencies each seeking to expand the admission of different types of entrants, the path of least resistance has been for Democrats to advocate for more of each, and more of the same.

The cold reality in the Trump era, though, was that the majority of Democrats just didn't think immigration is the most pressing issue confronting the United States. This was true before the COVID-19 pandemic, and it has been even more true since. Democrats have been far more concerned with inequality, climate change, health care, trade, racial justice, and gun control than immigration. As a result, the party and its officials have little interest in spending precious political capital to find a compromise, when compromise would require cooperation from intransigent Republican counterparts. Indeed, if the party does pursue an even more progressive immigration policy agenda, it will risk agitating and mobilizing legions of voters for whom immigration actually *is* the number one policy matter.

With their heads in the proverbial sand since 2013, Democrats would find this "ostrich" strategy of retreat politically savvy and more feasible if it weren't for the one immigration policy matter on which all Democrats *can* agree.

The Undocumented

The lingering purgatory of the approximately 11 million undocumented immigrants in the United States has united the otherwise unwieldy Democratic coalition like few other issues. Most undocumented immigrants have been present in the United States for decades, living in the shadows but contributing their labor, taxes, and disproportionately good citizenship without the formal citizenship rights that normally accompany those contributions. Their unresolved status becomes increasingly problematic for the inefficiencies and injustices it engenders every day it persists. Citing favorable public opinion data, Democrats have sought, unsuccessfully, to regularize the status of the undocumented, shield them from deportation, and legislate a pathway to naturalization. And the organizers of the immigrant rights movement have pressured lawmakers to prioritize these goals over any other immigration policy initiatives.

Doing so has been at the expense of modernizing admissions, because the plight of the undocumented also unites Republicans. For the Right, the phenomenon of undocumented immigrants is a failure of governance that reinforces perceptions of unguarded borders and lax oversight. To Republicans, their unresolved status becomes more problematic every day for the security risk they purportedly present, the state resources they consume, and their alteration of American demography. After Mitt Romney's 2012 election loss, many Republicans argued that supporting legalization was a way to woo Latino and Asian American voters, who were tilting toward Democratic candidates.[4] But since the rise of Donald Trump, Republicans instead have sought to transfer more resources to the U.S.-Mexico border and reduce the government's obligations to asylum seekers.

Under Trump, Republicans employed the plight of the undocumented as a bargaining chip to exchange for an extended border wall. They recently conditioned their acquiescence to the regularization of undocumented childhood arrivals on funding for such border reinforcement. In turn, Democrats were loath to give Trump his wall. They abhorred its symbolism at the gateway to Latin America, and they were disgusted by the way the youthful Dreamers were being held hostage. Besides, Democrats argued, the wall would do little to address undocumented migration. Illegal entry was less common than visa overstays, undocumented immigration had declined massively since the 1990s, and there were more sophisticated ways to secure the border. Thus no deal was ever made, and Trump unilaterally repurposed federal emergency funds to build the still-unfinished wall anyway.

As some analysts asked at the time, why did Democrats fear the failure of Trump's wall?[5] Its uselessness would be plain to see, and it was the cost of resolving the thorny problem of childhood arrivals' status or other thorny challenges. Why not call Trump's bluff and make him prove that the wall was the panacea? Inside the Democratic caucus, legislators aligned with the movement have resisted any compromises that involved allocating funding to border reinforcements, but they have also resisted Democratic-sponsored expansions of economic migration unless the plight of the undocumented is resolved too.

The result has been an impasse that ignores areas of bipartisan agreement and digs in on both sides of sacred causes—the wall and the undocumented. That distraction derails all attempts at compromise, riling up advocates on both sides of the aisle and making the prospects for reform—and modernization—ever more remote.

Falling Behind

The result of this paralysis is that, as I argue in a book I co-authored with Anna Boucher, the United States of America is an exception in the world of immigration.[6] We compiled data about citizenship and immigration flows—the number of foreigners a government admits each year—from thirty of the world's most prominent destination countries. Our study covers former settler states including the United States, Australia, Canada, and New Zealand. We also examine Japan and South Korea, the Nordic states, and all continental European countries from Germany westward. We include as well many countries from the developing world, where nearly half the world's migrants go today. These include Bahrain, Brazil, China, Kuwait, Mexico, Oman, Russia, Saudi Arabia, and Singapore. We have results for much of the past decade and complete data for 2011, a relatively ordinary year preceding the disruptions of the European migrant crisis.

With only a few exceptions, we find that three key features characterize most countries' immigration policies:

- *Temporary visas.* Immigrants enter on more temporary visas that—while often renewable—limit their residency entitlement to a short term.
- *Labor migration.* Most permanent visas admit immigrants for their labor or under regional free movement agreements designed to facilitate labor mobility.
- *Fewer naturalizations.* These policies mean fewer immigrants are able to access citizenship and the full set of freedoms, rights, and protections it entails.

With these priorities, other nations have evolved to recognize immigration as a crucial strategy to combat demographic aging, recruit innovators, attract highly skilled professionals, and fill labor gaps with limited new membership. Some, including Canada, Australia, and the United Kingdom, have devised points-based systems that admit migrants based on the extent to which they fulfill "merit" criteria related to language proficiency, skill, employment, and recognized educational credentials. Other countries, such as those on the Arabian Peninsula, have established overseas labor recruitment offices to promote and facilitate temporary migration. Many countries in

Europe and Latin America have struck agreements with each other to permit the mobility of human capital.

These governments have identified the specific ways that immigration benefits their economies and their populations, and they have proactively sought to design systems that deliver immigration in the manner they wish. The United States, in contrast, has failed to overcome the inertia around an outdated system and assumed that America's magnetic power will override the benefits of considered strategy for recruitment, admissions, and retention.

Policy Formaldehyde

Consequently, the United States has been stuck in a sort of policy formaldehyde since the reforms of the 1960s. For example, foreign students at American universities are forced to take their new skills and leave within a year of graduation if they cannot find a company to sponsor them. The United States has also rigidly capped the admission of highly skilled engineers, scientists, and programmers from China and India, and it is costly and difficult for companies to justify the hiring of foreign people with talent. Meanwhile, it is relatively easy for people to overstay their visas unbeknownst to the U.S. government. The U.S. economy is structurally reliant on the cheap, flexible labor of undocumented immigrants, particularly in the construction, agricultural, and service industries that build, nourish, and comfort American society. Congress has voted against laws that condition hiring on documented status checks and refused to implement a system of exit stamps that confirm the departure of immigrants at ports. Congress has also refused to adequately fund the agencies that process applications for citizenship and entry, as if the U.S. government were doing immigrants a favor and not redeeming any benefits of its own.

As a result, the United States stands out internationally. About 65 percent of our permanent visas are granted for the specific purpose of family reunification. No other country is higher than 50 percent, and the peer settler states of New Zealand, Australia, and Canada were at 37 percent, 25 percent, and 23 percent at the time of our measurement. In 2011, the share of all visas granted to family members and refugees was higher in the United States than in all other countries—more than 11 percentage points higher than the nearest countries, Ireland and Sweden. People who immigrate to the United States for non-economic reasons, such as family reunification, and those who arrive as refugees are typically fast-tracked on the path to citizenship; yet American naturalization rates are lower than numerous other countries with a greater emphasis on economic migrants, especially Canada. Further, while other countries have increasingly regularized undocumented immigrants, the United States has the highest estimates of undocumented immigrants in the world.

From the perspective of moderate Republicans and moderate Democrats alike, American policies are makeshift and haphazard. We turn away millions of highly skilled professionals, patent filers, and young contributors to the tax base. We are an anachronism that fails to compete at the international level for the best and the brightest and fails to manage flows responsibly. The costs are immeasurable because the counterfactual is unknown, but it is qualitatively clear that American economic admissions policies hinder high-skill migration more than those of other countries do.

Country of Dreams

On the other hand, many advanced countries have devalued humanitarianism, ignored the benefits of family migration and greater diversity, and pursued economic strategies without consideration for their ethical implications. Singapore deports certain classes of immigrants if they become pregnant. Countries on the Arabian Peninsula grant almost nobody citizenship and deport immigrants' children if they don't get a job by the time they are adults. And

European countries have refused to equally share the responsibility of resettling humanitarian migrants; the 2013 Dublin Regulation shifts all responsibility to the countries of first arrival on the Mediterranean Sea.

In recent decades—until the Trump administration's Muslim ban and 60 percent cut in refugee admissions—the U.S. government vetted, resettled, and promoted the integration of more refugees than any other country worldwide. American policies provided citizens with the right to reunify with their spouses, children of any age, parents, and siblings by sponsoring them for admission. Even though accepting these immigrants was not justified by the economic gains they were expected to bring, employment and entrepreneurship data do not suggest an appreciable difference between them and labor migrants. Though successive administrations have created and maintained obstacles to acquiring citizenship (such as tests, fees, bureaucratic drag, and waitlists), rates of naturalization remain higher than in many European peers, even if lower than in other settler states. The United States has also run a unique "diversity lottery" that vets and randomly selects qualified immigrants from underrepresented countries for admission—solidifying America's reputation as a country of dreams that is open to all peoples.[7]

From this perspective—shared by many liberal and mainstream Democrats—the United States' inability to evolve has meant that it has maintained one of the more humane admissions systems in the world. Prior to Trump's executive orders, the United States was a beacon of openness—a laissez-faire country that with each generation reinvents itself thanks to the infusion of innovative, intrepid, industrious new arrivals.

Snowballing

The problem is that our failure to modernize this relatively humane system has led to a snowball of unquantifiable, missed economic opportunities and gross inefficiencies that inflame political polarization and conflict.

- When the United States did not facilitate temporary work permits and seasonal visas for unskilled laborers, migrants chose to meet employer demand without authorization, and employers willfully ignored their legal status.
- When Congress did not act on the plight of the innocent "Dreamers" who accompanied these undocumented labor migrants, President Barack Obama issued an executive order that circumvented the legislative process. Separately, scores of municipalities refused to cooperate with federal immigration enforcement agents.
- When the public grew frustrated with a perceived inability to govern borders, many supported President Donald Trump and his promise of greater order. However, the Trump administration's draconian crackdown on undocumented immigrants and their families further retrenched the United States at a time when we needed to be catching up.

And yet, the United States could be both humane and economically sensible at the same time.

A First Draft

In spring 2019, President Trump briefly expressed interest in overhauling the immigration system so that it stopped favoring visa applicants with U.S. family ties and instead gave priority to highly skilled applicants and those with job offers.[8] The proposal was based on the assumption that immigrants' educational credentials—what the administration called "merit"—would lead to increased wages for American workers and attract immigrants who would better integrate into U.S. culture.

Immediately after it was announced, the proposal drew criticism from all sides in all the predictable ways. Many Republicans didn't think it went far enough to combat illegal immigration, while others on the Right wanted total immigrant admissions to be cut. Many Democrats, meanwhile, didn't want to roll back the system's humanitarian, family-oriented principles, and also wanted to resolve the status of America's undocumented before considering any other proposals for change.

The whole idea of "merit" is a lightning rod in a highly charged issue. But there's a smarter way for both sides to think about whom we let in, and why. The Trump administration was on to something when it said we need a new way to evaluate immigrants, one that predicts their future success as Americans. Indeed, considering future immigrants' potential contributions is now commonplace in immigration policies around the world. But the Trump administration's idea of how to do this was too crude. Many Democrats, for their part, are too quick to dismiss any type of systematic evaluation as anti-humanitarian. Done right, however, it actually would consider family and other humanitarian factors, and likely set new arrivals up for greater success in their new country.

Immigration Moneyball

Call it immigration Moneyball—a two-part plan that determines what factors matter to immigrant success and then selects immigrants accordingly.

For decades, baseball was managed according to hunches and instinct. For a sport that collects more statistics than any other, much of its recruiting and game-day decision-making was based on a highly subjective *je ne sais quoi*.

This all ended when the Oakland Athletics began incorporating evidence-based, analytical reasoning into decision-making, an approach documented in Michael Lewis's 2003 book *Moneyball*, and now adopted to some extent by every major league team.[9] Early adopters held a significant advantage before the rest of the game caught up.

Just as baseball was revolutionized with a multi-dimensional data-driven system for evaluating and selecting players, the United States could analyze far more information than it currently does to decide which immigrants will best thrive in American society and contribute to the economy—something people of all political persuasions should welcome.

Right now, both sides view immigrants in entirely one-dimensional ways. Imagine a system that instead considered immigrants more fully as individuals, rather than simply as skilled workers, unskilled workers, or family members, as our current immigration framework does. It might, for example, find merit in whether applicants made previous visits to the United States as a student, tourist, or temporary worker. Imagine a system that also tracked people's exits from our airports, harbors, and train stations, and then assigned value to an immigrant's previous on-time departures. The system might find "merit" in youth, in fluent multilingualism, in training or work experience in occupations that are in special demand at the moment, or in advanced degrees from American universities. It could prioritize immigrants who pledge to settle in rapidly depopulating regions for their first ten years after arrival; those admitted could even be matched to locales likely to produce their successful employment and integration.

Imagine if all this were considered alongside whether immigrants have family in the United States to receive them, help them adjust, and help them find work. That, too, is a predictor of likely success: research suggests that family migrants with close existing family ties have similar economic outcomes to migrants admitted on labor visas that screen for credentials and contracts.[10] In this light, family ties represent a powerful form of merit, too. And importantly—because welcoming people in need is a core American value—the criteria might include whether admission will rescue them from severe poverty, violence, or natural disaster in their home country.

We have the tools to discover what qualities and factors actually make immigrants most likely to succeed in the United States and then assess applicants for admission based on those criteria. To call the approach "Moneyball" is oversimplifying, of course; immigration, unlike baseball, doesn't deliver easily countable runs and wins, and an immigrant's success can and should be defined in manifold ways. It could mean law abidance, employment, economic mobility, business ownership, patents filed, sense of belonging, or political participation.

What qualities matter most should be determined by an independent immigration admissions council, as I detail below. While we can debate what constitutes successful integration, it would be better if we actually collected and consolidated information about the extent to which various types of admitted immigrants are making progress in specific ways. If we did that, we could see which attributes known at admission best predict these different forms of success and adjust our criteria accordingly in the future.

A Baseball Metaphor Extended

Today, U.S. immigration policy looks a lot like baseball once did. Most people orient their policy preferences around their gut feelings about foreigners. Many on the Left view immigrants as either hard workers who will reinforce shrinking populations or vulnerable people who must be welcomed in the spirit of humanitarianism. On the nationalist Right, many view immigrants as opportunists or even (as President Trump has regularly suggested) criminals, who come to exploit the resources of rich countries and whose presence threatens the national culture. The debate has mostly been argued from the extremes (for example, fearmongering about the gang MS-13 and calls to abolish ICE) and has become unmoored from any pretense of sober reasoning.

As countless studies have shown, immigrants on average are

powerful generators of economic growth who are disproportionately employed, innovative, entrepreneurial, and law-abiding—and who, on average, quickly integrate and do not compete with American-born workers for jobs, except for a minuscule group of workers at the lowest wages and educational levels. Immigration advocates have repeated these findings more than a pitcher rehearses his windup.

But the current system is also operating with a clunky, outdated selection strategy. This is where critics have an important point: The system we have is relatively indiscriminate, even arbitrary, and unconcerned with predicting good outcomes.

Data-Driven

Like baseball teams, governments and researchers already collect extensive data about admitted and prospective immigrants along multiple dimensions: employment and welfare consumption, criminality and civic engagement, language attainment and educational achievement, and more.

But the government doesn't use or consolidate all this data. It has not systematically crunched the numbers to determine the full range of qualities and factors that help an immigrant succeed and contribute—how much, for example, English-language skills upon entry matter for longer-term workforce participation, and whether younger skilled immigrants contribute more tax dollars before retirement than older skilled immigrants with more established expertise.

Furthermore, rather than evaluate the entirety of an admission applicant's qualifications, the U.S. government—like many others—limits consideration to a few factors and an arbitrary interview at an embassy. Visa types are designated by the primary "purpose" of entry, as if immigrants are either workers or family members, refugees or students. It reduces each immigrant, a person with unique potential and confluence of skills, attributes, and needs, to a single, artificial classification and then files her or him into a line. While particular H-1B visas, for example, might prioritize immigrants who have a specific skill and job, they take no account of humanitarian concerns, or whether that immigrant has family in the United States.

The result is a system that ignores many valuable indicators of immigrants' potential. Would you rather grant admission to an engineer based on no other information, or to an engineer who speaks fluent English, has a sister in Detroit, and was once a high school exchange student in Omaha? The answer seems obvious.

Perhaps less obvious: would you rather grant admission to a qualified engineer without family ties or demonstrated familiarity with the United States, or to an agricultural worker who speaks proficient English, has a sister in Detroit, and was once a high school exchange student in Omaha?

More difficult: would you rather admit that agricultural worker with family ties and English skills or one who already has a contract offer and has agreed to settle in a rapidly depopulating region but who doesn't have family in the United States?

An admissions system informed by statistical reasoning and criteria adjustable to current needs would be able to answer these questions, selecting optimal applicants for temporary or permanent visas based on reliable predictions about the applicants' productivity and social contributions, as well as the state of the U.S. economy at the time.

Backed by such reasoning, the engineer or agricultural worker doesn't just look good; we will have evidence-based assurances that she is likely to actually *be* good.

In Practice

Does all this require an overhaul of the existing admissions system? Yes, it would replace the way we currently admit people on labor visas and admit family members based on a different logic. In addition to verifying the data we already collect from applicants, we'd need to collect more—and then build the capacity to quickly process admissions decisions. It would also be useful to have a system that processes exits as well as entries and studies immigrants' progress once they are admitted.

Once built, the system could easily be adjusted to fill labor gaps, respond to new research findings, or accommodate new legislation with agility. Imagine if there were a shortage of nurses or programmers. Imagine if fertility rates dropped and Social Security neared insolvency. Imagine if there were a pool of immigrants already with American university credentials who were qualified for open jobs. All of these are known actualities, and a more advanced system would enable timely adjustments.

The most effective way to operationalize this would be to establish an independent immigration admissions council, onto which both parties may appoint three individuals for staggered five-year terms— an institution akin to the Federal Reserve Board of Governors. Like the Fed, the council would hold the power to adjust the distribution of point values on a quarterly basis to accommodate national interests. In contrast, the prioritization of immediate family members and the total number of immigrants admitted would need to be set by acts of Congress. The council could consider advocacy and evidence presented by large employers and industrial associations, but also by unions, governments, and universities monitoring trends, all of which might inform their decisions.

Such a system could also help the country incorporate more visas for circular migration, permitting workers to regularly or seasonally enter the United States for specific purposes and then return to their country of origin. If government agencies synchronized their data, renewing a visa for these and other temporary immigrants could be as simple as renewing a driver's license, subject to a variety of quick checks. This would dramatically reduce the incentive to cross the border without authorization or overstay a visa. Today, employers with low-skill or seasonal labor needs often rely on undocumented workers, who—if they return to their country of origin—cannot legally return to the United States, or who—if they are caught in the United States—are barred from returning for ten years thanks to "unlawful presence" rules.

The idea that what we know about immigrants when they apply for admission predicts their ultimate social and economic contributions has informed immigrant admissions in places such as Australia and Canada, whose point-based systems evaluate applicants based on such skill-oriented criteria. A more advanced alternative could solicit residency pledges for special applicants such as physicians and small business entrepreneurs, or even low-skill workers with family in regions with relevant labor shortages in agriculture or construction.

Prospects

As with any immigration policy, there will be political hurdles. Critics on the Left will worry that algorithms will replace the current system, which dedicates about two-thirds of all visas to family admissions. But algorithms could be weighted or overridden to continue to prioritize spouses and minor children without counting them toward quotas. And they could also be programmed to recognize more extended members of American families, who have been less likely to be admitted in recent decades.

Critics on the Right might worry that such a meritocratic system will lead to even greater annual flows of immigrants. However, the qualifications for entry could be raised or lowered to hit annual flow targets, and quotas—if desired—could still be applied. It is also worth acknowledging that the foreign-born represent about

14 percent of the American population. Compare this figure to those of Switzerland (30 percent of the population is foreign-born), Australia (29 percent), New Zealand (23 percent), Canada (22 percent), Austria (19 percent), Sweden (18 percent), Ireland (17 percent), and elsewhere.

Other critics may worry that a system based on algorithms and points may be less transparent than the current one, and more subject to bad-faith inputs driven by racism or xenophobia. As I have argued elsewhere, a side effect of established points-based systems has been preference for white applicants and others from countries with stronger education systems.[11] Giving credit for previous visits to the United States can have the same effect because it is easier to get visas from Western countries. But this could be offset if family ties were substantially taken into consideration. The system could also assign "merit" to people who hail from countries underrepresented in the United States—among the purposes of the diversity visa lottery that the Trump administration proposed eliminating. Furthermore, the current system is hardly transparent anyway. Consular officers and immigration judges possess enormous arbitrary power, and there have been reports of certain VIPs receiving special treatment and expedited processing.

Ideally, a system like this would appeal to many on both sides of the political divide. It would render a sense of control to those on the Right, while justifying a steady flow of newcomers, as the Left envisions.

As in baseball, there will be plenty of exceptions, when advanced reasoning still fails to predict good outcomes. Not every immigrant will create as many jobs as Elon Musk; some will commit crimes (although at lower rates than American citizens, according to U.S. government and other data).[12] And as in baseball, there will be holdouts who don't want to modernize the immigration system and prefer instead to maintain current flows, whether because of persistent prejudice or deep-seated mistrust. But as in baseball, such small-mindedness will ultimately mean losing out.

Trump got away with strategies as simplistic as a steel wall and tactics as barbaric as separating children from their parents because the debate has become symbolic rather than substantive, and thus subject to our most basic instincts, be they for humanity or for control.

The best way to simultaneously humanize immigrants and control their admission is to shift to a system that considers their humanity in the most complete way possible. Then, in regard to immigration, the Democrats could be the party of ideas and America could be the place of dreams once again.

Notes

1. Priscilla Alvarez, "Don't Bet on Comprehensive Immigration Reform in the New Congress," *The Atlantic*, Nov. 24, 2018.

2. Danielle Kurtzleben, "What the Latest Immigration Polls Do (And Don't) Say," NPR, Jan. 23, 2018; see also Gallup, "In Depth: Topics A to Z: Immigration," news.gallup.com/poll/1660/immigration.aspx.

3. Jia Lynn Jiang, *One Mighty and Irresistible Tide: The Epic Struggle over American Immigration, 1924–1965* (New York: W.W. Norton, 2020).

4. Henry Barbour et al., "Growth and Opportunity Project," Republican National Committee, assets.documentcloud.org/documents/623664/republican -national-committees-growth-and.pdf.

5. David Kampf, "Democrats Should Just Give Trump His Wall," *Politico*, Nov. 2, 2018.

6. Anna Boucher and Justin Gest, *Crossroads: Comparative Immigration Regimes in a World of Demographic Change* (Cambridge: Cambridge University Press, 2018).

7. Jason DeParle, *A Good Provider Is One Who Leaves: One Family and Migration in the 21st Century* (New York: Penguin, 2019).

8. Michael Shear, "Trump Immigration Proposal Emphasizes Immigrants' Skills over Family Ties," *New York Times*, May 15, 2019.

9. Michael Lewis, *Moneyball: The Art of Winning an Unfair Game* (New York: W.W. Norton, 2004).

10. See Guillermina Jasso and Mark R. Rosenzweig, "Do Immigrants Screened for Skills Do Better than Family Reunification Immigrants?," *International*

Migration Review 29, no. 1 (1995): 85–111.

11. Justin Gest, "Points-Based Immigration Was Meant to Reduce Racial Bias. It Doesn't," *The Guardian*, Jan. 19, 2018.

12. National Academies of Sciences, Engineering, and Medicine, *The Economic and Fiscal Consequences of Immigration* (Washington, DC: National Academies Press, 2017), www.nap.edu/catalog/23550/the-economic-and-fiscal-consequences-of-immigration; Anna Flagg, "Is There a Connection Between Undocumented Immigrants and Crime?," *New York Times*, May 13, 2019.

Keep It Moving

A "Future Flow" Agenda for the Immigrant Rights Movement

Amaha Kassa

———————

The U.S. immigrant rights movement faces the challenge of articulating an agenda for how to engage with global migration in an era of increasing human mobility. Part of this challenge is more clearly understanding the goals of immigration restrictionists, who made unprecedented gains under the Trump administration.

Restrictionists focused great effort on reshaping immigration policies that determine "future flows"—that is, the rules under which future generations of immigrants can enter the United States legally. Across a variety of specific arenas—from refugee resettlement and asylum, to family reunification admissions, to the Diversity Visa (DV) program—the Trump administration acted to block major pathways and drastically decrease *legal* migration, belying the rhetoric that they opposed only "illegal" immigration.

I argue here that the fight over future flows is a fight over the future of American citizenship. It is a fight that the immigrant rights movement is losing, largely because we have ceded the terrain by failing to prioritize future flow issues. The movement needs to articulate a "future flow agenda" that advances an expansive notion of citizenship and takes seriously our obligations not only to immigrants currently in the United States but also to those who seek to be Americans and those who will come after us.

Fighting Against the Future: Who Gets to Be a Citizen?

The Trump administration pursued sweeping changes to immigration policy. One prong of its strategy was mass illegalization, seeking to eliminate programs like Temporary Protected Status (TPS) and Deferred Action for Childhood Arrivals (DACA) that give undocumented immigrants some of the benefits of permanent status, including protection from deportation and work authorization, and provide "temporarily documented" immigrants with time to remain in the United States and seek a path to permanent status. By escalating enforcement and accelerating deportation, and specifically by rescinding previous immigration enforcement priorities, Trump created an atmosphere of fear in which all undocumented immigrants—and even many immigrants with status—felt they could be a target of enforcement at any time. By increasing detention, the administration also increased the barriers facing asylum seekers and undocumented immigrants fighting to remain in the United States.

These strategies aimed to control which types of immigrants can pursue permanent status and, eventually, citizenship. More directly, the Trump administration sought to slam the "front door" to the United States by throttling nearly every pathway to legal migration, including the Diversity Visa program, refugee resettlement, the legal right to seek asylum, and family reunification.

Mass Illegalization

Contrary to anti-immigrant rhetoric, immigrants are not divided neatly into "legal" and "illegal," or even "documented" and "undocumented," under U.S. immigration law. The complex legal patchwork includes multiple forms of temporary legal presence, work authorization, or both, generally under the exercise of the executive branch's prosecutorial discretion.[1] Many of the most harmful policy changes under Trump involved stripping "temporarily documented" immigrants of their legal status—illegalizing them, in the phrase of legal scholar Joel Sati—in a sharp break from prior policy and procedure.[2]

Trump's attempt to eliminate DACA—a signal, if inadequate, immigration program enacted by the Obama administration—was the most visible example, threatening hundreds of thousands of young undocumented immigrants. Similarly, Trump sought to terminate TPS for hundreds of thousands of Central American, Caribbean, Asian, and African immigrants, most of whom had resided for many years in the United States. TPS holders, who come from countries affected by some of the most severe humanitarian crises on the planet, were also the targets of Trump's infamous "shithole countries" slur, which contrasted immigrants from the global South with "desirable" immigrants such as those from Norway. That racialized slur signaled more clearly than any other Trump statement or policy the stakes in the battle over future flows.

Attempts to eliminate DACA and TPS were blocked by courts on grounds of administrative procedure, rather than as violations of fundamental rights, as in the *Ramos v. Nielsen* litigation, in which my organization is one of the plaintiffs. These attempts at illegalization succeeded, however, in making DACA and TPS beneficiaries less secure, more contingent, and further removed from the benefits of citizenship.

Escalation of Enforcement

Trump ramped up the already aggressive immigration enforcement practices of his predecessor—which had earned Obama the epithet "deporter-in-chief." Under the Trump administration, both the number of immigration arrests and the number of removals shot up from the Obama years. Trump ended Obama administration priorities that focused law enforcement resources on immigrants with criminal legal convictions, the recently arrived, and those with existing orders of removal. Instead, the doctrine of Immigration and Customs

Enforcement (ICE) under Trump was that any and every "removable alien" is a legitimate target.[3]

In practice, because ICE's resources are not unlimited, the overwhelming majority of deportations continued to fall into the previously articulated priority categories. Still, the elimination of enforcement priorities created fear and uncertainty among millions of undocumented immigrants about their risk of deportation—as it was intended to do.

Mass Detention

Trump largely delivered on his campaign promise to lock up more undocumented immigrants. He multiplied the capacity of immigrant detention centers and set a grim record by detaining more than fifty thousand immigrants, the largest number in U.S. history.[4] Disregarding its own policies on parole of detained immigrants, the Trump administration denied parole to 96 percent of arriving asylum applicants and pressured nominally independent immigration judges to deny parole or set exorbitant bond amounts, increasing the median immigration bond amount by 70 percent.[5] Most immigrants detained under these policies were held not for any criminal offense but solely for alleged immigration violations, including exercising their legal right to seek asylum, and the majority were deemed by ICE to pose no risk to the community.[6]

Trump's aggressive immigrant detention policies exploded into public awareness in 2018 with the spectacle of "kids in cages," as thousands of primarily Central American families from a caravan of asylum seekers were detained in squalid conditions that shocked the conscience of many Americans. However, this action drew praise from restrictionists seeking a "tough" policy against immigrants, including asylum seekers. As journalist Adam Serwer opined in regard to policies like child detention and family separation, "the cruelty is the point."[7]

Cruelty was not, however, the only point. One of the most significant effects of increased immigrant detention was to limit access to counsel. Detained immigrants are much less likely to be able to secure legal representation than those released pending a hearing, and unrepresented immigrants are far more likely to be deported, even when they are entitled to relief. Denial of effective due process through detention was essential to the Trump administration's strategy of placing immigrants, including those who may have a right to asylum, on a "fast track" toward deportation and away from permanent status and full citizenship.[8]

Cutting Off Humanitarian Immigration

Perhaps no area of U.S. immigration policy was as profoundly changed by the Trump administration as refugee resettlement. At the end of the Obama administration, the annual refugee resettlement goal stood at 110,000 per year. Even before the COVID-19 crisis, Trump slashed resettlement targets to just 18,000, the lowest in the history of the program.[9]

Less visible but just as significant was the erosion of the right to seek asylum, a right to which the United States nominally subscribes under international treaties. In addition to locking up asylum seekers, as noted earlier, the Trump administration sought to drastically reduce the number of asylum seekers who could become permanent residents through nearly every stratagem imaginable. It stripped away domestic violence and gang violence as grounds for granting asylum and attempted to block asylum eligibility for those who traveled to a third country before entering the United States. Customs and Border Patrol (CBP) arbitrarily limited the number of asylum applicants who could enter through official checkpoints, while the administration attempted to disqualify frustrated asylum seekers who crossed the U.S.-Mexico border between checkpoints. The administration also sought to punish asylum seekers financially, first with the jaw-dropping step of charging a fee to apply for humanitarian protection, and then by cutting off access to the right to work for asylum applicants, who may wait years for their cases to be adjudicated.[10]

Through all these methods, the Trump administration single-mindedly sought to drive down the number of humanitarian immigrants who might ultimately become American citizens.

Throttling Legal Migration Programs

While the Trump administration's most dramatic successes were in blocking avenues to humanitarian immigration, that was only one part of its effort to stifle legal immigration and control future flows. Trump's 2018 State of the Union address put forward "four pillars" for changing immigration policy. One pillar was Trump's much-touted "wall," another was a ten- to twelve-year path to citizenship for DACA beneficiaries, and the other two involved cutting off future flows of legal migration. Although the four pillars were never enacted, they were the most explicit articulation of the administration's immigration strategy.[11]

The proposed pillar limiting family reunification—which the administration attempted to rebrand as "chain migration"—would have eliminated the right of U.S. citizens to sponsor their parents and adult children for visas, and the right of permanent residents to reunite with their spouses and children. This would have blocked nearly a quarter of a million family members of American citizens and permanent residents from immigrating legally to the United States each year.[12]

The Four Pillars plan also sought to eliminate the Diversity Visa (DV) program, which permits 55,000 immigrants from countries with historically low levels of immigration to the United States to immigrate legally and obtain permanent status. While the program does not make headlines as often as other immigration programs do, it provided a path to permanent residence for more immigrants than the entire refugee resettlement program during the Trump years. This is precisely why the program is a perpetual target for nativist groups.

Because DV was established by statute, Trump's efforts to abolish it were largely stymied. But his administration did succeed in erecting procedural barriers to applying to the program, requiring applicants to have expensive and difficult-to-obtain passports before their application is even selected, and suspending DV application processing as part of the blanket ban on visa processing during the pandemic.[13]

Furthermore, many of the Trump administration's other targeted "bans" focused on categories of visas and immigration that are most likely to result in permanent residence and eventually citizenship. For example, immigrants from countries targeted by the Muslim ban, including Syria and Somalia, are among the top countries of origin for resettled refugees and asylum applicants in the United States.[14] While the alleged rationale of Trump's 2020 "Africa ban" was to enhance national security by excluding visitors from countries of origin that do not adequately screen travelers, the policy actually targeted family visa and DV visa immigrants, who undergo extensive vetting by the U.S. government itself, not tourists and other temporary visitors who might pose the greatest security risks. The ban prevented Nigerian and Eritrean citizens and permanent residents from sponsoring their family members (a major step toward undermining family reunification) and banned Sudanese and Tanzanian nationals from the DV program, thereby eliminating categories of visas that lead to permanent status.[15]

In short, the combined effect of the Trump administration's varied policies was to block off multiple paths by which immigrants may seek access to permanent status and, eventually, full legal citizenship.

Who Fights for the Future?

While immigration restrictionists have relentlessly focused on controlling future flows and who becomes a citizen, the same can hardly be said of pro-immigrant advocates. Few of the anti-future-flows policies just described have garnered widespread opposition on the

scale of the mass protests, litigation, major media coverage, and legislative responses to Trump policies such as the Muslim ban, efforts
to end DACA and TPS, and the caging of kids at the border. Slash-
ing refugee resettlement by more than eighty thousand people per
year represents a humanitarian disaster, but outside of a handful of
mobilizations, mostly by faith-based institutions, opposition has
been muted. Stripping American citizens of the right to sponsor their
own parents as legal immigrants is a shocking departure from long-
standing U.S. policy, but most Americans probably never even heard
about this proposal. And when my own organization sought to protect the DV program, one of the most significant pathways for legal
migration to the United States, we found few legal partners willing to
help defend the program.[16]

To some extent, this disjuncture is understandable. Detaining
Muslim visa holders at U.S. airports, stripping long-term U.S. residents of their status and putting them on a fast track to deportation, and building detention centers for immiserated children are
immediate, tangible, and personified harms, and prompt a fiercely
urgent response. By comparison, the harm of foreclosing a chance to
legally migrate to the United States might seem more remote and less
personal—even if such a policy harms many more people in the long
run. It is not surprising that there is not as robust a constituency for
future flow issues as for other immigration policies.

However, there should be. There are many moral arguments for
defending future flows: the United States has historically offered
sanctuary to persecuted immigrants; the nation should shoulder its
fair share of global responsibility for providing refuge to displaced
migrants; and current and future U.S. citizens and permanent residents should not forfeit the right enjoyed by their counterparts in
past generations to reunite with their family members.

There is also a significant pragmatic reason. Continuing legal
migration contributes to a more diverse, more globalized United
States. Together with native-born people of color (many of them

descendants of immigrants), legal immigrants are an essential part of an emerging, multi-racial American majority that supports broadly progressive values. Immigration contributes significantly to the growth of U.S. Latinx, Asian, and Arab communities—and increasingly, of Black communities as well. Since the 1990s, approximately 20 percent of the growth in the nation's Black population came from Black immigrants, including Africans, Afro-Caribbeans, and Afro-Latinos. As of 2015, 28 percent of New York City's Black population was foreign-born; in Miami, the figure was 34 percent.[17]

The xenophobic right wing understands the stakes. When white supremacists chanted "Jews will not replace us" in the streets of Charlottesville, Virginia, they articulated their belief that the alliance between progressive U.S. citizens (including those who support immigrants and refugees because of their faith and their own historical experience of persecution) and those seeking to become new American citizens and permanent residents is an existential threat to white supremacy.

People's Instinctive Travels and the Paths of Resistance: Toward a Progressive Future Flow Agenda

What follows are preliminary thoughts about the values and visionary demands that might underlie a progressive future flow agenda.

Migration Is Human Nature and a Human Right

The xenophobic right has advanced a bold narrative about migration: the United States is being "flooded" or "overrun" with migrants (legal and illegal); whether immigrants or refugees, these newcomers are imminently dangerous, because they are either terrorists, gang members, welfare parasites, job stealers, or (somehow) all of the above; and, unlike previous generations of European migrants, non-white migrants are fundamentally "not American" and cannot be integrated into U.S. society. Underlying this narrative, however, is the fear that new immigrants *will* integrate into American society, and in doing so fundamentally change it—the fear of "replacement" voiced by white supremacists in Charlottesville.

The immigrant rights movement needs an equally bold and compelling narrative about migration. One part of it should be an affirmation that the course of human civilization—indeed, the development of the human species—has been shaped by successive waves of migration: voluntary, forced, and in-between. Instead of solely spotlighting the contributions of "exceptional" immigrants or extraordinary cases of humanitarian hardship, we must also lift up the *ordinariness* of migration. We should affirm that the most common reasons for migration—to escape persecution, to find greater opportunity for economic advancement, to enjoy greater freedom and personal realization, to reunite with family and loved ones—are normal and natural human drives. Societies that seek to stifle the freedom of their citizens to move, or to isolate themselves from the flows of human migration (even while enjoying the flows of capital, goods, and culture), should bear the burden of moral justification, not migrants.

Refugee Protection Is a Moral Obligation, and the United States Must Do Its Fair Share

A fact known by those who pay attention to refugee policy—but unknown to most Americans—is that the West does little for refugees compared to developing countries. Worldwide, 85 percent of refugees are hosted by developing countries, often those neighboring the countries from which they were displaced: Palestinians in Lebanon, Sudanese in Ethiopia, Syrians in Turkey, and so forth.[18]

At the end of the Obama administration, the United States pledged to admit 110,000 refugees per year. During his 2020 campaign, Biden promised to exceed that goal and resettle 125,000 refugees per year, and to raise that number further over time. Such actions would place the United States above other high-income countries in the number of refugees admitted annually, as it had been throughout the history of the refugee resettlement program prior to the Trump years. However, even an increased commitment of 125,000 refugees resettled would represent only about 0.04 percent of the U.S. population—less than one refugee for every 1,000 U.S. residents. By contrast, in 2019 Ethiopia hosted 10 refugees for every 1,000 residents, Turkey 45, and Lebanon an astonishing 156 refugees per 1,000 residents.[19]

Imagine for a moment that the United States agreed to accept just one refugee for every 1,000 U.S. residents (or 1/10th of 1 percent of the U.S. population) each year. That would mean resettling 328,000 refugees in the United States annually, a number that may sound staggering relative to historical levels of refugee resettlement in the United States and most other developed Western nations. But it is modest compared to the scale of the need, or to what neighboring countries are doing already. Even over a decade, it would barely shift the percentage of the U.S. population that is foreign-born. A truly visionary future flow agenda would argue unapologetically that the United States can and should undertake a humanitarian commitment of this scale and boldness.

The good news is that the recent backlash against refugees has relatively shallow roots in American culture. In marked contrast with Europe and the United Kingdom, where anti-asylee and anti-refugee sentiment has been a central feature of immigration politics for decades, prior to the Trump administration only a handful of the most vocal immigration restrictionists considered it a priority. Indeed, America as a place of refuge continues to play a central role in our national story. Even some elements of the conservative coalition, such as evangelicals, are sympathetic to "genuine" refugees. Over 70 percent of Americans, including a majority of Republicans, consider it important to take in refugees escaping war and violence.[20]

The 2019 Liberian Refugee and Immigrant Fairness program, which granted permanent status to an estimated ten thousand undocumented African immigrants, many of whom had been in the

United States for decades, is a rare success story of legalization under the Trump administration. It could not have been enacted without quiet support from key Republican senators.[21]

Another hopeful example is that when Trump offered states the opportunity to "opt out" from resettlement of refugees in their states (an executive order later found to be illegal), only eight states took him up on the offer, and several solidly conservative states affirmed their continued acceptance of refugees.[22]

We can push for more, not less, refugee resettlement, and we can win.

Immigrants Are Entitled to Due Process

The only thing more absurd, cruel, or sickening than the spectacle of immigrant children representing themselves in life-and-death asylum proceedings is the pretense that this represents due process, rather than indifference or hostility to the rights of asylum seekers. The separation of families and caging of children at the U.S. border similarly shocks the conscience.

But the truth is that this sad drama has played out under both Democratic and Republican administrations. The response to the previous Central American caravan, led by Secretary of State Hillary Clinton during the Obama years, was less spectacularly cruel but was nearly as inhumane. The current U.S. asylum system permits only a small number of humanitarian migrants—those who can best articulate their experience of persecution in conformity with asylum law, those lucky enough to elude the barriers that keep them from presenting their claims, and those who manage to find legal representation—to gain permanent status and ultimately citizenship. Managing one of our country's most important humanitarian international commitments in this way does not comport with any defensible theory of justice.

We need a policy debate about the root causes and limits of migration, and how best to distribute opportunities for humanitarian admissions. For example, we may wish to encourage resettlement as a safer path for refugees than transcontinental migrant caravans.

But one cornerstone of any humanitarian immigration policy regime must be asylum proceedings that comport with due process, including meaningful notice, opportunity to be heard, and equality before the law. The most effective way to achieve this end is a guaranteed right to counsel, similar to that protected under U.S. criminal law. Asylum applicants unable to afford legal counsel should receive it free of charge, and courts should be adequately funded and staffed to ensure timely adjudication of claims—eliminating "rocket dockets" and other types of mass-processing or pro forma proceedings. Like criminal courts, immigration courts dispose of fundamental rights of life, freedom, and family unity. If they are not required to do so justly and fairly, they become simply extensions of ICE, and equally worthy of being abolished.

Equity Includes Diversity, Opportunity, and Fairness

Finally, a visionary future flow agenda should include a full-throated defense of the DV program and the values that underlie it. While the Trump administration focused relentlessly on attacking the program, demanding changes to it as part of any immigration deal, pro-immigrant elected officials and immigrant rights advocates alike have been tepid in its defense. In some cases, advocates have treated the DV program as a bargaining chip to be negotiated away for immigration priorities that are seen as more urgent: in 1997, when five thousand visas per year were reallocated from DV to the Nicaraguan Adjustment and Central American Relief Act program; in 2012, when DV elimination was offered up as part of "comprehensive immigration reform"; and most recently in 2018, as a gambit to save the DACA program.[23]

During the 2018 debate in the U.S. Senate over a "consensus" immigration proposal that would preserve DACA, some leaders in the Democratic caucus supported abolishing the "lottery" system for allocating applications to the DV program and replacing it with a preference for immigrants from Africa and other historically low-admission regions under other visa programs (including family reunification and employment-based visas).[24] The argument was that eliminating the "lottery," with its connotations of chance and gambling, would neutralize attacks from opponents of the DV program, and that the proposed family and employment preferences would maintain a geographic preference for Africa and other historically low-admission regions.

This debate, which took place largely behind closed doors, revealed deeply problematic understandings of the principles, purposes, and benefits of the DV program. The program is not merely a political concession to the African, Asian, European, and other countries and diasporas that disproportionately benefit from it. Rather, it is an opportunity for legal immigration from low-admission countries for people who have no access to existing family, employment, or humanitarian-based channels.

Family sponsorship requires immediate relatives in the United States, which immigrants from low-admission countries, by definition, are less likely to have, in part due to historical discrimination in immigration admissions. Similarly, African immigrants are much less likely than those from other parts of the world to have an offer of employment from a U.S. employer: as of 2018, only 3 percent of employment-based visas went to African immigrants. Employment-based discrimination against Black immigrants and the underdevelopment of African educational systems and infrastructure are major causes. From 2012 to 2017 approximately 100,000 Africans were admitted through the DV program, accounting for over 40 percent of all DV admissions. In the same time period, only 72,000 Africans were admitted through family preference visas and employer-sponsored visas *combined*.

The debate about where the DV program fits into future flows is difficult because it requires balancing competing claims to fairness.

Should H-1B visa holders and other immigrants whose labor is in demand by large corporations get the first shot at legal immigration opportunities? Or should claims by immigrants who have strong family ties to U.S. citizens and permanent residents take precedence—even if those family ties reflect historical patterns of discrimination? Does the United States have a particular obligation to migrants from neighboring countries in the Americas? What are its obligations to those from other regions where it has played an outsized role in the root causes of migration, such as the Persian Gulf, Liberia, and Somalia?

Without presuming to answer these questions, I argue that the principles underlying the DV program—correcting historical discrimination, equality of opportunity regardless of personal privilege, and global inclusion—merit strong consideration alongside other forms of distributional fairness in any future flows regime.

Conclusion

So who fights for the future, and for future flows? The elements of a coalition are already there. The traditional immigrant rights movement must embrace a focus on future flows at the same level as issues such as enforcement and a path to status for those already here. Moreover, any progressive concerned with the building of a durable electoral majority must put future flow issues on their agenda, alongside issues such as the Census, voter protection, and reenfranchisement.

We also urgently need to communicate with more unlikely allies, including moderate and conservative people of faith who are sympathetic to the right to seek refuge. There is room in the big tent as well for policymakers and businesses concerned with what declining global fertility rates and the growing needs of the aging American populace mean for caregiving.

But the fight over future flows must be led by those most affected. Millions of immigrants wait for years or even decades to be able to bring their relatives to the United States because of lengthy backlogs. We need to organize them to fight for higher annual admissions so that they can reunite with loved ones. Immigrants who have benefited from the DV program need the chance to tell their own stories and counter the false narratives deployed against the program. And we can no longer leave to official refugee resettlement agencies—whose hands are tied by dependence on government funding and the need for official cooperation—the work of fighting for refugee resettlement in the halls of government, in the courts, and in the streets.

White nationalists like those who marched in Charlottesville fear that future flows could fundamentally change America and threaten the idea of white supremacy. It is up to us to transform that threat into a promise, and a reality.

Notes

1. See, e.g., *Plyler v. Doe*, 457 U.S. 202 (1982); *Lozano v. City of Hazleton*, 496 F. Supp. 2d 477, 530-33 (M.D. Pa. 2007).

2. I am grateful to Joel Sati—who in addition to his legal scholarship is a former African Communities Together student organizer—for introducing me to the framework of illegalization, which he has developed in essays such as "Noncitizenship and the Case for Illegalized Persons," *Berkeley Blog*, Jan. 24, 2017, blogs .berkeley.edu/2017/01/24/noncitizenship-and-the-case-for-illegalized-persons.

3. For an overview of changes in immigration enforcement, see John Gramlich, "How Border Apprehensions, ICE Arrests and Deportations Have Changed Under Trump," Pew Research Center, Mar. 2, 2020; Guillermo Cantor, Emily Ryo, and Reed Humphrey, "Changing Patterns of Interior Enforcement in the United States, 2016–2018," American Immigration Council, June 2019.

4. For an overview of the escalation of immigrant detention, see Dara Lind, "'Catch and Release,' Explained: The Heart of Trump's New Border Agenda," *Vox*, Apr. 9, 2018; Nuria Marquez Martinez, "This Map Shows How Radically Trump Has Changed Immigration Detention," *Mother Jones*, Dec. 27, 2019. But see Emily Kassie, "How Trump Inherited His Expanding Detention System," The Marshall Project, Feb. 2, 2019, which demonstrates that immigrant detention has grown steadily over successive presidencies.

5. On trends in parole, bond, and immigration judge judicial independence, see "Parole vs. Bond in the Asylum System," Human Rights First, Sept. 5, 2018, www.humanrightsfirst.org/resource/parole-vs-bond-asylum-system; Dianne Solis and Jenny Manrique, "Could It Get Any Tougher for Immigrant Detainees?

High Bonds Are New Hurdle," *Dallas Morning News*, July 23, 2018; Daniel Bush, "Under Trump, Higher Immigration Bonds Mean Longer Family Separations," *PBS NewsHour*, June 28, 2018; Beth Fertig, "Presiding Under Pressure," WNYC, May 21, 2019.

6. See National Immigrant Justice Center, "ICE Released Its Most Comprehensive Immigration Detention Data Yet. It's Alarming," Mar. 13, 2018, immigrantjustice.org/staff/blog/ice-released-its-most-comprehensive-immigration -detention-data-yet.

7. Adam Serwer, "The Cruelty Is the Point," *The Atlantic*, Oct. 3, 2018.

8. On the difference that access to counsel makes to immigration case outcomes, see Ingrid Eagly and Steven Shafer, "Access to Counsel in Immigration Court," American Immigration Council, Sept. 28, 2016.

9. Muzaffar Chishti and Sarah Pierce, "Despite Trump Invitation to Stop Taking Refugees, Red and Blue States Alike Endorse Resettlement," Migration Policy Institute, Jan. 29, 2020.

10. See Anneliese Hermann, "Asylum in the Trump Era: The Quiet Dismantling of National and International Norms," Center for American Progress, June 13, 2018; National Immigrant Justice Center, "A Timeline of the Trump Administration's Efforts to End Asylum," Mar. 2020, immigrantjustice.org/sites/default/files /uploaded-files/no-content-type/2020-04/04-01-2020-asylumtimeline.pdf.

11. See Senate Republican Policy Committee, "Four Pillars: The Trump Administration Immigration Plan," Feb. 13, 2018, www.rpc.senate.gov/policy -papers/four-pillars-the-trump-administration-immigration-plan.

12. Ibid.; William A. Kandel, "U.S. Family-Based Immigration Policy," Congressional Research Service, Feb. 9, 2018.

13. On the DV program generally, see Congressional Research Service, "The Diversity Immigrant Visa Program," updated Oct. 2019. On the lawsuit challenging the "passport rule," *E.B. v. Dep't of State*, which African Communities Together partnered with the Georgetown University Law Center Institute for Constitutional Advocacy and Protection (ICAP) to bring, see ICAP, "Lawsuit Challenges Trump Administration's New Passport Requirement for Diversity Visa Lottery Applicants," Sept. 24, 2019. On the suspension of DV visa processing, see Exec. Order No. 10,052, 85 Fed. Reg. 38,263 (June 22, 2020); Danilo Zak, "President Trump's Proclamation Suspending Immigration," National Immigration Forum, June 23, 2020, immigrationforum.org/article/president-trumps-proclamation-suspending -immigration.

14. Department of Homeland Security, "Annual Flow Report: Refugees and Asylees 2017," Mar. 2019.

15. Exec. Order No. 9,983, 85 Fed. Reg. 6,699 (June 22, 2020).

16. I am grateful to the nonprofit legal advocates who have joined African Communities Together in defending DV, including ICAP, the International Refugee Assistance Project (IRAP), and the Lawyers' Committee for Civil Rights Under Law.

17. Mary Mederios Kent, "Immigration and America's Black Population," *Population Bulletin*, Dec. 2007, 4, www.prb.org/pdf07/62.4immigration.pdf; Monica Anderson, "A Rising Share of the U.S. Black Population Is Foreign Born," Pew Research Center, Apr. 9, 2015.

18. UN High Commissioner for Refugees, "Refugee Data Finder," www.unhcr.org/refugee-statistics; Amnesty International, "The World's Refugees in Numbers," www.amnesty.org/en/what-we-do/refugees-asylum-seekers-and-migrants/global-refugee-crisis-statistics-and-facts.

19. Amnesty International, "Refugee Data Finder"; Brittany Blizzard and Jeanne Batalova, "Refugees and Asylees in the United States," Migration Policy Institute, June 13, 2019; Joe Biden, "My Statement on World Refugee Day," *Medium*, June 20, 2020, medium.com/@JoeBiden/my-statement-on-world-refugee-day-fddb4abddfd5.

20. See Andrew Daniller, "Americans' Immigration Policy Priorities: Divisions Between—and Within—the Two Parties," Pew Research Center, Nov. 12, 2019.

21. Personal communication with Senate policy staff.

22. Muzaffar Chishti and Sarah Pierce, "Despite Trump Invitation to Stop Taking Refugees, Red and Blue States Alike Endorse Resettlement," Migration Policy Institute, Jan. 29, 2020.

23. The Congressional Black Caucus has been one of the program's few ardent defenders.

24. The comments that follow are drawn in part from my personal correspondence in 2018 with members of Congress about protecting the DV program. I am grateful to Patrice Lawrence, Co-Director of the UndocuBlack Network, with whom I worked closely on this advocacy, for her contributions to them.

Abolish ICE . . . and Then What?

Peter L. Markowitz

The movement to abolish the U.S. Immigration and Customs Enforcement agency (ICE) burst into the national consciousness in the summer of 2018.[1] The idea was the natural extension of years of thoughtful organizing by a loose coalition of grassroots immigrant rights groups.[2] They had become convinced that efforts to reform ICE were futile and that a more radical approach was needed. Prominent national politicians quickly lined up behind the idea.[3] But that initial rush of support has waned in the years that followed.

ICE's brutality and lawlessness have been well documented.[4] The one area where ICE has demonstrated startling success has been in garnering resources for itself. Its funding has risen from $3.3 billion in 2003, the year after its creation, to $7.5 billion in 2018—an increase of approximately 130 percent.[5] What has been gained from this enormous spending increase? Certainly, the number of deportations has skyrocketed.[6] But if the goal is to increase compliance with the law, the surge in funding has failed miserably. In 2000, just before the creation of ICE, the country's undocumented population stood at 7 million.[7] The Department of Homeland Security's (DHS) most recent estimate of the undocumented population is 12 million.[8] Thus, while ICE's resources have more than doubled, the undocumented population has grown by over 70 percent. Waste and mismanagement are part of the problem, but at base, these numbers demonstrate that ICE's ever-increasing investment in detention and deportation has simply failed to increase compliance with U.S. immigration law.[9] The failure of ICE's enforcement paradigm, however, merely begs the question whether there is a better way.

Scholars and movement leaders have proposed specific and thoughtful changes to our immigration enforcement paradigm.[10] These changes, however, focus almost exclusively on a negative vision of what we need to eliminate in our current enforcement scheme: detention, mass deportations,[11] and the entanglement of our criminal justice and immigration systems, among other flaws.[12] Lacking in the public discourse is a clear affirmative vision for a practical immigration enforcement system that is not dependent on mass detention and deportation.[13] This chapter seeks to offer such a vision for a new immigration enforcement paradigm that is both humane and effective but does not rely on mass detention and deportation.[14]

The Four Pillars of a Humane and Effective Immigration Enforcement System

Any successful proposal for a post-ICE immigration enforcement scheme must achieve two distinct goals. First, the new system must forswear and commit to cure the inhumanity and brutality that characterize immigration enforcement under ICE—most notably by eliminating immigration detention and mass deportation. Second, the new system must be more effective at promoting compliance with immigration law. Some critics of the Abolish ICE movement have suggested that the two goals are mutually inconsistent, but they need not be so.[15] In what follows I propose four pillars of a new immigration enforcement paradigm—one that would radically reshape immigration enforcement and create a humane system that could be both more effective at encouraging compliance with U.S. immigration laws and dramatically less expensive. The proposal draws lessons from our own and other nations' past immigration enforcement schemes, from mechanisms employed by other federal agencies, and from the expertise of the leaders of the movement to abolish ICE interviewed for this chapter.

Pillar One: Optimal Enforcement Scaling

DHS was founded with the mission of achieving a "100% removal rate."[16] Accordingly, ICE's goal from the outset was, and remains, to deport every person potentially subject to deportation.[17] This approach, which has driven the extraordinary increase in ICE's funding, is both wildly impractical and dramatically out of step with historical norms.[18] During the twentieth century, when the United States also had significant levels of noncompliance with immigration laws, the nation deported less than 25,000 people per year on average.[19] Thus far in the twenty-first century, the United States has deported more than 300,000 people per year on average—a startling 1,200 percent increase.[20] Accordingly, the first inquiry is to determine whether the current extraordinary levels of punitive enforcement are justified.

Any well-conceived enforcement scheme must identify its optimal scale by balancing the societal costs of punitive enforcement against the marginal additional compliance such enforcement can achieve and the societal benefits associated with that additional compliance. For example, extremely high levels of enforcement by the Nuclear Regulatory Commission are justified because even low levels of noncompliance risk grave societal harm. In other areas, such as the regulation of marijuana, sex work, or quality-of-life crimes, there is a growing consensus that the cost and collateral harms of high levels of enforcement, the low deterrent value of heavy-handed enforcement, and the relatively minor societal injuries associated with noncompliance militate in favor of low enforcement levels.

In the administrative arena, the approach of the Internal Revenue Service (IRS) stands out as an example of an intentionally low-level punitive enforcement strategy. Initially, the IRS was required to audit all tax returns.[21] Over time, this enforcement approach came to be seen as overzealous.[22] In response, Congress implemented reforms that caused punitive enforcement activity to decline significantly.[23] The IRS now employs a notably low level of punitive enforcement, annually auditing less than one percent of returns and prosecuting only a couple of hundred people for failure to file.[24] This shift away from punitive enforcement and toward compliance assistance has not undermined the IRS's enforcement of tax laws. Indeed, the United States now enjoys one of the world's highest tax compliance rates.[25]

In the immigration arena, the societal costs of the current high levels of punitive enforcement are profound. The destruction of family units, deaths, mistreatment, and the traumatization of entire communities are well documented. Further, the fiscal costs are extraordinary.[26] On the other side of the equation, the harms associated with noncompliance are hotly contested. Immigration restrictionists point principally to three categories of alleged harm: criminality of undocumented immigrants, the cost of providing public benefits and services to undocumented immigrants, and the harms that may flow from labor competition with undocumented workers.[27] However, the social science data establish that these alleged harms are either nonexistent or minor.

Study after study has concluded that undocumented immigrants pose no heightened risk of criminality.[28] Undocumented immigrants are also ineligible for virtually all federal benefits programs.[29] Indeed, many undocumented workers pay taxes and pay into Social Security and other benefits systems, notwithstanding their ineligibility to receive such benefits—leading some to argue that they are a net benefit to the public coffer.[30] Evidence on whether undocumented workers create increased labor competition in low-wage fields is more contested, but the overwhelming weight of the evidence demonstrates that undocumented workers are a critical net benefit to the U.S. economy.[31] Indeed, much of the literature demonstrates that the greatest harms of immigration noncompliance are suffered by the undocumented population itself.[32] Moreover, even if we were to assume some significant level of harm from noncompliance, high levels of enforcement are justified only if they actually reduce noncompliance. The weight of the evidence, however, suggests that ICE's heavy-handed tactics are of limited value in reducing noncompliance.[33]

Accordingly, the first pillar requires policymakers to scrutinize the level of punitive enforcement employed by ICE and to identify the optimal scale. In doing so, they will likely see that the current high level of punitive immigration enforcement is of limited utility in increasing compliance and carries significant fiscal and human costs that outweigh the relatively minor societal harms associated with the deterrable noncompliance. A humane and effective immigration enforcement scheme thus requires a radical reduction in the scale of punitive enforcement. This first pillar could be largely implemented through executive direction and without any change in law.

Pillar Two: Mandatory Preferences for Compliance Assistance

There are large categories of undocumented immigrants who are potentially subject to deportation but also eligible to obtain lawful status. For example, someone who came to the United States lawfully, overstayed their visa, and married a U.S. citizen may be either deported or allowed to obtain legal permanent residence. Immigration authorities have a choice between two enforcement pathways: punish the noncompliance through deportation or allow the individual to come into compliance by applying for permanent residence.

Administrative law scholars have widely praised the trend toward "cooperative enforcement," whereby administrative agencies outside the immigration context increasingly favor efforts to help entities come into compliance over deploying punitive measures.[34] When the regulated parties are corporations rather than immigrants, the government seems comfortable with this approach. It is the approach now favored by federal agencies such as the Occupational Safety and Health Administration, the Food and Drug Administration, the Environmental Protection Agency, and the Securities and Exchange

Commission.[35] Indeed, it is the approach that the IRS has favored in modern times, which has helped it successfully transition away from heavy-handed punitive enforcement.[36]

But when it comes to immigration, the government has done the opposite.[37] Instead of diverting people out of the punitive enforcement stream (ICE's deportation machine) and into compliance assistance mechanisms (United States Citizenship and Immigration Services [USCIS] application processes), it does the reverse. When an eligible-but-deportable individual applies for an immigration benefit, USCIS frequently declines to grant their application and diverts them into the deportation system.[38] There are large categories of undocumented individuals eligible to obtain lawful status right now.[39] There are other significant categories of people being pushed through the deportation pipeline who will, in time, become eligible for lawful status.[40] In addition, there are many more people eligible to obtain or maintain status through mechanisms that are currently only available defensively in deportation proceedings, such as cancelation or withholding of removal.[41]

Prosecutorial discretion is the mechanism that has generally been used to determine which enforcement pathway to pursue, and it has failed to deliver a reliable preference for compliance assistance. Accordingly, the second pillar of a humane and effective immigration enforcement scheme is to enact mandatory rules that give people the *right* to affirmatively pursue pathways to lawful status before they can be subject to any punitive enforcement action. This mandatory preference could be implemented through a rule or regulation and, like the first pillar, would not require any congressional action.[42] In addition, Congress should consider making compliance mechanisms that are presently only available defensively instead available on an affirmative basis. Most dramatically, if Congress created new affirmative pathways to citizenship for undocumented individuals, as it has done in the past, this pillar could address the majority of noncompliance.[43] With a significantly reduced investment in punitive enforcement, the

United States could increase compliance by redirecting resources to USCIS (or, if DHS were reformed, some successor agency in another department responsible for delivering immigration benefits) to speed up processing times, expand legal assistance, and reduce application fees for immigration benefits.

Pillar Three: A System of Proportional Consequences

Even if the United States dramatically reduces the scale of punitive enforcement and relies principally on compliance assistance, there will still be situations where individuals cannot be brought into compliance and where enforcement is warranted. Accordingly, there must be some consequences that can be triggered by noncompliance. The current regime relies only on a single penalty—deportation—which is grossly disproportionate to the overwhelming majority of immigration offenses. A binary choice between no penalty and the harshest possible penalty is not how other effective enforcement systems work. It is like a medieval criminal justice system where the only two choices were no penalty or the death penalty. Accordingly, implementing a new system of scalable penalties is the third pillar of a humane and effective immigration enforcement scheme.[44]

Fines are the most obvious option and are widely used across the administrative state. As recently as 2000, fines were also a critical part of the immigration enforcement system. Certain individuals who entered unlawfully were permitted to obtain lawful permanent residency if they paid a $1,000 penalty.[45] Any such fines would need to be of sufficient magnitude to be significant to the regulated population but also within their ability to pay. Other scalable penalties could include, for example, delayed access to immigration or other public benefits, lengthened pathways to citizenship, or mandated community service obligations. As with the former $1,000 penalty, any such scalable penalties would then unlock a previously unavailable pathway to status. New penalties and the ability to access lawful immigration status thereafter would require an act of Congress. As with other administrative schemes, the penalties could be offered as a negotiated resolution of noncompliance by USCIS or the successor services agency, and if no agreement could be reached, such penalties and any defenses thereto could be litigated through the immigration courts.

Pillar Four: Minimizing the Use of Physically Coercive State Power

Even with the reforms just outlined, there will be outlier cases where the agency is unsuccessful in bringing individuals into compliance or where an individual fails to comply with the imposed scalable penalty, and where thereafter the proportional punishment is deemed to be deportation.[46] In such cases, the United States has a legal and moral obligation to find mechanisms to ensure that people appear in court and comply with deportation orders without unnecessarily severe deprivations of liberty.

The first step in that effort must be to eliminate the use of preventative immigration detention. Virtually every other federal agency has found a way to enforce its civil administrative scheme without putting people in cages. There is no reason why deportation proceedings, or even the deportation process itself, must begin with handcuffs. For most of U.S. history, those processes began with notices.[47] The question then becomes, how can we more humanely ensure people's appearance in immigration court and ultimately, for some, their compliance with deportation orders?

The answer begins with due process. The data demonstrate that the most important thing we can do to improve appearance rates in immigration court is to provide lawyers. The most recent publicly available data show that virtually every family who was released from immigration detention and had a lawyer showed up for all of their immigration court hearings (99 percent).[48] Those without lawyers were significantly less likely to consistently appear (76 percent).[49] Lawyers help ensure that individuals have accurate information about the time and place of hearings. Lawyers also remove the terror of walking into an unfamiliar courtroom alone and litigating in one of the most complex arenas of American law, against trained government prosecutors, without any legal training, and often in an unfamiliar language. Moreover, the feasibility of a program of assigned immigration counsel has been robustly demonstrated in New York City and New York State, which have had universal appointed counsel programs dating back to 2013 and 2017, respectively.[50] To be sure, implementing such a program on a national scale would be costly, but the massive scale-down in punitive enforcement contemplated in pillar one would more than offset the costs. Providing lawyers is thus the first step toward ensuring that individuals know and comply with their obligations in immigration court.[51]

In addition, other countries such as Canada have engaged in promising experiments with inducements to improve compliance with deportation orders.[52] Canada used financial inducements of up to $2,000 to encourage voluntary compliance with deportation orders. With the United States spending an average of $12,000 per deportation, the cost-saving opportunities of such a program are significant.[53] Other inducements for those who promptly comply with deportation orders—such as reduced wait times for readmission and continued access to earned domestic benefits such as Social Security—could also be powerful tools to promote compliance.[54]

Finally, the immigration system can draw on lessons from the criminal justice reentry movement. It has become accepted wisdom that if we want individuals leaving prison to successfully reintegrate into society, we need to invest in reentry services. Those services include, for example, job training, housing assistance, health care planning, and mental health treatment. We provide these services to people coming out of prison because it is inhumane to deposit individuals on the street without the means to survive and thrive. But we also deliver these services because they are critical to ensuring that individuals do not reoffend. Reentry services for individuals being deported could serve these same purposes. They could be powerful tools to help individuals reintegrate into their countries of origin, thereby reducing the brutality of deportation and easing the terror that leads some to resist compliance with deportation orders. Successful integration, in turn, is critical to reducing the chances of unlawful return to the United States. As with the financial incentives discussed earlier, care would need to be taken to ensure that such services themselves do not become an incentive for noncompliance.

Conclusion

ICE has failed by every measure. It has brutalized communities, wasted billions of dollars, and failed to increase compliance with immigration laws. The four pillars set forth in this chapter provide a blueprint for how a radically new vision for immigration enforcement could increase compliance while simultaneously reducing the human and fiscal costs of enforcement. This blueprint would allow us to abolish ICE and to create an effective and humane enforcement system without the need for any dedicated agency of immigration police. In place of ICE, the United States would need to increase public investment in an immigration agency, such as USCIS, that delivers services to immigrants and that would be responsible for facilitating compliance assistance programs. Such an agency, however, should not be housed inside DHS. Instead, the immigration agency should be housed in a department, such as Health and Human Services, that has a mission consistent with appropriate immigration policy goals: to look after the well-being and economic vitality of immigrants and of the nation as a whole.

The ability to theorize a workable and humane immigration enforcement system is a necessary but insufficient precursor to realizing the reforms that our nation's immigration system desperately needs. Other aspects of the system, such as legalization pathways for undocumented immigrants and laws regulating the future flow of immigrants, are equally in need of reform. However, much good work has already been done to reimagine these aspects of the system, while comparatively little has been done to rethink the substantive rules or the mechanics of immigration enforcement. This chapter sets forth a framework for the mechanics of a just enforcement system. Additional work is needed to reimagine the substantive rules that should dictate who can be punished for immigration violations, and what types of punishments are appropriate. The proposal set forth here is intended as a starting point for the immigrant rights movement and for policymakers to use, critique, and improve upon.

Notes

This chapter is an excerpted version of an essay originally published by the Yale Law Journal Company, Incorporated in the *Yale Law Journal Forum*, Volume 129 (2019), pp. 130–148. A fuller presentation of the proposal set forth herein is published in Volume 55 of the *Wake Forest Law Review* (2020). I am grateful for the ideas and insights shared by the immigrant community leaders who generously participated in interviews for this project, including Silky Shah from Detention Watch Network; Mizue Aizeki and Marie Mark from the Immigrant Defense Project; Paromita Shah from Just Futures Law; Javier Valdés and Luba Cortes from Make the Road New York; Natalia Aristizabal from the Center for Popular Democracy; and Jacinta Gonzalez from Mijente.

1. Molly Hensley-Clancy and Nidhi Prakash, "'Abolish ICE' Was the Call of Last Summer. 2020 Democrats Have Moved On.," *Buzzfeed News*, May 15, 2019; Julianne Hing, "What Does It Mean to Abolish ICE? Activists and Politicians Want a Total Overhaul of Immigration Enforcement—but Do We Have a Real Plan?," *The Nation*, July 11, 2018.

2. JOMO, "Fighting Obama's Deportation Policies Without Papers—and Without Fear," *The Nation*, Apr. 24, 2014.

3. Hensley-Clancy and Prakash, "Abolish ICE"; Hing, "What Does It Mean to Abolish ICE?"

4. Madeline Buiano, "ICE Data: Tens of Thousands of Deported Parents Have U.S. Citizen Kids," Center for Public Integrity, Oct. 12, 2018, publicintegrity.org/immigration/ice-data-tens-of-thousands-of-deported-parents-have-u-s-citizen-kids; Office of Inspector General, U.S. Department of Homeland Security, "Concerns About ICE Detainee Treatment and Care at Four Detention Facilities," June 3, 2019, www.oig.dhs.gov/sites/default/files/assets/2019-06/OIG-19-47-Jun19.pdf; Alia Al-Khatib, "Putting a Hold on Ice: Why Law Enforcement Should Refuse to Honor Immigration Detainers," *American University Law Review* 64 (2014): 145–46; Bess Chiu et al., "Constitution on ICE: A Report on Immigration

Home Raid Operations," Cardozo Immigration Justice Clinic, 2009, larc.cardozo.yu.edu/faculty-articles/110.

5. American Immigration Council, "The Growth of the U.S. Deportation Machine: More Immigrants Are Being 'Removed' from the United States than Ever Before," Mar. 2014, 4, www.americanimmigrationcouncil.org/sites/default/files/research/the_growth_of_the_us_deportation_machine.pdf; U.S. Department of Homeland Security, "Budget-in-Brief: Fiscal Year 2020," www.dhs.gov/sites/default/files/publications/19_0318_MGMT_FY-2020-Budget-In-Brief.pdf.

6. *2017 Yearbook of Immigration Statistics*, prepared by Office of Immigration Statistics, U.S. Department of Homeland Security, 193, table 39, www.dhs.gov/sites/default/files/publications/yearbook_immigration_statistics_2017_0.pdf.

7. Office of Policy and Planning, U.S. Immigration and Naturalization Service, "Estimates of the Unauthorized Immigrant Population Residing in the United States: 1990 to 2000," 1, www.dhs.gov/sites/default/files/publications/Unauthorized%20Immigrant%20Population%20Estimates%20in%20the%20US%201990%20to%202000.pdf.

8. Office of Immigration Statistics, U.S. Department of Homeland Security, "Population Estimates: Illegal Alien Population Residing in the United States: January 2015," Dec. 2018, 2, www.dhs.gov/sites/default/files/publications/18_1214_PLCY_pops-est-report.pdf. Some nongovernmental actors have estimated that the undocumented population has declined somewhat in recent years. Relevant analysis can be found in Jeffrey S. Passel and D'Vera Cohn, "U.S. Unauthorized Immigrant Total Dips to Lowest Level in a Decade," Pew Research Center, Nov. 27, 2018, www.pewhispanic.org/2018/11/27/u-s-unauthorized-immigrant-total-dips-to-lowest-level-in-a-decade. However, such decline is generally understood to be the result of changes in the push and pull factors that drive immigration and is not believed to be attributable to ICE's enforcement strategy.

9. Detention Watch Network, "ICE's Fiscal Mismanagement: Deceit and Abuse," www.detentionwatchnetwork.org/sites/default/files/ICE%E2%80%99s%20Fiscal%20Mismanagement-%20Deceit%20and%20Abuse.pdf.

10. César Cuauhtémoc García Hernández, "Abolishing Immigration Prisons," *Boston University Law Review* 97 (2017): 292–300; Kari Hong, "10 Reasons Why Congress Should Defund ICE's Deportation Force," *New York University Review of Law and Social Change* 43 (2019): 40; Detention Watch Network, "Defund the Detention and Deportation Machine Campaign," Nov. 12, 2018, www.detentionwatchnetwork.org/sites/default/files/DefundHate%20Explainer_11.12.2018.pdf; Mijente, "Free Our Future: An Immigration Policy Platform for Beyond the Trump Era," June 20, 2018, mijente.net/wp-content/uploads/2018/06/Mijente-Immigration-Policy-Platform_0628.pdf.

11. The Immigration and Nationality Act (INA) uses the term "removal" rather than "deportation"; 8 U.S.C. § 1229a (2018). This term tends to sanitize the state violence associated with the physical separation of individuals from their families and communities. Accordingly, I use the term "deportation."

12. Detention Watch Network, "Defund the Detention"; Mijente, "Free Our Future."

13. For a discussion of legislation to abolish ICE that would create a commission to recommend a new immigration enforcement system, see Elliot Hannon, "House Democrats Preparing Legislation That Would Abolish ICE," *Slate*, July 10, 2018. Some proponents of abolishing ICE have rejected the idea of enforcement altogether, calling for an end to borders; see, e.g., California Immigrant Youth Justice Alliance, "First We Abolish ICE: A Manifesto for Immigrant Liberation," July 2, 2018, ciyja.org/wpcontent/uploads/2018/07/AbolishICE.pdf. However, the majority of the movement has not seen any utility in staking out a formal position. In contrast, the movement is united and clear in its goal to literally abolish ICE and any dedicated agency of immigration police. In recognition of the reality that borders are likely here to stay, they are interested in the practical effort of mitigating the pain that immigration enforcement visits upon their communities. I adopt this approach throughout. Assuming that rules will remain about who may enter and stay in the United States, I seek to envision the most just and humane way to enforce those rules.

14. "Enforcement" as used throughout this chapter is not limited to systems of punishment through coercive physical state power. Rather, the term is used broadly to describe any method to address noncompliance or encourage compliance.

15. Jeh Charles Johnson, "Abolishing ICE Is Not a Serious Policy Proposal," *Washington Post*, July 6, 2018.

16. U.S. Immigration and Customs Enforcement, "Endgame: Office of Detention and Removal Strategic Plan 2003–2012," June 27, 2003. fas.org/irp/agency/dhs/endgame.pdf.

17. Ibid.; Executive Order No. 13,768, 82 Fed. Reg. 8799, 8800 (Jan. 30, 2017); Secure Fence Act, Pub. L. No. 109-367, § 2(b), 120 Stat. 2638 (2006).

18. See Julia Preston et al., "What Would It Take for Donald Trump to Deport 11 Million and Build a Wall?," *New York Times*, May 19, 2016.

19. *2017 Yearbook of Immigration Statistics*.

20. Ibid.

21. Revenue Act of 1918, Pub. L. No. 65-254, § 250(b), 40 Stat. 1057, 1083 (1919); J.T. Manhire, "What Does Voluntary Tax Compliance Mean? A Government Perspective," *University of Pennsylvania Law Review Online* 164 (2015): 14 n. 17.

22. Leandra Lederman, "Tax Compliance and the Reformed IRS," *University of Kansas Law Review* 51 (2003): 972, 998.

23. Lederman, "Reformed IRS," 972, 983–1008.

24. U.S. Internal Revenue Service, "Internal Revenue Service Data Book, 2013," Mar. 2014, 21–24, www.irs.gov/pub/irs-soi/13databk.pdf; U.S. Internal Revenue Service, "Statistical Data—Non-filer Investigations," May 3, 2019, www.irs.gov/compliance/criminal-investigation/statistical-data-nonfiler-investigations.

25. Rene Chun, "Why Americans Don't Cheat on Their Taxes: The Weirdly Hopeful Story of How the U.S. Came to Be a Leader in Tax Compliance," *The Atlantic*, Apr. 2019, www.theatlantic.com/magazine/archive/2019/04/why-americans-dont-cheat-on-their-taxes/583222; Lederman, "Reformed IRS."

26. Department of Homeland Security, "Budget-in-Brief: Fiscal Year 2020."

27. See *Arizona v. United States,* 567 U.S. 387, 436 (2012) (Scalia, J., dissenting).

28. Anna Flagg, "Is There a Connection Between Undocumented Immigrants and Crime?," Marshall Project, May 13, 2019, www.themarshallproject.org/2019/05/13/is-there-a-connection-between-undocumented-immigrants-and-crime; Rubén G. Rumbaut and Walter A. Ewing, "The Myth of Immigrant Criminality and the Paradox of Assimilation: Incarceration Rates Among Native and Foreign-Born Men," Immigration Policy Center, 2007, 1–2, www.americanimmigrationcouncil.org/sites/default/files/research/Imm%20Criminality%20%28IPC%29.pdf.

29. Personal Responsibility and Work Opportunity Reconciliation Act of 1996, Pub. L. No. 104 193, §§ 401-420, 110 Stat. 2105, 2260-70 (codified at 42 U.S.C. § 601 (2018)).

30. See Hong, "Why Congress Should Defund ICE's Deportation Force," 52–54.

31. Julia Preston, "Immigrants Aren't Taking Americans' Jobs, New Study Finds," *New York Times*, Sept. 21, 2016; National Academies of Sciences, Engineering, and Medicine, *The Economic and Fiscal Consequences of Immigration*, eds. Francine D. Blau and Christopher Mackie (Washington, DC: National Academies Press, 2017), 80. Others disagree; cf. Christoph Albert, "The Labor Market Impact of Undocumented Immigrants: Job Creation vs. Job Competition," Universitat Pompeu Fabra, Apr. 3, 2017, www.upf.edu/documents/2963149/3253728/The_Labor_Market_Impact_of_Undocumented_Immigrants_Christoph_Albert_April2017.pdf.

32. See Regina Day Langhout et al., "Statement on the Effects of Deportation and Forced Separation on Immigrants, Their Families, and Communities," *American Journal of Community Psychology* 62 (2018): 3.

33. See Scott Borger and Leah Muse-Orlinoff, "Economic Crisis vs. Border Enforcement: What Matters Most to Prospective Migrants?," in *Mexican Migration and the U.S. Economic Crisis: A Transnational Perspective*, ed. Wayne A. Cornelius et al. (San Diego: University of California San Diego, Center for Comparative Immigration, 2010), 95, 97–102.

34. See Jody Freeman, "Collaborative Governance in the Administrative State," *UCLA Law Review* 45 (1997): 4–7; Bradley C. Karkkainen, "Environmental Lawyering in the Age of Collaboration," *Wisconsin Law Review* 2002 (2002): 557; Orly Lobel, "The Renew Deal: The Fall of Regulation and the Rise of Governance in Contemporary Legal Thought," *Minnesota Law Review* 89 (2004): 343.

35. Amanda Frost, "Cooperative Enforcement in Immigration Law," *Iowa Law Review* 103 (2017): 3–4.

36. U.S. Internal Revenue Service, "National Taxpayer Advocate Delivers Annual Report to Congress; Focuses on Taxpayer Bill of Rights and IRS Funding," Jan. 9, 2014, www.irs.gov/newsroom/national-taxpayer-advocate-delivers-annual-report-to-congress-focuses-on-taxpayer-bill-of-rights-and-irs-funding.

37. See Frost, "Cooperative Enforcement," 9–13.

38. "Policy Memorandum: Updated Guidance for the Referral of Cases and Issuance of Notices to Appear (NTAs) in Cases Involving Admissible and Deportable Aliens," prepared by U.S. Immigration and Customs Enforcement, U.S. Department of Homeland Security, June 28, 2018, www.uscis.gov/sites/default /files/USCIS/Laws/Memoranda/2018/2018-06-28-PM-602-0050.1-Guidance -for-Referral-of-Cases-and-Issuance-of-NTA.pdf; Noah Lanard, "Married Immigrants Seeking Green Cards Are Now Targets for Deportation," *Mother Jones*, Apr. 20, 2018.

39. See 8 U.S.C. §§ 1101(a)(15)(U), 1101(a)(27)(J), 1158(a), 1255 (2018).

40. See 8 U.S.C. § 1153(a) (2018); 8 C.F.R. § 245.1(g) (2019).

41. See 8 U.S.C. §§ 1229b, 1231(b)(3) (2018); 8 C.F.R. § 1208.16(c)(2) (2019).

42. For an example of a court interpreting the INA to forbid the use of an unadjudicated affirmative application as a mechanism to initiate removal and suggesting that an alternative reading of the statute would raise serious constitutional questions, see *You Xiu Qing v. Nielsen*, 321 F. Supp. 3d 451, 466 (S.D.N.Y. 2018). As noted earlier, however, the creation of any new affirmative pathways for legal status that do not currently exist would likely require legislation.

43. See Immigration Reform and Control Act of 1986, Pub. L. No. 99-603, 100 Stat. 3359, codified as amended in scattered sections of Title 8 of the U.S. Code (2018).

44. See Tom Jawetz, "Restoring the Rule of Law Through a Fair, Humane, and Workable Immigration System," Center for American Progress, July 22, 2019, www.americanprogress.org/issues/immigration/reports/2019/07/22/472378 /restoring-rule-law-fair-humane-workable-immigration-system; Michael J. Wishnie, "Immigration Law and the Proportionality Requirement," *UC Irvine Law Review* 2 (2012): 416.

45. For a description of such a system for certain individuals physically present in the United States on Dec. 21, 2000, see 8 U.S.C. § 1255(i)(1)(c) (2018).

46. For some in the movement to abolish ICE, deportation is never a proportionate penalty. They view the freedoms to move, stay, work, and thrive as sacrosanct and inviolable human rights. There is a strong case to be made that deportation is inherently inhumane and, like banishment, has no place in our modern society. However, as long as deportation remains a reality, we have an obligation to mitigate its brutality to the greatest extent possible. This final pillar is aimed at that goal.

47. See Lenni B. Benson, "By Hook or by Crook: Exploring the Legality of an INS Sting Operation," *San Diego Law Review* 31 (1994): 815 n. 12, 832; Mary Fan, "The Case for Crimmigration Reform," *North Carolina Law Review* 92 (2013): 130.

48. Transactional Records Access Clearinghouse, "Most Released Families Attend Immigration Court Hearings," June 18, 2019, trac.syr.edu/immigration /reports/562. These data are consistent with earlier studies, which also showed that

the presence of counsel is strongly correlated with appearance rates in immigration court, such as Ingrid V. Eagly and Steven Shafer, "A National Study of Access to Counsel in Immigration Court," *University of Pennsylvania Law Review* 164 (2015): 73.

49. Transactional Records Access Clearinghouse, "Families Attend Immigration Court."

50. See Jennifer Stave et al., "Evaluation of the New York Immigrant Family Unity Project: Assessing the Impact of Legal Representation on Family and Community Unity," Vera Institute of Justice, Nov. 2017, storage.googleapis.com /vera-web-assets/downloads/Publications/new-york-immigrant-family-unity -project-evaluation/legacy_downloads/new-york-immigrant-family-unity-project -evaluation.pdf.

51. There are also a host of reasons why appointing counsel in deportation proceedings is sound policy (and, arguably, required) that are wholly unrelated to promoting compliance. For an example of such an argument, see Johan Fatemi, "A Constitutional Case for Appointed Counsel in Immigration Proceedings: Revisiting Franco-Gonzalez," *St. John's Law Review* 90 (2016): 917.

52. See Richard Black et al., "Pay-to-Go Schemes and Other Non-Coercive Return Programs: Is Scale Possible?," Migration Policy Institute, Apr. 2011, 2, www.migrationpolicy.org/research/pay-go-schemes-and-other-noncoercive-return -programs.

53. See Frost, "Cooperative Enforcement," 5; Ben Gitis, "The Personnel and Infrastructure Needed to Remove All Undocumented Immigrants in Two Years," American Action Forum, Feb. 28, 2016, www..americanactionforum.org /research/the-personnel-and-infrastructure-needed-to-remove-all-undocumented -immigrants-in-two-years.

54. 42 U.S.C. § 402(n) (2018), for example, terminates Social Security benefits upon the deportation of the primary beneficiary.

Immigrants Are Essential

A Manifesto for the COVID-19 and Climate Change Era

Saket Soni

The COVID-19 crisis plunged us into the future. At first it was an eerie realization. As we greeted masked strangers, stopped hugging, and learned to work from home, we had the inescapable sense that an old way of life was ending, a new one beginning.

At home, in the respite forced by the menace, we were brought to sudden awareness of the things we took for granted before. Awareness, for example, of our dependence on "essential" workers. In the new way of life, some people risked everything to work, so that the rest of us could stay home.

Gratitude poured out. Overnight, millions of homebound Americans were applauding those workers. Celebrating them on social media. Hanging handmade banners of praise and thanks. Literally shouting from the rooftops in gratitude, from coast to coast and at countless points in between.

Claps raining down from roofs on nurses and doctors at shift change would have been remarkable enough. But even more astonishingly, the applause wasn't just for health care workers. Suddenly, Americans who rarely so much as looked low-wage workers in the eye were recognizing them. Farmworkers, grocery store clerks, care workers, janitors and cleaners, delivery drivers, warehouse workers, and many more.

The applause wasn't the result of marketing or messaging. It was organic. Facing grave threats to our health and the breakdown of life as we knew it, ordinary people suddenly understood that they literally couldn't live without the workers they'd always overlooked. The people previously deemed "unskilled" and relegated to invisibility had their value reappraised.

They received a new name. They were "essential."

In the early days of the crisis, it struck me how profound this recognition was. I'm a labor organizer. For years, I had been trying to win recognition for workers—particularly workers of color, immigrant workers, southern workers, people trapped on the bottom rungs of America's caste system. For years, I was advised by pollsters and communications consultants that the key to winning for workers was to avoid calling them "workers." Let's try not to say that word so much. Think more "hardworking mothers and fathers." We don't want to lead with worker identity—it's deadening.

Now we couldn't have been in a more different reality. The whole country was talking about worker identity—not as deadening but as the reason that we were still alive.

The applause was appreciated. But to many—certainly to the essential workers themselves—it wasn't enough. Even as they fed us, healed us, and helped us stay home, essential workers scrambled desperately for their own economic survival. Essential workers needed real protections. Without those, many who had been gratified by the applause became justifiably dubious. If applause is a salve, they said, a way to let people off the hook for injustice, you can keep it.

It's a fair point. Appreciation, however heartfelt, can't replace gloves and N95 masks. Or hazard pay. Or access to health care. Or paid sick days. That's what essential workers need. In a pandemic, their lives depend on it. So do ours.

And millions of essential workers need one other thing. Immigration status.

Here is one of the fundamental paradoxes of the COVID-19 response: a vast proportion of the workers suddenly deemed essential are immigrants. Many of them are undocumented. Many others have temporary, provisional status that gives them only a tenuous foothold in the United States. America's survival depends on workers who have yet to be recognized as American.

Even President Trump agreed—in his own way—when he deployed the Defense Production Act to allow meat processing companies to keep their plants open, even after COVID-19 outbreaks. He deemed meatpacking a critical American industry. The workers at the heart of the meatpacking industry include the undocumented, resettled refugees, asylees, and holders of TPS (Temporary Protected Status). That's true of other front-line industries as well. In fact, 69 percent of immigrant workers toil in industries deemed essential.[1]

Immigrants are essential. We must turn the applause they are getting into the systems they need. We must recognize them as the Americans they already are. That means granting them full legal status, immediately and permanently. Call it citizenship. Call it amnesty. Call it public health. The more secure immigrant workers are, the more resilient we all are in the COVID-19 future.

Future Shock

How did COVID-19 reveal our future? The pandemic was prologue. A dress rehearsal for how we must prepare for an even greater threat—one that has been with us for decades, and is objectively more catastrophic.

That threat is climate change. How we will overcome it is the most profound and consequential question about humanity's future. For a long time, most in the political establishment refused to face it, even as climate scientists warned about radical disruptions to our lives, our economies, and our political systems.

Then one day a warm wind rose over the Bahamas. It turned into a tempest in Miami, uprooting trees. Then it took a turn and lurched toward the Gulf Coast with enough force to earn it a name: Hurricane Katrina. We could have been prepared, but we weren't. Katrina was the first time most Americans saw the climate disaster unfold. A threat that had seemed abstract coming from scientists became quite real when the levees broke in New Orleans. More than a thousand people were killed. More than a million were displaced. Like COVID-19, Katrina (and the government's response to it) laid bare the racial disparities that some political commentators insisted America had overcome. And, like COVID-19, Katrina opened a window into the future. Climate change, unchecked, would force us all into a new way of life shaped by volatility, destruction, and death.

That future is already here. Since Hurricane Katrina, there have been more than 160 climate disasters in the United States that have caused more than $1 billion in damage each. Following the trend decade by decade, the acceleration is frightfully clear. There were 29 billion-dollar disasters during the 1980s, 53 during the 1990s, 62 during the 2000s, and 119 during the 2010s.[2] The economic toll of Hurricane Harvey alone, which hit Texas in 2017, was $125 billion.[3]

Because of climate change, the projected frequency of such storms has skyrocketed.[4] Four of the five largest wildfires in California history have taken place this decade.[5] And the six hottest years on record in human history have been the six most recent, from 2014 to 2019.[6] In the climate change era too, recovery and rebuilding depend on essential workers. After floods, fires, and hurricanes, they go to work so we can come home. As a labor organizer in the aftermath of Hurricane Katrina, I watched this workforce as it first took shape. In the shadow of a statue of Robert E. Lee in New Orleans, workers would gather early each morning: immigrants from Central and South America, often undocumented, who did the most hazardous recovery work without proper protections or pay. They pulled decomposing bodies out of Ninth Ward homes without safety gear, climbed onto roofs to repair them without harnesses. And on payday, their employers often called Immigration and Customs Enforcement to apprehend them as they lined up to collect their checks.

Katrina marked the beginning of a new era. Each year new disasters struck and new epicenters of trauma opened up. Sandy. Florence. Irma. Maria. Harvey. Michael. Floods in the Midwest. Fires in

Paradise, California. Each time, resilience workers arrived, ready to rebuild. "We are America's white blood cells," one of them once told me. And even as they rebuilt, demagogues attacked them, culture warriors demonized them, and immigration agents hunted them.

But inside the epicenters, people depended on them. They were essential. Many expressed gratitude for the role they were playing—even conservative Republicans. Mayor Pamn Henderson of Callaway, Florida, spoke for many when she declared after Hurricane Michael: "We've had a lot of Spanish-speaking workers. I say, 'Thank Heaven for them.' We'd be a lot further from recovering if it weren't for them."[7]

She's right. And she should know. Imagine her position. In October 2018, Hurricane Michael made landfall, the second hurricane in two years, snapping oaks and pines in two, spinning off tornadoes, and damaging nearly 80 percent of the housing stock, including the mayor's own house. A clock started running. She had a year to get those homes rebuilt back to code. If she couldn't, her constituents faced fines they couldn't afford. They would lose their foothold in their hometown. Those sheltering elsewhere wouldn't come back. Those living in "tiny homes"—disaster sheds outside their damaged homes—would move away. The tax base would shrink. Without tax revenue, the mayor's city, already poor before the hurricane, would collapse. The immigrants on the rooftops in Callaway helped her constituents come home and made the city whole. Who could be more essential?

"Rapid repair," the rebuilding of homes in the one to three years following a disaster—by the millions in an epicenter like Houston—is only one of the many essential roles that immigrant resilience workers play. In an era of climate change, our safety, our security, and our very lives require the building of resilient infrastructure, social and physical—not just restoring what was there before, but building better infrastructure, more capable of facing the next fire, or storm, or flood. At scale, true American resilience would require the federal government to invest significant amounts of money in this workforce, and to legalize it. Mayor Henderson and the immigrants on her rooftops agree.

But what would convince Washington to spend trillions of dollars on American disaster resilience and grant a new status to the undocumented whose labor helps build it? It would take a new magnitude of disaster to make the government even consider that.

A disaster like COVID-19. Amid the pandemic, the federal government did what it alone can do, and what it hasn't done in more than a generation. It spent $2 trillion in a matter of days. And even in Washington, the idea of legal status for immigrant essential workers moved out of the margins. The Democratic Party leadership proposed an immediate path to citizenship for essential workers. Then-candidate Joe Biden included it in his list of immigration reforms.[8]

If these measures are crucial to COVID-19 resiliency, they are even more crucial as we face and fight climate change. We need a new federal playbook for climate resilience. It must include, at its center, legal protections and an immediate path to citizenship for the unrecognized Americans whose heart, talent, and labor builds and rebuilds this country.

A New Beginning

Our work doesn't end with winning legal status for essential immigrant workers. That's where it begins. Once their immigration status is the least important thing in their lives, the formerly undocumented will be free to work without fear on our nation's most important priority: resilience.

As climate change makes disasters more frequent and destructive, the majority of Americans are abandoning complacency, denial, and panic and joining a new conversation about resilience. They are realizing that our security and our very lives depend on making sure that our homes, cities, and communities are made smarter and stronger, better able to withstand the next storm or fire or quake or drought, and the next. There is also a growing recognition of the need to rebuild not only the physical structures we inhabit but the social structures as well.

To do that, the organization I lead, Resilience Force, is proposing the formation of a nationwide public Resilience Corps, a program that creates millions of good jobs for the workers who are making America more resilient in the era of climate change.

The Resilience Corps would rebuild America in body and soul, through a spirit and practice of radical inclusion. The Corps would target all those who have been historically locked into exploitative working conditions or locked out of work altogether. The formerly undocumented. The formerly incarcerated. Those barred from good jobs because of bad credit. Those who lost access to trade schools and training centers when budgets shrank. Those whose gender, race, or immigration status trapped them at the bottom of their industries. People in rural America whose unemployment crisis was compounded by the opioid crisis. People in urban America where manufacturing hubs were hollowed out and replaced by minimum-wage service sector jobs.

The Resilience Corps would perform lifesaving work. Workers would train to become home rebuilders and dam repairers. Community health workers and caregivers. Emergency navigators and social workers.

As the Corps rebuilds homes and cities, it can also build new social cohesion. Those bonds would become the new DNA for American citizenship; the cooperation, a new basis for American freedom.

The program would be modeled after the New Deal's Works Progress Administration, which employed 8.5 million people and supported 30 million of their dependents. This twenty-first-century version, however, would be different in one crucial way: most WPA workers were white men.

The New Deal, too, was a disaster recovery measure. Staring into collapse, America conceived a new bargain to build the foundation for the broadest expansion of prosperity in history. And like today's recoveries, it widened inequality. In order to get the New Deal passed, Congress had to overcome a veto by southern Democrats. It did so by agreeing to exclude the workers who powered the southern economy—including Black workers, day laborers, farmworkers, domestic workers, tipped workers, and others.[9] The exclusions hardened America's racial caste system for generations to come.

To be fully realized, the Resilience Corps must disrupt that legacy, not continue it. Congress's current rules of disaster recovery and resilience are hidden engines of inequality. As they are currently carried out, recoveries widen the racial wealth gap and leave many of the workers who power them poorer than when they started work. But with high wages, benefits, labor standards, and the right to organize, the Corps could reverse that. It would deliver opportunity and security for millions of Americans as they work to recover. America's resilience workforce, like auto workers of an earlier era, could rise to become the new middle class of the cities they are rebuilding.

The Resilience Corps should be at the heart of the Green New Deal. It's our moonshot for this moment, and it will need all the talent, all the heart, all the labor our communities have to give. The resilience workforce will make America anew. Not restore it to the way it was before the disasters, but make it strong enough to face the future.

In the beginning of this era, in post-Katrina New Orleans, I found a new mentor in Dr. Vincent Harding, a preeminent American moral philosopher and the author of Dr. Martin Luther King Jr.'s transcendent 1967 speech, "Beyond Vietnam."[10]

I sat with him one day and shared my despair over the latest low point in the American story. How can we go to the people the American government had left to die, I asked, to the people who were rebuilding not because of the American government but despite it, and recruit them to have faith in American democracy?

"America," Dr. Harding said, "is a country that is yet to be born."

In the climate crisis, the America we need is waiting to be built. Together, we can build it.

Facing the Future

May 2020 brought America the first climate disaster of the COVID-19 era. Record rains came, not in Florida, not in North Carolina, but to an unlikely place: Michigan. Two months into the pandemic, the torrent burst two massive, antiquated dams. Downstream, more than ten thousand people were faced with the choice that tens of millions of immigrants understand only too well: to stay or to leave? As floodwaters filled their homes, they gathered what they could and left. "If only I had known," one resident told me, "I'd have prepared."

In the coming decades, most Americans will need to prepare for climate change. And that will include preparing for migration. Many will become migrants, because one day the floods or fires will reach them. Many others will receive migrants.

We're seeing it already, in coastal areas vulnerable to ever-fiercer hurricanes, in forested states with constant wildfires, in Sun Belt communities where life-threatening temperatures have become the new normal. Even the climate science skeptics in these communities measure time by counting floods and fires. They need to prepare for the day the dam breaks and they become climate migrants—American-born, but migrants all the same.

But our internal climate migrant flows are only a shadow of the far larger, far more disruptive global climate migration that will transform the world in the coming decades. The predictions are dire. The area of the globe designated "a barely livable hot zone" is projected to rise from 1 percent currently to 19 percent by 2070—displacing billions of residents.[11] Compounding the extreme weather in these areas will be economic desperation and political instability—or even state collapse. In Central America alone, millions will face the same choice as the climate migrants in Michigan. And they will head north, seeking refuge.

That is why we need an immigration policy that confronts the reality of climate change. The first step is simple and obvious: U.S. immigration policy must include a new legal status for climate refugees. This may sound far-fetched given our current public debate, but it has plenty of precedents. Past administrations have resettled refugees fleeing wars and granted Temporary Protected Status to victims of natural disasters. But climate change is a blind spot in American immigration policy. An immigrant seeking asylum in the United States is required to prove a "well-founded fear" of returning home. There could not be a better-founded fear than that of climate change, but the asylum system is not set up to accept it.

The legal status I propose wouldn't involve America rescuing the climate refugees. It would involve climate refugees rescuing America's immigration policy. Rather than locating our immigration priorities in a larger conversation about the reasons for global migrant flows, including economic incentives and the impact of U.S. foreign policy, we have responded to whoever is at the border in the moment that they arrive. That has allowed our public debate to fall prey to racist opportunism, as nativist politicians have recast safety-seekers as criminals, not only unjustly harming desperate refugees but also sowing the seeds of division among Americans.

But this year, next year, and the year after that, climate refugees will continue to arrive. Our climate future is already here. A 2018 World Bank report projected that without concerted global action, 143 million people in sub-Saharan Africa, South Asia, and Latin America could be forced from their homes by climate change by 2050. With measures of prevention and resilience, that number could be cut by 80 percent.[12] America must be part of the global cooperation that achieves that.

Creating a legal status for climate refugees is not benevolence but rather climate reparations. The Guatemalan farm families movingly profiled in a *New York Times* analysis of climate migration are leaving home because of heat produced largely by U.S. carbon emissions, not Central America's.[13] Our debt has come due.

Our laws, no less than our aging dams and archaic bridges, are concrete expressions of their time. Just as our homes, hospitals, and schools need to be retrofitted or even rebuilt completely to face the climate crisis, our legal regimes need to be reconceived to meet the current moment—starting with our immigration system.

Just as properly addressing the needs of essential workers could make immigration status the least salient fact of their lives rather than the most, properly planning for climate refugees can make them an integral part of a just immigration system, rather than a series of crises to be managed.

We need a reform as sweeping as the 1965 Hart-Celler Act, which eliminated racist immigration quotas, allowing millions of talented people to find a home here and build new lives. A visionary climate justice movement must ensure that our immigration policy, like our dams and bridges, is radically reconceived to meet a world on the move.

Notes

1. Donald Kerwin, Mike Nicholson, Daniela Alulema, and Robert Warren, "US Foreign-Born Essential Workers by Status and State, and the Global Pandemic," Center for Migration Studies, May 2020, cmsny.org/wp-content/uploads/2020/05/US-Essential-Workers-Printable.pdf.

2. NOAA National Centers for Environmental Information (NCEI), "U.S. Billion-Dollar Weather and Climate Disasters," 2020, www.ncdc.noaa.gov/billions.

3. Ibid.

4. Kerry Emanuel, "Assessing the Present and Future Possibility of Hurricane Harvey's Rainfall," *Proceedings of the National Academy of Sciences* 114, no. 48 (2017): 12681–4.

5. State of California, CalFire, "Top 20 Largest California Wildfires," www.fire.ca.gov/media/5510/top20_acres.pdf.

6. Jeff Masters, "Earth Had Its Second Warmest Year in Recorded History in 2019," *Eye of the Storm* (*Scientific American* blog), Jan. 15, 2020, blogs.scientificamerican.com/eye-of-the-storm/earth-had-its-second-warmest-year-in-recorded-history-in-2019.

7. Miriam Jordan, "Hurricane Chasers: An Immigrant Work Force on the Trail of Extreme Weather," *New York Times*, Oct. 6, 2019, A13.

8. See Biden-Sanders Unity Task Force Recommendations, joebiden.com/wp-content/uploads/2020/07/UNITY-TASK-FORCE-RECOMMENDATIONS.pdf.

9. See Ira Katznelson, *When Affirmative Action Was White* (New York: W.W. Norton, 2005).

10. Martin Luther King Jr., "Beyond Vietnam," Apr. 4, 1967, kinginstitute.stanford.edu/king-papers/documents/beyond-vietnam.

11. Abrahm Lustgarten, "The Great Climate Migration," *New York Times Magazine*, July 23, 2020.

12. World Bank, "Groundswell: Preparing for Internal Climate Migration" (infographic), Mar. 19, 2018, www.worldbank.org/en/news/infographic/2018/03/19/groundswell---preparing-for-internal-climate-migration.

13. Mengpin Ge and Johannes Friedrich, "4 Charts Explain Greenhouse Gas Emissions by Countries and Sectors," World Resources Institute, Feb. 6, 2020, www.wri.org/blog/2020/02/greenhouse-gas-emissions-by-country-sector.

Part IV

STRATEGIES FOR CHANGE

The Progressive Path Forward on Immigration Policy

Pramila Jayapal

M y parents believed that America was the place where my sister and I would have the best education and the most opportunity. They scrimped and saved to send both of us to the United States for college at tremendous sacrifice. Shortly before my high school graduation, after my sister was already in America, my father lost his job. Still, he was determined that I should make it to America, and he used his last $5,000 in savings to make sure I too could study in an American university.

In 1982, just before I turned seventeen, I started my undergraduate studies at Georgetown University on an international student visa. Almost eighteen years later—after being on an alphabet soup of visas and having a constantly palpitating heart every time I stood before a U.S. immigration official—I finally became a U.S. citizen in 2000. When I took my oath, hand over heart, surrounded by hundreds of other immigrants from all over the world speaking dozens of languages, I understood all over again the privilege and responsibility of U.S. citizenship, offered to so few and desired by so many. I felt the deep unyielding belief in the *idea* of America—a shining city on a hill for millions around the world, governed by the will of the people of every race, religion, and color.

One year after I took that oath, in the wake of the September 11, 2001, terrorist attacks, I founded Washington State's largest immigrant and civil rights advocacy organization, originally called Hate Free Zone and later renamed One America. That began my two decades of work as an immigrant advocate at the local, state, and federal levels. We successfully sued the Bush administration and prevented the deportation of thousands of Somalis across the country, fought the early Muslim bans of the post-9/11 era, and organized for humane immigration reform. We registered tens of thousands of new American voters, passed progressive state and local laws on immigration, and led civil disobedience protests against both Republican and Democratic presidents for failing to address the immigration crisis in our country. I was inspired daily by the resilience of immigrants I worked with, who gave everything they had to cross deserts, oceans, and borders to get themselves and their families to safety and a better life—only to then live in the shadow of uncertainty, detention, or deportation, having to prepare safety plans in case they were suddenly separated from children, fearing every knock on the door even as they contributed all their labors to this country they had struggled to get to.

What I have learned from these decades of work is that our immigration laws are extremely complex, disjointed, arcane, and perpetually outdated. They are deeply rooted in negative stereotypes and have over time criminalized more and more types of immigrants, enabling politicians to divide Americans and create a false "us versus them" narrative.

At the end of the day, I believe that immigration has never been simply an issue of policy; it has always been about who we are as a country and what we stand for. Any positive changes in immigration policy have occurred because there was a movement of immigrants who pushed to change the narrative with their personal stories—and because there were elected leaders who had the courage and took leadership to move forward a different narrative, sometimes despite popular opinion.

As one of only fourteen naturalized citizens to serve in Congress, I am the first South Asian American woman to serve in the House of Representatives. As a lifelong organizer now in Congress, I see the challenges—but also the renewed urgency—of defining a new moral vision of immigration and fixing our broken and inhumane immigration laws. To do so will require political leaders who use our platforms and our power to help educate and lead those who might be fearful into a new place of understanding and acceptance, leaders who understand that having a functioning immigration system undergirds every other piece of progress we need to make in a country—from health care for all to education to jobs.

Addressing the systemic injustices that are built into both policy and politics will be possible only if we build a deep and intersectional, multi-generational, multi-racial coalition that also addresses the concerns of our U.S.-born brothers and sisters. Any solution that benefits immigrants must be framed and conceived in a way that also benefits those who were here before and yet still suffer unspeakable injustices.

Immigrants and the U.S.-born work, live, and play side by side. We depend on each other, whether we acknowledge it or not. Reimagining our immigration policy must work in tandem with reimagining all aspects of social justice—one patch in a tapestry of a greater progressive project. In 2020, COVID-19 illuminated anew the truth that our fates are tied together; the question now is whether we will have the courage to lead as we must.

Donald Trump: Symptom and Cause

When Donald Trump was elected president in 2016, we were already living in a time of staggering income inequality, a health care crisis that had 87 million Americans uninsured or underinsured, and a minimum wage that had stagnated for decades.

Trump's election was both a *symptom* of America's failure to bring economic security and opportunity to working people—allowing for a populist anger to explode—and a *cause* of unspeakable brutality, cruelty, and destruction that emerged over the following four years.

We cannot successfully reform immigration without understanding the three major (and interrelated) themes of Trump's presidency. First, he used popular economic discontent to shift blame away from his efforts to maintain the concentration of wealth in the hands of the few, to enable the largest corporations to continue to pillage the American people, and to ensure that he personally would benefit every step of the way. Second, Trump's base was fired up by the idea of ending legal immigration as we know it, and Trump surrounded himself with the people who could help him do that, Stephen Miller among them. Third, Trump used the tools provided to him by previous administrations, both Republican and Democratic, who had laid the groundwork for the criminalization of immigration, the expansive enforcement network, and the exploitation of the administrative powers of the presidency.

Unlike any president before him, Trump aimed to undermine the very idea of immigration as a positive force. He urged Americans to reject the idea that the nation's identity is deeply linked to generations of immigrants who have come to our soil, instead leaning into the "us-versus-them" narrative to divide and conquer. What began as a diatribe against "illegal" immigration quickly led to efforts to reduce *all* immigration. His administration worked quickly to undermine every legal avenue for immigration, including zeroing in on eliminating admissions based on family reunification—the cornerstone of U.S. immigration policy for decades—in favor of a "merit-based" system where wealth and class would become determinants of who is allowed into America. And, in order to stoke the economic discontent of Americans suffering from policies that favor the wealthiest individuals and corporations, he promoted the most negative stereotypes of immigrants as the takers of benefits rather than contributors. Far better to have U.S.-born individuals turn against immigrants than against the money and power of corporations and the wealthiest—including Trump himself.

Trump utilized the powerful platform of the White House, along with all the levers of executive and administrative power, to slow every means of immigration to a trickle and to inflict terror on immigrant communities. He tried to terminate the status of millions of

DACA (Deferred Action for Childhood Arrivals) and TPS (Temporary Protected Status) recipients; introduced discriminatory bans on Muslims, Africans, people seeking asylum, and refugees; undercut judicial discretion and fairness to turn immigration courts into deportation assembly lines; and refused to send aid to struggling countries or acknowledge the effects of climate change, both of which are essential root causes of migration.

Perhaps the cruel confidence of Trump and DHS will be most remembered for the caging of children and the separation of families. In the summer of 2018, I became the first member of Congress to visit hundreds of parents who had been separated from their children and were being held in a top-level-security federal prison just south of my district in Seattle, Washington, that typically holds people awaiting trial as well as those who have been convicted of a federal crime.

What I saw and heard there that day will haunt me forever. The majority of these mothers and fathers were asylum seekers. Many of them had come with children, some as young as six months old, and the U.S. Border Patrol had forcibly taken those children away from them. None of them had a chance to say goodbye to their children, and most did not even know where their children were. They wept inconsolably and told stories of being demeaned and humiliated by Immigration and Customs Enforcement (ICE) and Border Patrol agents who called them "filthy" and "disgusting" and told them they would never see their children again. While it is true that Trump doubled down on cruelty toward immigrants—the cause of incredible suffering—he did so with tools that had been provided to him over the years by presidents and members of Congress from both parties.

He immediately weaponized the giant, sprawling Department of Homeland Security (DHS) toward his ends. Created after 9/11, ostensibly to emphasize national security and create more coordination, DHS had become the third-largest cabinet agency, just after the Department of Defense. It combined immigration services with interior and border enforcement of immigration laws, under the rubric of protecting the homeland. Under the Trump administration, DHS went to new depths of cruelty, from implementing the infamous family separation policy to evaluating the efficacy of border policies not just by the number of people apprehended but also by the number of people who died entering the United States.[1] Trump escalated his use of DHS as a tool of his cruelty and overriding of constitutional rights: by the summer of 2020, SWAT teams from Customs and Border Protection were being sent into cities including Portland, Seattle, and Chicago—without the consent of mayors or governors—to crack down on protesters calling for racial justice, using unmarked vehicles to pick up protesters and refusing to show identity badges.

Trump inherited the tools for criminalizing and incarcerating immigrants from President Bill Clinton. In 1996, Congress passed and Clinton signed the Illegal Immigrant Reform and Immigrant Responsibility Act (IIRIRA), which expanded detention and deportation of immigrants while taking away discretion from the courts and undermining due process for immigrants.[2] Spending on immigration enforcement increased every year since then, and by 2018 it exceeded *combined* federal spending on five other federal law enforcement agencies by nearly 35 percent.[3] Paradoxically, decades of an enforcement-only approach has not made us safer or improved compliance with immigration laws.[4] And yet Congress and various presidents have refused to stop pouring money into failed border and interior enforcement measures.

In 2016, the last year of President Barack Obama's presidency, America detained approximately 360,000 people in a sprawling system of more than two hundred immigration jails across the country,[5] 70 percent of them in private, for-profit prisons operated primarily by two companies that have poured money into President Trump's campaign as well as the campaign of other elected officials.[6] In 2018, taxpayers paid an average of $208 per person per night for these detention centers and significantly more for children and families.[7] Within these facilities, there are few accountability or oversight measures, little to no transparency, and unlimited funding for private contractors that provide substandard food, supplies, and health care.[8]

Most Americans do not know that, unlike the criminal justice system, immigration is a complex civil system, which 90 percent of immigrants navigate without legal representation.[9] The vast majority of immigrants held in detention have never been charged with a crime, much less committed one, and for the rest the bulk of such "crimes" are offenses like marijuana possession, now legal in a majority of states.[10] They are often detained for no specific reason, simply pending review by immigration judges or prior to deportation.

And while most immigration advocates have spent enormous time fighting against detention and deportation, we all understand that this would be largely moot if we passed true humane and comprehensive immigration reform to establish a system that allows people to enter in an orderly and compassionate way, to be with their families and loved ones, and to contribute their full selves to an economy that desperately needs their labor and talents.

Perhaps the most surprising fact for most Americans who are new to thinking about immigration is that we actually do not have a functioning immigration "system" and that the laws we do have in place have not been updated for decades. Millions of immigrants are stuck in legal limbo, and many others of all statuses are excluded from access to numerous safety net programs.

It is easy to despair at the complexities of the politics and the policies of immigration. But if the next president does not lead on the issue, the cleavages will only deepen. We must not allow racists and xenophobes to use immigrants as a political football, and most importantly, we must restore the vision of America as a beacon of light, a place of refuge. Indeed, our status as a refuge is already being destroyed: a Canadian judge ruled in July 2020 that the United States is not a safe country for people seeking asylum, because the asylum seekers in America are "immediately and automatically imprisoned," often under inhumane conditions.[11]

Yet Trump's cruelty toward immigrants has pushed more Democrats, independents, and even some Republicans to stand up for immigration reform. The next administration and Congress must create a functioning system of immigration laws that is humane and effective. It is time to rethink the rhetoric and politics of exclusion and disband the structures that have stymied progress on multiple fronts, while building the foundations of a just and humane immigration policy.

The Path Forward: Undo, Rebuild, Reform

While passing legislation is easiest if Democrats control the White House as well as both chambers of Congress, it is still possible and no less urgent if Democrats control only the White House and the House of Representatives, with Republicans controlling the Senate by a slim majority. That is because, surprisingly, Trump's right-wing immigration policies may have backfired, his cruelty triggering an opposite response from Americans and bringing more Americans to support immigration. In June 2020, Gallup's national polling found that support for increased immigration was at an all-time high among Democrats and independent voters. Nearly eight in ten Americans said they believe immigration is good for America, while a new low of 28 percent favored decreased immigration.[12]

COVID-19 also brought new opportunities to challenge the notion of immigrants as unnecessary to the functioning of America. As advocates, we tried for decades to help Americans understand that the work of immigrants is essential. COVID-19 highlighted our dependence on those very essential workers, from those in the food supply chain to those in the health care industry on the front lines of the pandemic response. They were subjected to such cruel contradictions as "essential but deportable," or essential but unable to access relief in legislation that excluded them based on immigration status, or essential but uncovered for COVID-19 treatment, protective equipment, or workplace rights.

Trump showed the tremendous administrative powers of the presidency and how they can be abused. Reforms must focus on limiting the power of future presidents to use bad immigration policy as a political tool. But until new laws can be passed, the next administration should immediately deploy all the current powers of the president to reverse and implement protections to the maximum extent possible.

While the next president's initial focus must be on undoing the damage, rebuilding and reforming can also begin immediately. These should be seen not as separate items but rather as simultaneous efforts to quickly and urgently resolve the many immigration issues that face the country.

Undoing the Damage

Our next president must immediately reverse all of Trump's immigration executive orders and purge all departments of the white nationalist operatives that were installed on his watch. This enormous task can be undertaken immediately and will have huge consequences for communities across the country: reinstating DACA; restoring refugee admissions; reversing the Muslim, African, and asylum bans; abandoning the border wall; reversing the wealth tests for immigrants under Trump's interpretation of the "public charge" rule; and ending his unjust border policies.[13] The next president can also immediately roll back administrative changes that expanded interior enforcement and restore prosecutorial and judicial discretion as well as the ability to fairly and expeditiously process immigration benefit applications.

In the midst of the ongoing COVID-19 pandemic, the next administration can also immediately invest in alternatives to detention and review all the cases of those in detention to reduce the population that is held there, releasing the most vulnerable populations—including caregivers, asylum seekers, pregnant people, and LGBTQ immigrants.

The next president should immediately appoint a task force solely dedicated to making reparations for the unfathomable cruelty and unfairness of Trump-era policies, which should start with ensuring that every single child torn from a family member under President Trump's zero-tolerance, zero-humanity family separation policy is reunited with their parents and other loved ones.

Rebuilding

The president and Congress must fundamentally restructure the Department of Homeland Security, bringing accountability to what has become a sprawling, completely unaccountable, and economically wasteful agency that has only been in place since 2002.[14] Since DHS was created through congressional action, it will require congressional action to break it up. This process must start immediately, because it speaks to the fundamental values of our country and will provide a framework in which to push forward important policy reforms with accountability. The president can establish this vision through his first budget proposal and break up DHS as follows.

First, FEMA, Cyber-Security, and TSA can be separated and returned to other appropriate existing agencies, as they were prior to the creation of DHS. This will allow them to function more effectively and separate from the consequences of being lumped in with agencies that do not share their mission.

Second, to elevate the moral importance of immigration to our country's values and ideals, the next president should create a cabinet-level department for immigration services and integration. We have a Department of Labor to advocate for workers and a Department of Agriculture to advocate for farmers. Imagine an entire immigration and citizenship services agency dedicated to advocating for, helping process, and integrating into society our newest Americans. It could oversee refugee resettlement, efficiently process visas and citizenship applications with fully resourced personnel, invest in legal counsel to assist immigrants through the process, and broaden the scope of citizenship services to oversee a new suite of integration programs, from citizenship and English language learning to job training and development. Imagine the message it would send to immigrants about their worth and to the moral psyche of a unified America that values the contributions of everyone.

Third, we should separate enforcement from immigration services, creating a separate enforcement agency for interior and border enforcement, as was the case prior to the creation of DHS. With a functioning immigration system, interior enforcement would constitute a much smaller part of the whole. Wherever it is placed, immigration enforcement must immediately be refocused on only the few who pose a true risk to public safety. We need to develop a menu of scaled consequences to immigration violations.[15] Further, we must immediately restore judicial discretion, staff the immigration courts with knowledgeable professionals, and invest in legal resources that protect due process for immigrants within the system.

Installing excellent and knowledgeable personnel to administer every level of immigration policy is critical, including individuals who were not in previous administrations and who can bring a new and updated perspective to the issue. We need new eyes that can see and undo the harms of previous laws, whether passed under Democratic or Republican administrations.

Reform

The next president must do as much as possible within the scope of his powers, but ultimately the president and Congress will need to collaborate on an immediate push for comprehensive, humane immigration reform. As recently as 2013, the U.S. Senate passed—with a remarkable sixty-eight bipartisan votes—a comprehensive immigration reform bill that would have fixed many of the most outdated parts of the system.[16] Some components of that bill would not be satisfactory today, so it is critical that we not simply try to pass the 2013 bill wholesale, but rather reevaluate it and add provisions to address the many injustices of the 1996 laws that have created so many problems ever since.

The president should take the lead in setting forth a comprehensive vision to create a fair, humane immigration system. This proposal will set markers for Congress's work, whether legislation moves in connected pieces as part of a package or in one bill. Two immigration reform measures that would provide a path to citizenship for key categories of immigrants who have been residing in the country are already in the pipeline: the Farm Workforce Modernization Act and the Dream and Promise Act, both of which were passed by the House of Representatives in 2019, would immediately provide a road to citizenship for at least 4 million agricultural workers, Dreamers, and recipients of Temporary Protected Status and deferred action.[17] A sustained campaign outside of Congress highlighting the stories, abuses, and successes of immigrants who obtain legal status, to flip the negative narratives that Trump put forward, would also immediately boost immigrants and advocates, as well as the economy, and minimize the ability of people to vilify immigrants as "takers" rather than contributors.

However, these two bills are not sufficient. Congress and the president must quickly focus on implementing the larger, comprehensive vision as early in 2021 as possible. Legislation must tackle other critical pieces of immigration reform, including family immigration, detention and enforcement, and employment-based immigration. Such foundational reform of the dysfunctional system's interconnected pieces is critical to avoid problems in the future.

The tragedies of family separation at the border and during COVID-19 have elevated the need to immediately strengthen our family-based immigration system and to affirm the value of the family unit to our country. We can immediately pass Representative Chu's Reuniting Families Act, which would raise the nation's per-country immigration limits for family-based categories and eliminate per-country or categorical caps. This would eliminate the enormous family backlogs that have kept parents from their adult children, sometimes for more than two decades depending on their country of origin. Family immigration was the strength of the American project since the nation's founding. Family support is essential for many new Americans' integration and enables them to reach their full potential.

Congress should also create an independent court system that ensures immigration judges are independent of political pressure, and it should replace politically appointed judges with no expertise in immigration law and policy with knowledgeable professionals.

It will be necessary to work with Congress to ensure that the entire detention system is overhauled. We do not need to incarcerate tens of thousands of immigrants in jails, prisons, and detention centers, and there should be no profit-making motive in incarceration—period. The administration can immediately begin eliminating DHS's use of for-profit detention facilities while Congress works to move comprehensive legislation to overhaul the detention system. In 2019, I reintroduced the Dignity for Detained Immigrants Act, which lays out a plan to accomplish much of this.[18] It would permanently transition away from the use of private, for-profit immigrant prisons and create a humane system that operates with accountability and transparency. It would also eliminate mandatory detention, and it would dramatically reduce the number of detainees through cost-effective case management and legal assistance.

Similarly, there must be a massive shift in the approach to border enforcement. The militarization of the southern border has continued, to the enormous detriment of the communities who live there, who have long-established cross-border relationships that recognize the history of Mexicans being pushed out by white settlers as well as the reality that communities on both sides of the border rely on each other for business and economic benefits. The next administration must fundamentally reform how the border is managed: tearing down Trump's monument to himself—the wall—and establishing non-invasive technologies and other basic security measures instead; shrinking the 100-mile Constitution-free zone that defines the border; establishing humane asylum policies at the border; and modernizing processing facilities and resources at the border. Most important, as the protests against anti-Blackness and white supremacy have shown us, we must stop relying on military tactics and dramatically reduce funding as well as the way funding is utilized for border enforcement.

Restoring our global place in the world under the next presidency also must include rebuilding international coalitions to address migration and climate change with our international partners, increasing U.S. aid to struggling countries, shoring up economies around the world, and reducing our reliance on military solutions and war that devastate other countries and force people to move. We must make sure America remains a beacon for the tired, the poor, and the persecuted, just as the Statue of Liberty promises. America has a long history of opening her doors to those fleeing violence. A useful precedent is the Lautenberg Amendment, passed in 1990 as part of the U.S. foreign operations budget, which allowed tens of thousands of Jews from the former Soviet Union to resettle here, and later other persecuted religious minorities such as Jews, Christians, and Baha'is from Iran.[19] We should create a similar program for people from Latin American countries in crisis to apply and be resettled in America. These are our nearest neighbors, and so many there suffer, in part because of the adverse effects of our own foreign policy.[20]

Perhaps the hardest piece of immigration policy in a time of extremely high unemployment will be that of future flows of workers. Our employment-based immigration system must prioritize sectors, such as home care and domestic work, that are projected to be the fastest-growing source of jobs in the coming decades, while at the same time maintaining the ability of the United States to attract creative and innovative thinkers who can help build our economy. Bills around future flows of workers should be written in a way that ties future immigration levels to economic needs and unemployment levels, but also prioritizes training and workforce investment.

Conclusion

Any president, given the way that politics operates, will need to be pushed and supported by organizers and advocates. To help call in our president and all elected leaders who have the power to shape legislation, we may need new tactics, new courage, and new resolve to change the full narrative, just as the Dreamers did under Obama. Depending on the receptivity and the political margins, there may be a point where we will need to challenge even our friends with a new scale of protest, supported by serious dedication and by training that mirrors that of the 1960s civil rights community or the suffragettes.

Reforming immigration will take courage, conviction, bold leadership, and sustained effort. It should be done as quickly as possible, whether in consecutive pieces or in a comprehensive bill, with the full backing and investment of the White House. We will likely only have one strong shot at this within the first term of a new president, and if we do not fix this, it will continue to be used to divide us and to further the cruelty that Donald Trump unleashed. Fixing immigration will take away the political leverage of a small and shrinking base of xenophobes and racists and allow us to bring forward a new focus on a vibrant and unified America where all cultures and contributions are respected.

Alongside the heartbreak of the broken and unjust immigration system is a deep and unshakeable faith in the American psyche about the value of immigrants. Under Trump, this faith was subjected to some of the worst racist attacks in our history, but instead of being diminished, it was only strengthened. In 1978, the Greek poet Dinos Christianopoulos wrote a small couplet that was later translated into English and has been used by various recent movements in Mexico and the United States: *"What didn't you do to bury me / But you forgot that I was a seed."*[21]

Let our seeds flourish as we do the work, with a new adminis-tration and a new Congress, to rebuild America as a more just and humane country that still beams a shining light of possibility around the world.

That will continue the great American project. Every generation is charged with bringing the country closer to its founding ideals by writing the next chapter in the story of American freedom. In the era of climate change, American cooperation can reduce emissions and expand resilience, making us free to stay. And when the dams break, expanded immigration can make us free to move.

Notes

1. Caitlin Dickerson, "A Rare Look Inside Trump's Immigration Crackdown Draws Legal Threats," *New York Times,* July 23, 2020.

2. See Roger Daniels, *Guarding the Golden Door* (New York: Hill and Wang, 2004); National Immigrant Justice Center, "A Legacy of Injustice: The U.S. Criminalization of Migration," July 2020, immigrantjustice.org/sites/default/files /uploaded-files/no-content-type/2020-07/NIJC-Legacy-of-Injustice-report_2020 -07-22_FINAL.pdf.

3. Daniel Costa, "Immigration Enforcement Is Funded at a Much Higher Rate than Labor Standards Enforcement—and the Gap Is Widening," Economic Policy Institute, Working Economics (blog), June 20, 2019.

4. Tom Jawetz, "Restoring the Rule of Law Through a Fair, Humane, and Workable Immigration System," Center for American Progress, July 22, 2019, www .americanprogress.org/issues/immigration/reports/2019/07/22/472378/restoring -rule-law-fair-humane-workable-immigration-system.

5. Detention Watch Network, "Immigration Detention 101," www .detentionwatchnetwork.org/issues/detention-101.

6. Livia Luan, "Profiting from Enforcement: The Role of Private Prisons in U.S. Immigration Detention," Migration Policy Institute, May 2, 2018, www .migrationpolicy.org/article/profiting-enforcement-role-private-prisons-us -immigration-detention.

7. Laurence Benenson, "The Math of Immigration Detention, 2018 Update: Costs Continue to Multiply," National Immigration Forum, May 9, 2019, immigra-tionforum.org/article/math-immigration-detention-2018-update-costs-continue -mulitply.

8. Eunice Cho, "Justice Free Zones," American Civil Liberties Union, Apr. 30, 2020, immigrantjustice.org/sites/default/files/content-type/research -item/documents/2020-04/Justice-Free%20Zones_Immigrant_Detention_ Report_ACLU-HRW-NIJC_April-2020.pdf; Eunice Cho, "ICE's Lack of Transparency About COVID-19 in Detention Will Cost Lives," American Civil Liberties Union, May 22, 2020, www.aclu.org/news/immigrants-rights/ices-lack-of -transparency-about-covid-19-in-detention-will-cost-lives.

9. Maria Benevento, "Without a Lawyer, Immigrants Lost," *National Catholic Reporter,* Dec. 15, 2017.

10. Jordan Cunnings, "Nonserious Marijuana Offenses and Noncitizens," *UCLA Law Review* 62 (2015): 510–69; John Gramlich, "Four-in-Ten U.S. Drug Arrests in 2018 for Marijuana Offenses," Pew Research Center, Jan. 22, 2020, www .pewresearch.org/fact-tank/2020/01/22/four-in-ten-u-s-drug-arrests-in-2018 -were-for-marijuana-offenses-mostly-possession.

11. Matthew S. Schwartz, "U.S.-Canada Asylum Treaty Unconstitutional, Judge Finds, Citing 'Cruel' U.S. Behavior," NPR, July 23, 2020.

12. Mohamed Younis, "Americans Want More, Not Less, Immigration for First Time," Gallup, July 1, 2020, news.gallup.com/poll/313106/americans-not-less -immigration-first-time.aspx.

13. In 1882, Congress established a rule allowing the U.S. government to deny admission to any immigrant who "is likely at any time to become a public charge," but without defining the term. The Trump administration advanced an interpretation defining any non-citizen who has received one or more public benefits (such as Medicaid, food stamps, or Temporary Assistance to Needy Families) for more than twelve months within any thirty-six-month period as a "public charge," but in July 2020 this interpretation was enjoined by a federal court.

14. Miriam Jordan, "Soviet-Era Program Gives Even Unoppressed Immigrants an Edge," *New York Times*, Aug. 26, 2017.

15. See Peter Markowitz's chapter in this volume.

16. U.S. Senate, Roll Call Vote 168, S. 744, the Border Security, Economic Opportunity, and Immigration Modernization Act, July 27, 2020, www.senate.gov /legislative/LIS/roll_call_lists/roll_call_vote_cfm.cfm?congress=113&session=1 &vote=00168.

17. House Judiciary Committee, Subcommittee on Immigration and Citizenship (approximately 1.5 to 2 million people would be eligible for relief under H.R. 5038); Nicole Prchal Svajlenka, "The American Dream and Promise Act of 2019: State-by-State Fact Sheets," Center for American Progress, May 28, 2020, www .americanprogress.org/issues/immigration/news/2019/05/28/470181/american -dream-promise-act-2019-state-state-fact-sheets (2.5 million immigrants would be eligible for protection under H.R. 6).

18. H.R. 2415, Dignity for Detained Immigrants Act of 2019, 116th Cong., 2019, www.congress.gov/bill/116th-congress/house-bill/2415?s=1&r=15.

19. Jordan, "Soviet-Era Program."

20. Deirdre Shesgreen, "How U.S. Foreign Policy in Central America May Have Fueled the Migrant Crisis," *USA Today*, Dec. 21, 2018.

21. An Xiao, "On the Origins of 'They Tried to Bury Us, They Didn't Know We Were Seeds,'" Hyperallergic, July 3, 2018, hyperallergic.com/449930/on-the-origins-of-they-tried-to-bury-us-they-didnt-know-we-were-seeds.

The Border and Beyond

Cecilia Muñoz

I f there is any single constant in the public discourse about immigration in this nation of immigrants, it's that emotion is the most powerful driver of the conversation. For better or worse, Americans have views about their ancestors' immigrant history (or lack of it), and about today's immigrants as they see them on the news or in the neighborhood. Immigration is baked into the mythology of who we are as a nation, though much of what we think we know about it turns out to be inaccurate. We think we know how it worked a century or more ago (we insist that our forebears came through an orderly, regulated system and didn't need help once they got here, neither of which is entirely true). We think we know how it works now (we're sure that there's an orderly, fair line where people can wait their turn, and we assume that unauthorized immigrants stubbornly refuse to get in it—but there isn't a line, and that's the problem). Most of what we "know" isn't true, but that doesn't seem to matter. Indeed, the facts about immigration and immigrants, even when they're well established and easily quantifiable (how many are there? Where do they come from? How do they get here? How much government help do they actually use?) are either absent from the conversation entirely or stubbornly unpersuasive if they come up at all.

Because this is such an emotion-laden debate, the most fertile terrain on which to have it has long been a landscape driven by values. Immigration is so central to our understanding of ourselves as a nation, to the individual histories of so many Americans as well as our national myths, that appeals to our emotions around immigration as a source of our identity and strength are powerful and often effective. Since 1965, these appeals have been used in the service of a relatively generous legal immigration policy, which focuses on allowing Americans to bring close family members from abroad and provides avenues for employers to bring in the talent and skills they need, in each case with important limits.

But values are also a driver of anti-immigrant policy and sentiment, as richly demonstrated by the Trump era, in which the most potent emotional appeals were focused on persuading us that we have been too generous, that immigration is out of control, and that extreme measures are needed, especially at the border, to protect the country from what is described as the threat and menace of those seeking to enter. As ugly as this debate has been, it is also arguably a values-focused debate, at least on the surface. While there's plenty of evidence that racism and even white supremacy were motivating values for the Trump era, much of Trump's rhetoric was about law and order, about rules and the expectation that people follow them, and about the necessity of taking drastic action to protect the integrity of our borders. It is important and necessary to challenge outright racism as a basis for policy. At the same time, that response has elided the fact that the racists have claimed the mantle of lawfulness, orderliness, and integrity, even as they foment chaos. Anti-racism is only part of the antidote; the pro-immigrant side of the debate must also present a coherent vision of how an orderly, humane, and rational immigration system can function in the future.

Nowhere is this more true than in the situation at the U.S.-Mexico border. The border is not only a literal entryway for people coming to the United States; it is also the de facto entry point into the debate about immigrants of all kinds, documented and undocumented, whether or not they entered at our southern border. It's not possible to have a successful discussion about legal immigrants, about enforcement in the interior of the country, about refugees, or about any related topic as long as the public is convinced that the border is out of control.

This is true regardless of what is actually happening at the border itself. We have been having variants of the same discussion about walls, detention facilities, and the size of the Border Patrol for more than 40 years. With the notable exception of 2019, the number of people attempting to enter during the last decade has declined precipitously.[1] The intensity of the debate has nothing to do with the actual intensity of the pressure at the border. It's as if we immediately enter a fact-free zone as soon as the border is mentioned.

It is easy to make the mistake of assuming that any conversation about addressing the U.S.-Mexico border is a concession to the Right, especially when a demagogue is stoking fears (in the ugliest possible terms) of migrants coming from the South. And the organizations that focus attention on the devastating impacts of the Trump administration's policies are absolutely right to do so. Unfortunately, however, what this argument looks like to the general public is a debate on *whether* there should be rules at the border, rather than *what* these rules should be and how they should be enforced.

The pro-immigrant advocacy community is getting really good at fighting against the policies that it opposes. Tragically, the Trump administration's actions provided more than enough to push back on, twenty-four hours a day, seven days a week. This is vital work, but it also prevents engagement in the much more difficult but necessary task of envisioning what the laws, policies, and infrastructure at the border should look like over a longer time horizon. If we expect to rebalance the government's approach to its various tasks at the border, which include maintaining the integrity of our national boundaries while also abiding by our values as a nation of laws and a nation of immigrants, advocates need to be able to articulate what they are *for*, and persuade the American people that they are for it too.

I say this as a policymaker, someone who has worked for decades as an advocate and also spent eight years at the highest levels of government attempting to find this balance. As we enter the era of a new administration that is trying to get it right, the people sitting at those tables will need allies and ideas, particularly when there are intense and complex pressures to be managed at the border, which is likely to be true for the foreseeable future.

Framing the Debate

The harm to immigrants, their families, and the larger U.S. community as a result of Trump-era policies has been incalculable and devastating. Yet for all of the damage that his administration caused, President Trump claimed the mantle of action. As the immigration advocacy world reacted, they reinforced his argument that he was battling mightily for change while his opponents care only about stopping him. Tragically, the necessity of reacting to his damaging policies had the perverse effect of undermining the ability of the immigration advocacy community to advance a narrative that digs the country out of the morass created by the Trump administration. Indeed, by engaging a debate on his terms, our side lost considerable ground. Even if the Trump era is followed by a less xenophobic one, it is not a foregone conclusion that the damage can be easily undone, or that a new immigration regime can be put in place. In the policy world, having a plan always beats not having one. And responding to the assaults of the Trump administration on immigrants, as important as that is, is not the same thing as having a plan.

Americans recognize that the country would benefit from an update of its immigration laws and policies; indeed, it can be argued that President Trump capitalized on the failure of Congress to act by taking matters into his own hands. Many Americans find action preferable to inaction, even when those actions are extreme. But there is some evidence that the excesses of the Trump administration got the country's attention and that a majority of the public is uncomfortable with extreme tactics such as separating families at the border.[2] This may be enough to reverse the most harmful policies as the political winds shift, but it will not be sufficient to change the circumstances that leave undocumented immigrants vulnerable, to update the laws governing asylum, or to repair a badly backlogged legal immigration system.

Americans are capable of supporting increases in legal immigration and the provision of a pathway to legal status for undocumented immigrants at the same time that they expect a secure border.[3] Their feelings about removing undocumented immigrants from the interior of the country are more nuanced. This is not simply a debate about whether immigrants are good or bad. Getting to a good policy with broad support requires finding a way to meet the public where it is, which means defining a new approach that feels orderly, fair, and generous. It may feel unsatisfying to build an approach that capitalizes on whatever limited political space is available in the short to medium term, knowing that it will take time to build toward the broader set of reforms that we need. But assuming that decision-makers in the here and now cannot speak up for a politics for which there is not yet broad support is at best a recipe for accomplishing nothing, and at worst could generate a backlash. The challenge for those seeking change is to define what is possible given current constraints, while expanding the space for broader reforms in the longer term.

President Trump and his ilk framed the debate as a choice between toughness and generosity. He pointed to a crisis, and while this involved wild exaggeration, it contained a kernel of truth: the pressures at the U.S.-Mexico border are undeniably real. This set up a dynamic in which his opponents were forced to respond on his terms. The framing looks something like this:

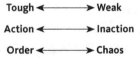

Response to a crisis:

Tough ⟵⟶ Weak

Action ⟵⟶ Inaction

Order ⟵⟶ Chaos

As long as the discussion is structured along these axes, the pro-immigrant world will be on the losing side. The louder their efforts, the more they reinforce this positioning. The ability to protect immigrants and the nation's best interests depends on being able to shift to a different framework, aligned along a different set of values. In recent decades, the moments during which the immigration advocacy community has succeeded in shaping public opinion and even winning the occasional policy debate have involved insisting on a frame of our own making, one that acknowledges the appetite among Americans for a system that is orderly and fair, and creates the space for a set of laws that are generous, humane, and effective. The alternative framing looks something like this:

We all agree that the status quo is unacceptable:

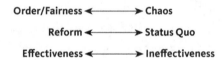

In this formulation, the organizations defending immigrants are squarely on the side of creating a system that is orderly and fair, and that moves the country away from an unacceptable status quo. This framework is achievable, and it positions Trump and his allies where they belong—as incapable of managing the challenges we face, creating chaos that harms immigrants as well as the rest of us while benefiting politically from the chaos they foment.

This requires accepting and acknowledging that what happens at the border is indeed a challenge. It requires reinforcing for the public that the integrity of the border is a legitimate concern, while also reminding them that these challenges can be met in a manner consistent with our nation's best values. It means rejecting the frame that works for the restrictionists, and forcing them to respond on very different terms.

Meeting the Challenge of Managing the Border

The administration that follows Trump is not starting from some neutral place from which they will be able to build. They face an immediate humanitarian crisis that was created in the Trump era, and the tools available to fix it are severely limited. A pro-immigrant administration, trying to find its way toward protecting the vulnerable, will very likely face the following tensions:

- The COVID-19 pandemic has slowed migration in the short term, but in the longer term, the economic dislocation it caused will likely contribute to migration.
- Restrictionists in Congress as well as civil society will continue to use the pandemic as a justification for their arguments to close borders.
- The tens of thousands of asylum seekers trapped in Mexico present an immediate humanitarian crisis. Continued public health fears sparked by the pandemic will likely complicate the possibility of their entering the United States.
- New migrants will continue to approach the U.S.-Mexico border, many from Central America, but also from places such as Brazil, Haiti, and Venezuela. Some will be fleeing violence, others will be fleeing dire economic circumstances, including the effects of climate change.
- The law as it stands today is inadequate for meeting this challenge: it provides only limited opportunities for asylum in a deeply backlogged system, and almost no options for economic migrants.
- Without a substantial change in the law, the facilities, personnel, and legal regime applied to this challenge will be those created to police the border we had a quarter century ago, when we had much larger levels of migration, mostly single adults coming from Mexico.

- A growing number of migrants are children, many of whom travel alone or in the hands of smugglers. They are in need of special protection.
- The economic dislocation within the United States in the aftermath of the COVID-19 pandemic will strengthen fears that migrants attempting to cross the southern border will compete with Americans for scarce jobs.
- This will feel like a crisis, both because of the trauma faced by the migrants themselves and because any unregulated pressure at the border is likely to be portrayed in dramatic terms in the media and in policy circles.
- This crisis-like atmosphere will be met with criticism from the Left and the Right, both of which will attack the administration attempting to manage it, albeit for different reasons.
- All of this could be exacerbated by unexpected future surges in migration due to, say, a natural disaster in the region.

The administration entering this situation must face questions like the following:

- The personnel currently available at the border are Border Patrol officials. The facilities at the border itself are essentially lockups. What should change about how and whether they are used? Is it possible to ensure that existing personnel implement those changes? The Border Patrol union will likely object to reforms; how should that challenge be managed?
- What are the conditions in border facilities now, and how should they change? Which changes are implementable in the short term, and which are not?
- What should the process be when border personnel encounter, say, a family from Central America?

- What is the next step for those who pass the first hurdle for the asylum process?
- What is the next step for those who don't?
- The waiting period for asylum hearings is currently several years. What happens to applicants, including families, in the interim?
- There's no budget for the government to provide legal assistance to asylum seekers. What steps should be taken to attempt to provide it?
- What happens when personnel at the border encounter an unaccompanied child? What facilities are needed at the border? What is needed once a child is transferred to Department of Health and Human Services (HHS) shelter care? Is there a better approach than a Border Patrol transfer to HHS? What about the fact that both the Left and the Right object to housing children at all?

Without a substantial majority in Congress, the new Democratic administration can expect a recalcitrant legislature that neither undertakes institutional reforms nor appropriates funds for managing the crisis. This means addressing the border with only the existing tools and resources, which are wholly inadequate.

A divided Congress, or one that displays some willingness to enact reforms without similar enthusiasm for appropriating the necessary funds, may create opportunities for some progress. A clear set of priorities would help guide policymakers in this scenario, as well as in a rosier scenario in which Congress is ready for reform and for major spending. Even in this most promising of scenarios, it is essential to provide clarity on where reforms and resources are most needed, as well as a set of priorities for how to manage while legislation winds its way through the process, followed by years of work for the federal government to promulgate regulations under a new set of laws.

What these scenarios suggest is that even the most well-intentioned administration will have a lot on its hands managing the U.S.-Mexico border, and the results are likely to be unsatisfying. Even in the best circumstance, in which there is a receptive, reform-minded Congress, there will be enormous management challenges while reforms are developed, legislated, and implemented.

Two truths are inescapable. First, whatever is happening at the border will determine how comfortable Americans are that the government can do the fundamentals of its job. Their comfort—or lack of it—will in turn have an impact on how much political space there is to address other immigration policy matters, such as reforms to the legal immigration system, asylum policy, enforcement of immigration laws in the interior of the country, and rules governing immigrants' access to public services.

Second, an administration grappling with these challenges, using the inadequate tools likely to be available, is likely to draw criticism from both the Right and the Left. This, in turn, will continue to reinforce the general public's impression that the system is broken and that solutions are elusive. In short, the situation will continue to feel like a crisis. If the pro-immigrant world has not done its homework and developed approaches that can convince the public that there is a way out of the morass that brings order, fairness, and humanity to the border, if it fails to neutralize the "we are tough and they are not" framing of the Trump era, it will be difficult to gain the political support needed for badly needed reforms. And if the pro-immigrant world focuses public attention only on what must be fixed—important as that is—without a vision of what a system looks like when it is working well, it is unlikely to meet its goals.

Toward a New Vision: The Border and Beyond

As challenging as it is to develop a new vision of border management that is effective, humane, and convincing to the American public, the good news is that there are some excellent sources of ideas for addressing some of the most vexing problems. Doris Meissner of the Migration Policy Institute (MPI), who designed a series of effective reforms to the asylum system in the 1990s, and her colleagues Faye Hipsman and T. Alexander Aleinikoff have developed a comprehensive set of recommendations for reforming the asylum system that are coherent, workable, and provide a pathway for fairness, order, and protection for those fleeing to the United States.[4]

Their proposal reminds us that the U.S. government succeeded for many years in delivering timely and well-informed decisions on asylum cases and deterring non-meritorious claims. Noting that tens of thousands of potential asylees are referred to the immigration courts each year, contributing to a massive backlog that can lead to a delay of several years before a hearing is scheduled, they recommend shifting the bulk of the adjudication process to the specially trained asylum corps that already conducts the first stage of the process to determine whether a claimant has a "significant possibility" of establishing eligibility for asylum. Meissner and her colleagues make the case that the asylum process can be both more efficient and effective in a non-adversarial process run by the asylum corps rather than the immigration court system, and that the ranks of asylum officers could be expanded to address the current backlog so as to return to an environment in which an answer can be delivered within six months. This is the rare situation in which a reform can be implemented by the agency without having to turn to Congress.

A reinvigorated, efficient, and humane asylum process would go a long way toward restoring a sense of order and fairness to the system, and could serve as the backbone to an entirely reenvisioned approach to the border. The current infrastructure that greets migrants, from the personnel to the facilities, was designed for a different set of demands than we currently face. The typical family coming from Central America, if they are able to cross at all, looks for the Border

Patrol to turn themselves in and begin the asylum process. The typical facility in which they are processed is a cinder-block structure with desks for the Border Patrol officers to process migrants and holding cells that were built for adult males. What if we envisioned a different type of facility altogether, designed based on the needs of migrants and the personnel who encounter them? The job of the government at the point of entry is to sort migrants who have the potential to enter from those who do not. What if we were to use some of the billions of dollars currently being pumped into detention facilities to create or adapt structures suitable for this function? They could house a Border Patrol with much better training—along with an expanded asylum corps, the FEMA personnel who have been deployed in previous times of crisis to help make sure migrants have sufficient food, water, and blankets, and even members of the Public Health Service to address the needs of those who are ill, injured, or traumatized. What if we were to host a design process to create facilities suitable for families with children—facilities that are expandable for use at times of unusual demand? These are not particularly challenging questions; rather, the challenge is that policymakers have seldom bothered—or dared—to ask them.

Once a migrant family leaves the facilities at the border, the next step in the process varies. Sometimes migrants are released and required to appear later at a removal hearing; in some cases this involves an ankle bracelet to guarantee their compliance. Congress funds tens of thousands of detention beds every year, and migrants are transferred to detention facilities to await the next step of the removal process, which may or may not involve an asylum petition. In the Obama years, DHS partnered with a handful of NGOs to create pilot family case management projects that allowed migrants to be released into the community in the care of organizations who would meet their immediate needs and facilitate their participation in their upcoming hearings. These projects were small but successful in that migrants' basic needs were largely met and they were better able to participate in their immigration court proceedings, often with legal representation. Though these efforts were canceled by the Trump administration, they could be revived, with a renewed focus on developing this capacity at a greater scale. The NGO sector may not be able to develop sufficient capacity to manage what is likely to be an enormous caseload, but it is likely to be both more cost effective and more humane to scale this kind of effort alongside other approaches such as ankle bracelets.

The debate on detention, which is being carried out in the courts as well as the civic commons, should include independent and in-depth analysis to lay to rest the question of what, if anything, detention accomplishes for people awaiting immigration proceedings, particularly as compared to other alternatives such as ankle bracelets or community monitoring. For over a decade Congress has effectively required the use of detention for tens of thousands of migrants, and there are long-standing requirements for detention of those with serious criminal violations who are awaiting removal. The use of detention for potential asylees is more controversial, particularly for parents with small children. Those who support its use argue that it is an important tool in the arsenal that creates high barriers to entry, reducing the likelihood that migrants will file asylum claims as a strategy to allow them to disappear into the United States while they wait years for a hearing. A reformed asylum process that delivers a fair answer in a shorter time frame could address much of this argument. And while there is a high emotional need among some policymakers to use detention as a show of toughness, to convince migrants that the doorway to the United States is not simply open, there is not much evidence to show that even the harshest treatment at the hands of U.S. officials does much to deter migration.

Yet it can be more satisfying for policymakers to pull the levers they have at hand—effective or not—than to develop new ones. The levers that are not currently in the grasp of U.S. policymakers may be the most important. Much of the solution to the situation at the

U.S.-Mexico border doesn't have anything to do with the border itself. Tactics focused on what happens at the border cannot be effective in addressing migration without measures to address the reasons people migrate in the first place. Even if our asylum system were functioning efficiently and effectively, which is far from the case, its Cold War–era design is ill-suited for twenty-first-century challenges, and it is unlikely ever to be sufficient for all of those in need of protection who manage the difficult and dangerous journey to the United States. As the United Nations High Commissioner for Refugees has pointed out, there is urgent need for a regional approach, in which nations collaborate to provide safe havens for those seeking protection.[5]

The answer to the refugee crisis in Central America is never going to be that everyone fleeing violence or economic insecurity ends up in the United States. The United States has a special obligation to provide resources and to partner with Central American governments, NGOs, and multilateral organizations to address violence, corruption, and economic instability in the region, both because of our stature as a global and regional superpower and also because our own policies have contributed mightily to the reasons that people migrate. Our policy of removing foreign nationals convicted of serious crimes, for example, has seeded the drug smuggling and gang violence that are contributing to migration.[6] More generally, U.S. foreign policy has shortchanged Latin America in a way that has allowed the proliferation of the conditions behind the current crisis.

A regional approach must also recognize that there is a refugee crisis in our hemisphere. The United States must mobilize itself, our regional partners, and the multilateral community in a more robust version of the effort that began in the waning years of the Obama administration to expand capacity across the region to accept those who flee their homes, provide refugee processing and opportunities for resettlement along with a more robust asylum infrastructure, stand up for local integration programs, expand resettlement within and outside the region, and arrange for safe and dignified return of those who do not qualify for international protection.

This will require strong leadership from the United States, which in turn will require an expansive conversation about migration. At present, the infrastructure focused on immigration—which includes policy and advocacy groups, congressional committees, and the federal agencies charged with implementation—is almost entirely separate from the advocacy, legislative, and implementation infrastructure focused on refugee resettlement and international development. In Congress, for example, the foreign affairs committee infrastructure is separate from the committees that focus on immigration and refugees. The federal government is similarly divided, with the State Department, the Department of Homeland Security, and to a lesser extent the Department of Justice sharing a range of responsibilities related to immigrants and refugees, while the State Department directs foreign affairs.

The advocacy world mirrors this institutional fragmentation: by and large, organizations focused on the border, immigration, and immigrants are different than those focused on refugee policy. The immigrant-focused groups have expertise on the experience of the foreign-born within the United States, although a subgroup focuses on the border and the plight of would-be asylees. There are human rights groups focused on foreign affairs and refugees, and there is an infrastructure of refugee organizations, typically faith-based groups that get substantial parts of their funding through their work resettling refugees within the United States—funding that was decimated by drastic reductions in the number of refugees under the Trump administration.

The result of this bifurcated setup is that, by and large, immigration and international engagement are separate spheres of U.S. policymaking, advocacy, and practice. This, in turn, almost guarantees that we have a robust conversation about what happens at the border with a set of players who are largely disconnected from the conversation about what we must do in the region to address the causes of migration. There are some notable exceptions among advocacy organizations (Kids in Need of Defense, Human Rights First) and think tanks (Migration Policy Institute, Center on Migration Studies), but most organizations working on immigration in the United States don't do international policy, and most groups doing international policy don't work on domestic immigration issues. This structural problem was not as critical when economically motivated migration from Mexico was the major migration policy concern in the United States, but it is potentially catastrophic for the future.

These structural challenges in the congressional, executive branch, and advocacy infrastructures are not easily remedied. In my own experience in the Obama administration, the strongest alignment of the various federal agencies with jurisdiction over immigration, refugee, and international issues occurred in 2014, to address the unexpected spike in the number of children arriving in the United States alone or with smugglers from Central America. The response to that crisis, organized initially to ensure adequate protection for the children, eventually became a multi-dimensional effort that included teams focused on sheltering children, managing border admissions, dispersing funds and expertise to the Northern Triangle countries to address the causes of migration, and engaging multilateral organizations and other nations in providing protection in the region for those facing danger. It took a crisis for that level of coordination to take root; the effort was quickly disassembled by the Trump administration, with disastrous results.

We cannot simply rely on the government to coordinate efforts to address the causes of migration while managing the border in a humane, orderly, and effective way, let alone to develop a vision for a world in which migration will be a growing challenge. Meeting the challenges of the coming era will require a more robust think tank and advocacy infrastructure with the capacity to address these issues in all their dimensions. This will require considerable effort and investment from the philanthropic community to build and strengthen the few organizations with the necessary capabilities and to create the space for advocates and experts to step back and build a strategic vision that is more global (or at least regional) than domestic. We are very far from having this capacity now, which will hinder any future efforts to craft a new vision for migration.

Migration will only grow as a global challenge, and the United States' history as a nation of immigrants that also became a superpower gives it unique global standing to lead the international conversation, for better or worse. Our history on this issue is replete with atrocities, including in the Trump years, but it also contains moments in which we have recognized the benefits of migration, accepted a leadership role in protecting the vulnerable, and brought a civil rights lens to the development of immigration policy within our own borders. We are positioned to lead, for good or for ill; the better we understand the values that we bring to the debate, and the sharper we are about developing a strategic vision that the American people can embrace, the greater will be our capacity to address these problems in a way that is once again a beacon to the world.

Notes

1. Jessica Bolter and Doris Meissner, "Crisis at the Border? Not by the Numbers," Migration Policy Institute, June 2018, www.migrationpolicy.org/news/crisis -border-not-numbers.

2. Blair Guild, "Poll: Most Americans Oppose Immigrant Family Separation," CBS News, June 18, 2018; Matthew Yglesias, "Support for Immigration Is Surging in the Trump era," *Vox*, July 5, 2018, www.vox.com/policy-and-politics/2018/7/5 /17527734/trump-immigration-poll.

3. Andrew Daniller, "Americans' Immigration Policy Priorities: Divisions Between—and Among—the Two Parties," Pew Research Center, Nov. 12, 2019, www.pewresearch.org/fact-tank/2019/11/12/americans-immigration-policy -priorities-divisions-between-and-within-the-two-parties.

4. Doris Meissner, Faye Hipsman, and T. Alexander Aleinikoff, "The U.S. Asylum System in Crisis: Charting a Way Forward," Migration Policy Institute, Sept. 2018, www.migrationpolicy.org/research/us-asylum-system-crisis-charting -way-forward.

5. "UNHCR Appeals for Regional Talks on Central American Displacement," June 12, 2019, www.unhcr.org/news/press/2019/6/5d0132624/unhcr-appeals-regional-talks-central-america-displacement.html.

6. International Crisis Group, "Mafia of the Poor: Gang Violence and Extortion in Central America," Apr. 6, 2017, www.crisisgroup.org/latin-america-caribbean/central-america/62-mafia-poor-gang-violence-and-extortion-central-america.

"We Have Found the Enemy and It Is Not Each Other"

Deep Canvassing to Change Hearts and Minds on Immigration in Rural and Small-Town America

Mehrdad Azemun and Adam Kruggel

Among the lessons of Trump's stunning 2016 election victory was the fact that he easily carried most small towns and rural areas. Anti-immigrant narratives and policies were at the center of his campaign strategy. Years after his victory, many progressives continue to write off rural areas, in effect ceding the issue of immigration to the Right, at least in those parts of the country. People's Action and our member organizations have begun to chart a different path by doing slow and patient listening and engagement with rural Americans, work centered around shifting worldviews around race and the economy. If we hope to build a durable progressive majority, progressives must contest the narratives about immigration and scarcity in a way that can authentically speak to working-class communities that have been marginalized and left behind.

In the summer of 2018, Jeremiah Jaynes traveled from the hills of Appalachia, where he grew up planting tobacco and raising chickens, to Washington, DC. A seventh-generation resident of Haywood County, North Carolina, Jeremiah is also a member of Down Home North Carolina (DHNC), a grassroots membership-based organization that is part of People's Action, a national racial and economic justice organization. Across from the White House, he spoke at a Families Belong Together march protesting the Trump administration's actions against immigrant families. He recounted the evolution of his thinking on immigration. "When I was a kid, I didn't see the big picture," he said in a gentle southern accent. "I used to think immigrants were a burden on the economy. I used to think it was us against them. But I now know that's just a big con."[1]

Analyzing Jeremiah's journey offers insights as to how organizers can meet the demographic, political, and cultural headwinds that progressives face in red states and rural areas and the challenges involved in building an enduring pro-immigrant majority. The process begins with a knock on the door, listening to each other, and invoking the mantra of Gale Cincotta, a longtime organizer from Chicago and a co-founder of National People's Action: "We have met the enemy and it is not each other."

Jeremiah first became involved in DHNC because of his struggles with addiction. The organization was working to help find solutions to the opioid crisis and was going door-to-door distributing naloxone to help prevent overdoses.[2] As he became more engaged in the group, Jeremiah, who is white, slowly built relationships with Black residents and immigrants in the region. When the separation of children from their families at the border became a national news story, he began processing the experiences with a local organizer and other members of DHNC. He had been incarcerated for three months for driving his wife to work with a suspended license. "This experience nearly destroyed me," he wrote in an op-ed for the local paper. "So when I see the forced separation of children at the southern border, or families indefinitely jailed just for seeking protection, I don't just feel heartbroken. I also feel a deep sense of connection—as a father, and as a human being. I understand what it's like to want to do everything in your power to keep your child safe from harm but lack the freedom to hug them when they're in pain or comfort them when they are scared."[3]

Jeremiah's transformation involved both being deeply engaged around his own self-interest and building a sense of agency. Being in relationships where he felt a sense of belonging allowed him to create a bridge of empathy that spanned racial differences and helped him to link his own suffering with that of migrant families in detention camps at the border.

In the aftermath of the 2016 election, People's Action and our member organizations recognized the need to wrestle with the deep divisions across race, class, and place plaguing our country. DHNC was a founding member of our Rural and Small-Town Organizing Strategy, which we used to build new chapters in more than forty communities in fifteen states, creating one of the largest progressive rural organizing efforts in the country. This work generated many stories of transformation like Jeremiah's.

Kari Snyder of Michigan United is another example. "I've lived in Wyandotte, Michigan, my whole life, and we were hit hard by the recession," she declared. "In my grandfather's generation, almost everyone worked in the auto industry. But I don't know anybody my age—I'm thirty-two—who works for auto. I've known what it's like to be hungry. A lot of people find it's easier to blame people who look different from them. . . . Race is a huge wedge that the other side uses to keep us apart so we don't get anything done."

Although we have had success in individual cases of transformation like Jeremiah's and Kari's, we wrestled with the idea of scaling these transformations in a meaningful way to help reshape the national balance of power and meet the challenges of progressive organizing in rural areas around immigration.

Those challenges were highlighted by Donald Trump's resounding success in rural counties and small towns in 2016, along with Hillary Clinton's underperformance, especially in the Midwest. Trump carried 206 "pivot counties" that Obama had won in both 2008 and 2012. In nearly all of them, however, Obama's victory margin had declined between 2008 and 2012, foreshadowing the 2016 results. As many commentators have noted, many of the areas where Trump performed better than expected had a long history of economic distress, declining life expectancy, and deteriorating social conditions.[4]

To reduce racial resentment in America, people's understanding of their suffering must be centered on the massive economic inequalities that have devastated communities. Only then can their moral and strategic interest in defeating racism, xenophobia, and nativism come to the foreground. This requires exposing who is causing—and who is benefiting from—surging inequalities. As People's Action director George Goehl puts it, "Did Muslims crash the economy? Are Black people pushing opioids into this part of the state? Did undocumented immigrants stash a bunch of money in offshore tax havens? No. We have found that the enemy is not each other; let's focus on the real enemy."[5]

It is critical to address the anxiety about the changing racial demographics of America, which further contributed to Trump's success among white Americans whose race/ethnicity is central to their identity.[6] White working-class voters who feel like "a stranger in their own country" and who believe the United States needs protection against foreign influence were 3.5 times more likely to support Trump than those who did not share those concerns. Moreover, white working-class voters who favored deporting immigrants living in the country illegally were 3.3 times more likely to express a preference for Trump than those who did not.[7] A 2017 poll found that rural residents were far more likely than city dwellers to consider immigrants a burden to the United States—42 percent compared to 16 percent.[8]

Political scientist Katherine J. Cramer's study of rural and small-town communities in Wisconsin exposed what she calls the "politics of resentment," in which people blame a "less deserving" social group, rather than broader social forces, for the economic decline they have experienced.[9] As Cramer shows, this reinforces cultural and racial antagonism and erodes public confidence in the value of government.

The neglect and marginalization that many working-class whites have experienced in some respects recapitulate what people of color have endured for generations. But instead of finding common ground, they all too often embrace the "dog-whistle politics" that fueled the growth of Republican Party power.[10] Yet they have a fluid, mixed consciousness, open to a variety of narratives, some of which may seem contradictory. Indeed, many organizers in rural areas have come to believe that "whoever is first on the front porch" will win.[11] The decline of organized labor and the erosion of progressive organizing in rural and small-town communities have created a vacuum into which right-wing media and white nationalist groups have stepped, helping to fuel widespread scapegoating around race and immigration.

As a study by Unbound Philanthropy of public attitudes toward immigration reform found, many Americans believe that there are not enough resources or space for immigrants and refugees to be in the United States.[12] Progressives "have not provided an alternative to the prevailing mental model of scarcity," the authors state. "Simply telling people that there is enough to go around for more and more people, when they are getting less and less in life generally, will seem counter-factual." That mental model of scarcity is particularly resilient in rural and small-town communities.

We have been exploring this problem in recent years with two innovative methodologies, "deep listening" surveys and a more intensive "deep canvass."

Deep Listening

We conducted deep listening surveys in ten states, involving conversations with nearly ten thousand respondents over the period from September 2017 through April 2018.[13] We created a standardized tool that we used across all ten states, so that we could conduct a rigorous analysis. The goal was to understand how people responded to conservative and progressive narratives regarding who should be held responsible for the conditions in each community.

We asked respondents to answer broad questions about the problems facing them and their communities, as catalysts for deeper conversations. First, we asked them to identify the problems that most concerned them, in their own words, without prompting. Then we read them a curated list of issues and asked them to indicate how much they were worried about each. That was followed by a list of groups that might be responsible for the problems they had identified, and asking respondents to apportion shares of responsibility to each group. Next, they were presented with a list of solutions and asked to rate how much impact each would have. Finally, we asked whether respondents believed that people acting together can achieve significant change, and we invited them to a local meeting to work on the issues they care about.

A content analysis found that the most common word that respondents used in identifying the problems facing their communities was "lack" (e.g., lack of jobs, lack of health care, lack of resources), confirming the ubiquity of the mental model of scarcity. This analysis also revealed the pervasiveness of financial insecurity, accompanied by instability, stress, health problems, and drug and alcohol abuse.

Results from the part of the deep listening survey in which respondents indicated which groups they held responsible for the problems in their communities are summarized in Figure 1. The group most frequently named was "government controlled by big money donors and corporate lobbyists," which 56 percent rated "very responsible," and another 25 percent rated "somewhat responsible." Ranked next was "big corporations and Wall Street," followed by "rich and powerful individuals." Many respondents expressed feelings of betrayal and anger toward a government that they felt had abandoned them and had been co-opted by the rich, as well as concerns about the "division of the country." Stagnant wages and the "uneven distribution of wealth in the community" were also mentioned frequently.

However, the villains featured in conservative populist narratives also received their share of blame: 55 percent of respondents saw "people who depend on government programs" as "very" or "somewhat" responsible for the problems in their communities. Moreover, a substantial proportion of respondents indicated that immigrants were either "very responsible" (15 percent) or "somewhat responsible" (28 percent) for those problems. On the other hand, in another section of the survey, one-third of respondents indicated that "not being welcoming to immigrants" concerned them "a great deal" or "often," while one in five expressed support for deporting immigrants as a "solution" to their problems.

These findings expose the resonance of both progressive and conservative forms of populism in rural communities. Although the progressive narrative blaming the wealthy and big corporations ranks first in the data shown in Figure 1, the narrative that immigrants and people of color were drivers of scarcity was also highly salient, reflecting palpable racial and nativist resentments. Overall, the findings reflect the mixed consciousness characteristic of rural and small-town residents, validating the previously mentioned observation that whoever is "first on the porch" will prevail.

In reviewing the results of the listening survey, we were struck by the salience of health care as a major issue, along with the mental model of scarcity. In the spring of 2019, to explore this further with a particular focus on immigration, we launched a deep canvass

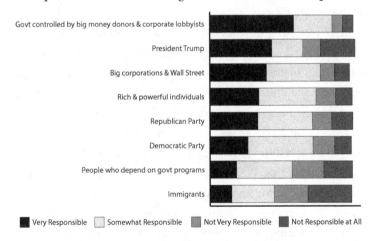

Figure 1: "How responsible are these groups for the problems in your community?"

project in three states: Michigan, North Carolina, and Pennsylvania. The research was developed and implemented by our member organizations Down Home North Carolina, Michigan United, and Pennsylvania Stands Up, with support from the New Conversation Initiative, which pioneered deep canvass methodology.

The Deep Canvass

The goal of this research was to explore the roots of mental models around scarcity and immigration and test the power of "solidarity narratives" to "build a bigger we" that includes immigrants, specifically the "Race-Class Narrative" developed by Anat Shenker-Osorio and Ian Haney López.[14] That narrative aims to persuade people to reject right-wing populism and instead embrace progressive solutions and forms of government that could implement those solutions. It explicitly names specific actors—wealthy elites and large corporations—and exposes their attempts to use racial divisions to further their own interests. In addition, the Race-Class Narrative evokes specific moments in U.S. history when people have joined together across racial lines (e.g., the New Deal and civil rights eras) to address massive social problems.

Three core insights from the Race-Class Narrative were incorporated into our deep canvass scripts. The first is the need to discuss race overtly. Our opposition is constantly talking about race, and if we fail to do so explicitly, the right-wing framing will prevail uncontested. Second is the importance of explaining how racism is used to divide us, redirecting people's anger about their conditions away from people of color and immigrants and toward the wealthy elites who profit from their suffering. Finally, we must make the case that racial justice is a path to economic prosperity, and that if we come together we can ensure that everyone could get the care that they need and deserve.

Deep canvassing is a powerful tool that aims to non-judgmentally solicit respondents' views and then pose follow-up questions about relevant, emotionally significant experiences. In candid, two-way conversations the canvassers share their own personal experiences as well.[15] Previous deep canvassing efforts have generated increased support for transgender-inclusive non-discrimination laws, and for a path to citizenship for undocumented immigrants and more humane immigration policies.[16]

Individuals who resist direct persuasion (because yielding to it threatens their self-image) are often more amenable to the deep canvassing approach. It is often difficult for people to admit that there are errors or inconsistencies in their views, or to recognize that they have been victims of manipulation. Deep canvassing aims to overcome these challenges through non-judgmental, respectful listening and active participation in a two-way conversation that is open to alternative viewpoints. The practice of sharing personal experiences creates an emotional connection and tends to be perceived as less manipulative and more engaging than simply presenting facts or talking points. Our experiment fused the deep canvass methodology of non-judgmental listening and story sharing with core messages from the Race-Class Narrative to explore the mixed consciousness of rural and small-town residents and to expose the ways in which strategic racism divided communities.

Other researchers have already conducted deep canvass research projects on immigration policy.[17] Our goal was to build on those with a study focused on the mental model of scarcity. In the context of ongoing debate about Medicare for All and other universal health care plans, we probed voters' feelings about opening up universal health care to undocumented immigrants.

The project began with a mailed pre-survey of registered voters in rural areas and small towns in the three states (Michigan, North Carolina, and Pennsylvania). That survey found that only 21 percent of those responding supported including undocumented immigrants in universal health care plans. The next stage involved paid organizers trained in the deep canvass methodology of asking questions in a non-judgmental manner along with techniques to elicit narratives from respondents about their experiences. Canvassers rigorously followed an established script, which the research team developed in consultation with Anat Shenker-Osorio as well as allies in the immigrant rights movement. Training involved role-playing and viewing videos of past canvass conversations, with particular emphasis on developing skills in vulnerable storytelling and compassionate curiosity. Forty-four percent of the canvassers were U.S.-born people of color, and 16 percent were immigrants. Among those who responded to the pre-survey and then had a follow-up deep canvass conversation, 56 percent were white. Nearly half of them (47 percent) were college-educated. Politically, 43 percent of respondents self-identified as conservative, 30 percent as moderate, and 27 percent as liberal; 44 percent of them expressed approval of Trump.

To enable us to assess the impact of the deep canvass conversations, researchers Joshua Kalla and David Broockman designed a randomized controlled trial in conjunction with our efforts. They mailed an invitation to registered voters in rural areas and small towns in the three targeted states to participate in a series of ostensibly unrelated, university-sponsored online opinion surveys covering a range of topics, including immigration and health care. A total of 369,319 invitations were mailed, and 8,925 people completed the online survey.

Canvassers then contacted 2,838 of the survey respondents, who were randomly assigned to three groups. Each group had similar demographic composition in regard to race, gender, income level, and educational attainment, as well as preexisting political views and media consumption habits.

The canvassers used a different script for each group. In the first one, they shared stories about their experiences with immigrants as well as stories about a time in their lives when the canvassers themselves really needed access to health care. The second script only included the stories about immigrants, and the third was a placebo script about an issue unrelated to immigration (e.g., the minimum wage).

The intervention began with efforts to elicit participants' opinions in a non-judgmental manner. In the first two groups, canvassers informed voters that they were at the door to discuss universal health care. They asked voters about their opinion on the policy (on a scale of 0 to 10, from not supportive at all to fully supportive) and then asked them to explain their position. This was followed (for the first two groups) by a more specific question about including unauthorized immigrants in a universal health care plan (again on a scale of 0 to 10). The canvasser and voter then exchanged stories about their personal experience with immigrants. Next the canvasser asked the voter if they knew anyone from outside the United States, and, in particular an undocumented immigrant. If so, the canvasser would have the voter talk in detail about how they knew this person, the person's immigration history, and about how it must feel to be an immigrant. Whether or not the voter knew an immigrant, for these two groups the canvasser would always share an immigration story of their own—either a personal story or one about a friend or family member—and then ask if the voter could relate to anything about the story.

For the first group, the canvasser then proceeded to exchange stories with the voter about a personal experience at "a time when you or a loved one struggled to pay for access to health care." Canvassers would also share their own stories, aiming for a non-judgmental exchange of narratives, and encouraging respondents to articulate the implications of the narratives—especially if there were contradictions with previously stated attitudes. The conversation then transitioned to a "making the case" segment aligned with the Race-Class Narrative, in which the canvasser shared the perspective that elected officials and the wealthy elite are strategically using racism to divide people who have worked together to solve problems in the past.

The next section of the script (for both the first and second groups) was especially significant, focusing on conflicting mental models and lived experiences. Here the canvasser would note any contradictions in the voter's opinions and comments, and probe further. For example, a canvasser might say, "It sounds like on the one hand you think that immigrants do a lot to benefit this country, and on the other hand you think it is more important to take care of our own citizens first. What is on your mind now that we have been talking?"

At this point, the canvasser would return to any concerns about undocumented immigrants and universal health care that the voter had mentioned earlier, invite further discussion, and, where applicable, provide facts and talking points to refute them. Canvassers were trained not to address such concerns until this late point in the conversation, to minimize the likelihood that voters would feel threatened. The intervention ended with canvassers returning to the 0 to 10 scale they had used at the beginning of the script, to assess whether or not the conversation had changed the voter's attitude about including unauthorized immigrants in a universal health care system.

In the final part of the experiment, voters received online opinion surveys one week, seven weeks, and five months after the canvass visit (with no explicit indication provided that the surveys were related to the canvass). About 1,700 voters responded to each round of post-canvass surveys.

Kalla and Broockman analyzed the responses to survey questions about immigrants and immigration after the canvass, comparing the two deep-canvassed groups to the placebo group. The surveys asked respondents to indicate their level of agreement with statements such as "Low-income undocumented immigrants in [state] should be allowed to receive Medicaid" or "Undocumented immigrants are a burden on our community." The results suggest that the deep canvass (for both non-placebo groups) had large and lasting effects on voters' immigration attitudes:

- The canvasses generated an 8 percent increase in support for including undocumented immigrants in an expanded health care social safety net, and this effect persisted for five months. It is rare for observed effects of political communication to persist for more than a couple of weeks. The magnitude of this shift—generating eight new supporters for every one hundred conversations—is larger than the shift in voter share away from Democrats between the 2012 and 2016 elections.

- The canvassing appears to have caused a broader shift in voters' attitudes, not limited to including immigrants in universal health care. For example, for every one hundred deep canvass conversations, there were five new supporters of including undocumented immigrants in food stamps—even though this was not discussed in the conversations.

- There is also evidence that the deep canvass conversations—despite not mentioning any political party or candidate—decreased respondents' approval ratings of Trump and their projections of his 2020 vote share. Democrats, Republicans, and independents; men and women; and voters from all three states became more critical of Trump (albeit to varying degrees) following the deep canvass.

- Another important finding was that the race of the canvasser and voter did not make any statistically significant difference in the results of the conversations, meaning that people were able to have these conversations in an impactful way regardless of their own (or the interviewer's) racial identity.[18]

Conclusion

Our findings from both the listening campaign and the deep canvass on immigration and health care build on a growing body of research suggesting that such interventions can significantly shift voters' worldviews. In our deep canvass experiment, a fifteen-minute conversation rooted in the Race-Class Narrative created significant and lasting change. These conversations also helped voters make new meaning out of their own life experiences. The exchanges effectively encouraged a sense of linked fate and mutual interest with groups—in this instance, immigrants—that are often the target of racial scapegoating.

We also learned that it is essential to name a culprit—wealthy elites and the elected officials they control—who is responsible for the current state of our local communities and our country. Voters named the "rich and powerful" as well as large corporations in our listening survey, and this is a key element in the Race-Class Narrative as well. Without naming those who are responsible, we risk sliding into a vague liberalism that probably would not pass muster in the rural and small-town communities where we are organizing.

By directly engaging with voters about topics that on the surface may seem difficult, and with voters who are themselves conflicted, we enter into a contest for meaning. Progressives write off rural counties at our own peril, leaving millions of people on the table for the Right to organize. Our work suggests the power of using class as a unifying narrative across race and immigration status, provided we take enough time to engage deeply with voters.

Although we are encouraged and inspired by these results, we also must be clear-eyed about the need for sustained work on this front. We must consistently build deeper solidarity across race if we hope to build a movement powerful enough to create lasting progressive change, and to build a path to citizenship and inclusion for immigrants in our country. We need to invest in narratives that center immigrants in the broader movement for racial and economic justice. And we need a strategy to confront the corporate power that has pitted us against each other for decades.

In short, we need to expose the "big con" that Jeremiah articulated before tens of thousands of people assembled under the sweltering sun that day in Washington, DC: "I know who is really hurting my community, and it certainly isn't desperate families and toddlers in cages." With a narrative of radical empathy that fuses race and class, we can build power to both advance justice for immigrants and transform our society and economy over the rest of the twenty-first century.

Notes

1. "Activist at Immigration Rally: 'Pitting Us Against Each Other Is Not the Solution,'" C-SPAN, June 30, 2018, www.c-span.org/video/?c4738179/activist -immigration-rally-pitting-solution.

2. "Down Home NC Launches Local Harm Reduction Hub," *The Mountaineer*, Aug. 17, 2018, www.themountaineer.com/life/health/down-home-nc-launches -local-harm-reduction-hub/article_9cc3f212-a08d-11e8-a875-c701ac3fc895.html.

3. Jeremiah Jaynes, "Being Separated from My Child Nearly Killed Me," *Herald Sun*, June 27, 2018, www.heraldsun.com/opinion/article213948689.html.

4. Shannon M. Monnat and David L. Brown, "More than a Rural Revolt: Landscapes of Despair and the 2016 Presidential Election," *Journal of Rural Studies* 55 (2017): 227–36. See also Arlie Russell Hochschild, *Strangers in Their Own Land: Anger and Mourning on the American Right* (New York: The New Press, 2018); Justin Gest, *The New Minority: White Working-Class Politics in an Age of Immigration and Inequality* (New York: Oxford University Press, 2016).

5. "Organizing to Defeat White Nationalism United States, S4 E2," YouTube, posted by People's Action, June 17, 2019, www.youtube.com /watch?v=Y52F5B7miEE.

6. Brenda Major, Alison Blodorn, and Gregory Major Blascovich, "The Threat of Increasing Diversity: Why Many White Americans Support Trump in the 2016 Presidential Election," *Group Processes and Intergroup Relations* 21, no. 6 (2018): 931–40.

7. Daniel Cox, Rachel Lienesch, and Robert P. Jones, "Beyond Economics: Fears of Cultural Displacement Pushed the White Working Class to Trump," PRRI/The Atlantic Report, May 9, 2017, www.prri.org/research/white-working -class-attitudes-economy-trade-immigration-election-donald-trump.

8. Washington Post and Kaiser Family Foundation, "Rural and Small Town America Poll," June 2017, apps.washingtonpost.com/g/page/national/washington -post-kaiser-family-foundation-rural-and-small-town-america-poll/2217.

9. Katherine J. Cramer, *The Politics of Resentment: Rural Consciousness in Wisconsin and the Rise of Scott Walker* (Chicago: University of Chicago Press, 2016).

10. Ian Haney López, *Dog Whistle Politics: Strategic Racism, Fake Populism, and the Dividing of America* (New York: Oxford University Press, 2018).

11. Jordan Green, "'We Get There First or White Supremacists Do': How These Rural Canvassers Disrupt Racist Narratives," *In These Times*, July 13, 2020.

12. Ryan Senser and Eleanor Morison, "New Insights: Winning on Immigration: Research Findings and Analysis," Oct. 2018, commissioned by Unbound Philanthropy.

13. Adam Kruggel and Jessica Juarez-Scruggs, "The Promise of a Progressive Populist Movement: Building a Multiracial, Race-Conscious Movement for Bold Change in Rural and Small-Town America," People's Action, Apr. 24, 2018, www.peoplesaction.org/wp-content/uploads/2018/04/PA_Report_Final_digital.pdf.

14. See raceclassnarrativeaction.com for more details on this research.

15. We based our deep canvassing work on recent experiments led by the California Immigration Policy Center and the Immigrant Strategic Messaging Project. See caimmigrant.org/immigrant-strategic-messaging-project-information.

16. Joshua L. Kalla and David E. Broockman, "The Minimal Persuasive Effects of Campaign Contact in General Elections: Evidence from 49 Field Experiments," *American Political Science Review* 112, no. 1 (2018): 148–66.

17. For example, California Immigrant Policy Center, "Research Brief: Deep Canvass, Deep Change," Mar. 2019, caimmigrant.org/wp-content/uploads/2019/05/Canvass-Research-Brief-FINAL2-1.pdf.

18. For a more detailed analysis of the experiment results, see peoplesaction.org/wp-content/uploads/2020/07/PA-Deep-Canvass-Final-Report-v5.pdf.

The Statue of Liberty Plan

Vision and Strategy for the Immigrant Rights Movement in
the Twenty-First Century

Deepak Bhargava

W e often confront a chasm between our dreams for the world
as it should be and the hard realities of the world as it is.
Nowhere is that gap more evident, painful, or consequential than in
the area of immigration. Compelling moral claims about the inher-
ent and equal worth of all human beings irrespective of national origin run up against a wall of public support for limits on migration.
Because immigration has become such a political lightning rod, the
stakes are high—not only for immigrants but for everyone. To bridge
the gap, we must yoke visionary idealism with sober pragmatism. This
concluding chapter proposes a "Statue of Liberty plan," an ambitious
agenda for a radically more welcoming immigration system, and four
strategies for immigrant rights movement leaders to generate the
power needed to realize that vision.

Power Creates Possibilities: Learning from Stephen Miller's Hops Across the Pond

Paradoxically, the immigration policymaker who most clearly points
the way to a new strategy for the left is Stephen Miller, Trump's senior
advisor. Many observers have described the viciousness and racism
of the Trump administration's immigration agenda.[1] Less often
have they dissected the cold, calculating, and sinister logic underlying it, most of which was Miller's handiwork. Miller is a strange

character—driven, ruthless, and racist. A cache of emails obtained by the Southern Poverty Law Center exposed his ties to white nationalist groups and ideas, and his obsession with the threat of "demographic replacement" of white people by people of color.[2]

The source of Miller's rage is the massive growth in immigration that followed passage of the 1965 Immigration Act. The foreign-born share of the U.S. population grew from a low of 4.7 percent in 1970 to 13.7 percent in 2018.[3] Many view the "browning of America"—the demographic revolution that could turn America into a majority-of-color nation by 2045—as inevitable.[4] Miller aimed to reverse the tide by driving down immigration from Asia, Africa, and Latin America. His efforts were remarkably successful: the net increase in the size of the immigrant population fell 70 percent from 2017 to 2018, and net immigration between 2018 and 2019 was only 595,348, a level not seen since the 1980s.[5] These reductions are all the more remarkable given the booming economy of this period. Miller achieved this with a multi-pronged approach, from imposing hurdles to make legal immigration harder to increasing immigration enforcement, from the "Muslim ban" to dramatically reducing refugee admissions.

While Trump was preoccupied with the symbolic victory of a wall at the border with Mexico, Miller was laser-focused on stopping the flow not only of undocumented immigrants but also of *legal* immigration. Later he used the COVID-19 crisis as a pretext to impose a hiatus on all new migration to the United States, celebrating in a private call with donors, "The first and most important thing is to turn off the faucet of new immigrant labor. Mission accomplished."[6] The final frontier of the strategy was to revoke citizenship from immigrants who have obtained it: in 2020, the Justice Department established a Denaturalization Section to review cases of fraud or crime that might result in revocations of U.S. citizenship. The ultimate goal is "undoing the naturalization of the more than twenty million naturalized citizens in the American population by taking away their assumption of permanence" and thereby making them "second class citizens."[7]

Morally, there is everything to deplore about what Stephen Miller has done. Strategically, however, we can learn from how he advanced the cause of white supremacy by implementing nativist policies with a ruthless, Leninist zeal. His long wish list of anti-immigrant policies constituted a master plan that he systematically pursued with an astonishing drive, resulting in over four hundred executive actions designed to reduce immigration.[8] Even when sloppy implementation resulted in visible chaos and backlash, the administration rarely backtracked, in contrast to what Miller contemptuously called the "apology-retreat cycle" of previous Republican administrations.[9] Although he suffered occasional setbacks in the courts, as with the first two iterations of the Muslim ban, he persisted and usually prevailed.

Trump and Miller used incendiary, racist rhetoric to dehumanize immigrants and to stoke fear. Not only the policy but the incitement to hatred discouraged migration by sending a chilling message to prospective migrants. When Adam Purinton murdered Srinivas Kuchibhotla, an engineer and immigrant from India, at a Kansas bar in February 2017—after calling him a "terrorist" and demanding that he "get out of my country"—he echoed the rhetoric of the newly inaugurated president and the right-wing media and alt-right groups Trump had whipped into a frenzy during the campaign. The murder created a firestorm in the Indian media and forced a conversation in millions of Indian households about whether America was still a safe place to seek a better life.[10]

Miller deployed the mechanisms of government itself to advance the immigrant threat narrative—for example, by elevating stories of crime by immigrants, and by forcing government agencies to supply false propaganda about the negative impact of immigrants on public services, jobs, and budgets. Although open racism surfaced at times (think of Trump's use of the phrase "shithole countries"), the official argument was about "protecting American workers" and the "harm" and "cost" of immigration. This frame provided a larger umbrella that people uncomfortable with explicit racism could stand beneath.

This tension between barely veiled racist intent and public rhetoric about protecting American workers reflected the gap between Miller's ultimate goals and his power. Like a frog trying to cross a pond to a destination in which white power is preserved and enhanced, he couldn't hop to the far shore in one giant leap, by openly declaring the desire for a white nationalist republic. Instead he invoked the frame of "protecting American workers" to legitimate incremental policies that lowered the flow of migrants from non-white countries to the United States. The result was to deter new immigration, delegalize existing immigrants, embolden white supremacists outside government, terrify immigrants themselves, and normalize a discourse that associated immigration with economic and cultural loss. As Miller hopped from lily pad to lily pad, each success had feedback effects that weakened pro-immigrant forces and strengthened nativists, altering the balance of power. Each extreme policy proposal—even when it faced intense backlash—moved the center of gravity and paved the way for even more radical policies. Miller relished what he called "constructive controversy—with the purpose of enlightenment."[11] The policies were often gratuitously cruel, but for Miller, white power was always the end, and stopping migration from non-white countries was the means.

While the nativist right is unified about the means and ends, pro-immigrant forces have often been bitterly divided about both. Leftists accuse liberals of selling out basic principles, and liberals accuse leftists of tilting at windmills. At times communication breaks down altogether and skirmishes with near-ideological neighbors seem more important than uniting to prosecute the war against common nativist foes. Part of the conflict reflects differences in vision (for example, about limits on migration), while another part involves time horizons. Leftists with a long-term vision of free movement of people may object to any action that violates that principle, while centrist and liberal immigration advocates focus on short-term tactical maneuvering in the name of realpolitik.

Instead we need a medium-term strategic orientation that honestly recognizes political realities yet does not abandon long-term values. The aim should be to expand the parameters of the possible without indulging in magical thinking. Stephen Miller was a canny operator in this middle range—committed to a long-term white nationalist vision but pushing up against political constraints and often moving them.

Four concepts, three from the liberal and left traditions and one from conservative thinkers, can help pro-immigrant forces chart a path forward. The first is the "united front," a concept that some socialists developed in response to fascism, which might now be productively applied to the threat of white nationalist nativism.[12] The idea is that when facing an existential threat, alliances must be made between groups who disagree about many things but have a shared interest in defeating the opponent. This does not require groups to abandon their deeply held principles. Rather, it forges unity on the basis of shared proximate goals. Leftists might seek to go from the lobby of an apartment building to its roof on the thirtieth floor, while liberals only want to go to the eighth floor. The two groups share a common imperative to overpower the nativists blocking ascent to the seventh floor, in full knowledge that they might start fighting again should they succeed.

Second is the academic concept of "policy feedback loops," which posits that some policies alter relations of power once enacted, creating new possibilities and foreclosing other paths. For example, after Social Security was established, a formidable constituency of beneficiaries emerged that resisted later efforts to cut benefits. Similarly, the 1965 Immigration and Nationality Act dramatically increased the number of immigrants from Asia and Latin America to the United States, creating a powerful constituency for more generous policies (and intense opposition from nativist opponents).[13]

Third is French Marxist André Gorz's concept of "non-reformist reforms," demands that prefigure what a decent society might look like and that if achieved would gradually undermine capitalism. Examples include policies such as universal basic income and Medicare for All, which would decommodify large parts of the economy. Applied to this context, we would pursue reforms that, when achieved, would both prefigure a just immigration system and simultaneously break the back of white nationalist nativism.

Finally, the idea of the "Overton window," developed by a conservative theorist, posits that the skillful introduction of ideas that are far outside the mainstream of political discourse may make other bold policies seem less extreme. The demand to "defund the police," for example, has expanded the realm of the possible in the debate over policing.[14]

The Statue of Liberty Plan: Making America the Most Welcoming Nation on Earth for Migrants and Refugees

Stephen Miller was clear about his long-term goal of white power. What is the north star for the immigrant rights movement? I propose one crucial aim: making the United States the most welcoming country on earth for immigrants and refugees.

Morally, the argument that we owe allegiance only to people from our own nation is flawed. The nation-state is a construct of relatively recent origin. Most progressive traditions of thought, from the religious and spiritual to the secular, liberal, and socialist, proceed from the idea of the equal dignity of all human beings. This is impossible to reconcile with a politics of walls, separating children from their parents, or banning migrants because of their faith or the color of their skin. Nor can it be reconciled with the idea that the country where you are born should determine your life outcomes. Moreover, because U.S. foreign and economic policy often creates conditions that force migration, the United States is implicated rather than innocent. Evoking the legacy of colonialism, European immigrant activists have adopted the slogan "We are here because you were there."

The coronavirus crisis has exposed the deep interdependence of all life on earth not only at the level of morality but also practically. It is no longer plausible to protect "our" tribe, build a wall around "our" nation, and hold at bay the suffering and chaos outside. Forces of technology, transport, and commerce connect us in a single field, so health, economic, or political crises in one area impact the entire world sooner or later. We are connected, as Dr. Martin Luther King Jr. famously said, in a "single garment of destiny." Our fates are linked. What's new is that a narrow conception of our moral obligations and self-interest could actually kill us. As climate change makes larger areas of the earth uninhabitable, migration from the global South to the North (in response to emissions overwhelmingly *from* the North) will grow exponentially. In extreme climate scenarios, more than 30 million climate refugees are projected to head to the U.S. border in the next thirty years.[15] Without an immigration policy that welcomes many more people, we will become a fortress democracy—which is no democracy at all.

Some argue that over the very long term, the world will require both more global governance and more local governance, with a smaller role for the nation-state.[16] Yet the actual response to COVID-19 has been overwhelmingly nationalist. Borders closed all around the world, and even existing regional and global bodies such as the World Health Organization came under attack. Borders may need to wither away in the far future, but in the meantime we will need to make many hops to many lily pads.

As we prepare for the world to come, a more promising approach is to move the "Overton window," making ideas that are currently unthinkable acceptable and eventually popular. The immigrant rights movement should advance a broad, bold, simple proposal for a more welcoming immigration system, what I call the "Statue of Liberty plan." It would set a standard for the United States to be the *most welcoming country on earth for immigrants and refugees*. The foreign-born share of the U.S. population, 13.7 percent in 2018, is near the historic high of a century ago, yet it is less than half the share in Switzerland, which is 28.2 percent, and well below that in Australia (21.0 percent) and Canada (17.2 percent).[17]

Under the Statue of Liberty plan, admission of immigrants to the United States would increase dramatically. If the plan were in effect today, the number of foreign-born residents would rise from the current 45 million to 92.6 million (using Switzerland as a benchmark), or perhaps to 69 million (using Australia as the standard). Over the past decade, the net increase in the foreign-born population averaged only 477,286 per year—so achieving such targets over a decade would require admitting millions more people to the United States each year.

Under this plan, we could welcome economic migrants but also substantially expand migration through the established family, humanitarian, and diversity pathways. Those non-economic criteria are a distinctly positive feature of U.S. immigration policy and are rare in the rest of the world, as Gest points out in this volume. The Statue of Liberty plan could launch a national civic project to welcome and integrate millions of new immigrants into communities, stimulate the economy, and reweave the social fabric in our deeply polarized society.

Such a proposal, while far beyond the parameters of the current policy discourse, is consistent with one deep strand of U.S. immigration history. Attitudes and policies toward immigration have been "a perfect sine wave, periods of welcoming inclusiveness alternating with years of scowling antipathy."[18] Racism is the country's original sin, but the nation's accidental genius has been its ability to renew itself through immigration. This proposal would align the reality of U.S. policy and practice with its most flattering (if not fully accurate) self-image. As Ngai points out in this volume, second-generation immigrants often power periods of progressive reform—and the current demographic wave could do so again.

There is every reason to believe that an extended immigration boom would be good for the country—and not only as a means to break the toxic stranglehold of white nationalism. It is well documented that immigration has a net positive effect on the U.S. economy. Employers seeking to increase profits, not immigration, have driven the degradation of labor standards, as Milkman shows in this volume. The most economically vital U.S. regions are those with the highest share of immigrants. An aging society needs caregivers and population renewal, and climate change necessitates massive investments and an expanded resilience workforce, as Soni argues in this volume. Immigration is essential to achieve these national imperatives. And for all the right-wing hysteria about immigration's negative cultural impact, most immigrants have lives and concerns that are similar to those of native-born people, belying sensational media coverage of the issue.[19] The ubiquitous "We Are America" signs at the immigrant rights marches in 2006 and 2007 had it right. It is time to directly challenge the scarcity model on which Trump, Miller, and other nativists have feasted (Trump famously said, "our country is full"). We should replace it with a narrative that emphasizes immigrants as crucial to U.S. identity and to national renewal, highlighting the shared interests of immigrant and native-born workers.[20]

The unifying and galvanizing demand of the U.S. immigrant rights movement for the past twenty years has been for a path to citizenship for the 11 million undocumented immigrants. That must remain a central plank in our program, as the impact of the broken system on undocumented people and their families remains one of the great injustices of our time. Our culture and democracy are deeply tainted by the hypocrisy of reliance on undocumented labor alongside a failure to recognize immigrants' full humanity. But as Kassa argues in this volume, the movement can continue to push for legalization while also embracing a bold vision of future migration.

Immigrant leaders and their allies should launch a campaign for dramatically increasing admissions of immigrants and refugees. Centrist and some liberal forces may not join, at least initially. We should remember that while legalization is part of mainstream politics now, that was not always so—as recently as the late 1990s the conventional inside-the-Beltway wisdom was to talk only about "deserving" (legal) immigrants. In 2006, Ted Kennedy was the only U.S. senator to show up at marches of hundreds of thousands of people for immigrant rights, while the rest feared backlash. But grassroots organizing opened the Overton window, moving legalization from the margins to the center of the discourse. Legalization has not yet been accomplished, but it *has* been normalized. A similar transformation of our sense of the possible should begin now with respect to future migration. As Miller demonstrated, being on offense, setting the terms of the debate, and forcing your opponents to react—putting them in a defensive crouch—is a far stronger position than arguing against hostile frameworks.

The Statue of Liberty plan cannot stand alone. Without economic security for all workers, welcoming policies won't be sustainable and will provide fodder for demagogues. Both Democratic and Republican administrations have pursued neoliberal economic policies for decades that have pushed many working people, native-born and immigrant, to the brink. Therefore, a necessary condition for greater immigration is economic security for the current population. Paradoxically, the greatest variable driving immigration policy has little to do with immigration per se. Since immigrants themselves are already a large share of the U.S. working class, they too will benefit from a new social contract that includes expanded labor rights, income security, racial justice, health care, and job creation.

The Bridge Connecting Current Reality and Future Vision: Four Essential Strategies

Movements need bold north star goals, but as old-school community organizers say, "Rocks are hard, and water is wet." Whatever the substantive or moral strength of a case for a radically more welcoming immigration system, the majority of the public does not yet support it. Public opinion research shows that passionate pro-immigration supporters are few in number and isolated from much of the country.[21] To acknowledge this reality is not to capitulate to it. As Perry Anderson put it: "A resistance that dispenses with consolations is always stronger than one that relies on them."[22] Pretending that you have more support than you do is tempting—but in politics, it's an unforgivable sin. Social change requires not only lofty visions but also practical routes to travel.

What, then, is to be done? I propose four core strategies, and while they are not entirely sequential, progress in each area will build momentum for the others.

A United Front

First, moderates, liberals, and leftists must join in a united front to defeat white nationalist nativism. Recent decades suggest that nativists are at their most resourceful and effective when they seem to be on their knees. After a crushing defeat in the 2012 elections, the Republican National Committee issued an autopsy arguing that in order to have any prospect of winning again, the party had to embrace immigration reform. Just a few years later, a comprehensive immigration reform bill lay in ruins after a skillful and ferocious campaign by nativists to win the Republican Party back, marked by a primary in which an anti-immigrant zealot unexpectedly defeated House majority leader Eric Cantor (R-VA).

It follows that *actually* defeating nativism means much more than undoing the harms perpetrated by Trump and Miller. Without a real shift in the balance of power, progress will be temporary. Pro-immigrant forces from the center to the left must prioritize the defeat of white nationalist nativism as their common goal and then choose their battles carefully. If a united front pursues a disciplined agenda, nativists can be banished to the fringes of politics.

Two difficult concessions are needed for such a united front to coalesce. Leftists will have to acknowledge that order, control, and limits—as Muñoz suggests in this volume—will be part of the discussion. Given the state of public opinion, this will be necessary to achieve the reforms that will allow the constituency that supports expanded migration to grow over time. Leftists do not have to say things they don't believe, but they must allow liberal and centrist allies to support limits without demonizing them. This will require enormous discipline—but the reward will be far greater power for immigrants themselves to set the terms of the debate. Centrists and liberals, on the other hand, will have to abandon the notion that a never-ending spiral of immigration enforcement is a necessary "price to be paid" for legalization, as Hincapié and Jiménez argue in this volume. This strategy has been widely criticized on moral grounds. But it is also terrible power politics, because acquiescence to a massive enforcement apparatus normalizes roundups and detention that demobilize immigrants, and fuels the growth of formidable constituencies that benefit economically and use their power to advocate even harsher immigration policies.

Moreover, concessions on enforcement will never bring "sensible" Republicans to the table. Only a series of crushing and repeated electoral defeats might break the nativists' death grip on the party. When Republicans come to bargain under those circumstances—which may happen quickly but could take years, given the Trumpification of the party at the grassroots—devastating concessions will not be needed. The habit of acceding to greater enforcement—"the great flinch," one might call it—needs to be unlearned. Just as Stephen Miller deliberately broke what he called the "apology-retreat" cycle in the Republican Party and made nativism mainstream, Democratic complicity with spiraling enforcement also must end.

Non-Reformist Reforms

Second, this united front must focus its limited leverage on key "non-reformist reforms" that alter the balance of power between pro-immigrant and nativist forces in the country. Miller's ferocity came not from confidence but from panic that he was running out of time to reverse the arc of demographic change, which threatened a death blow to white nativist nationalism. The immigrant movement has some power, but it is limited. How it spends its capital when it is in a position to affect national policy again will have enormous consequences. A simple criterion must govern policy priorities in the future: the movement must focus its power on measures that grow further power.

Staying focused on a few key reforms will be hard because there is so much damage to undo after the Trump years. But we must avoid a dispersion of energy across long lists of policy changes, however meritorious. Instead, a united front should focus its limited leverage in ways that generate feedback effects, by enabling immigrants themselves to *be* and *feel* more powerful in driving the debate.

Policies that reduce fear of detention, deportation, and use of social programs will encourage greater civic engagement. Mass marches of immigrants didn't happen under Trump as they did in 2006, 2007, and the early Obama years. It's no coincidence that the groups that mobilized first as the "resistance" under Trump—disproportionately white urban middle-class women—were those that felt a measure of security.

A moratorium on deportations and interior enforcement would begin to de-weaponize the enforcement machinery, and it should continue until a mass legalization is enacted by Congress. A moratorium would reverse the flawed logic of the Obama years that tough enforcement would encourage Republicans to come to the table; in fact, it had precisely the opposite effect. An extended moratorium will force conservatives to pay the price of delaying immigration reform. Immigrants would have space to breathe, live without fear, and organize.

The new president and Congress should also terminate the programs that enable cooperation between ICE and local police forces and radically reduce the budget for immigration enforcement, as Markowitz proposes in this volume. This would immediately reduce fear in immigrant communities. The new administration will need to rapidly deploy administrative action and engage in hand-to-hand bureaucratic combat against the DHS machinery (and the ICE and CBP unions) that have been terrorizing vulnerable immigrant workers and families. Miller used "shock and awe" to overwhelm the resistance of the bureaucracy to sweeping change and had to "burrow in" deeply to the details of policy administration to make changes stick.[23] Pro-immigrant forces will need to be just as relentless if high-flying rhetoric is to translate into freedom on the ground for immigrant communities. A dramatic reconstruction of the immigration bureaucracy of the kind that Jayapal proposes in this volume would also have a transformative effect.

The full range of executive powers should be used to protect immigrants already residing in the United States—Temporary Protected Status (TPS), Deferred Action for Childhood Arrivals (DACA), parole in place, and more. As Miller understood, the scope for executive action in the area of immigration is vast—and just as it has been used to harm, it can also be used to protect immigrants. The ability to change the composition of the Supreme Court may determine the fate of more ambitious initiatives (such as Deferred Action for Parents of Americans, which was rejected on a 4–4 vote and would have protected about 5 million people from deportation). Regardless, a new administration can restore and expand TPS and DACA, among other executive actions. That will not only give immigrants a greater sense of security but also give U.S. citizens in mixed-status families a compelling reason to mobilize in 2022 and 2024 to protect those gains.

Whenever a window for legislation opens up, a united front should prioritize creating a path to citizenship for the 11 million undocumented people now living in the United States. Equally critical are measures to expand future migration, including clearing family backlogs that would allow millions of people to reunite with loved ones. The Trump years showed the potential of executive action but also its limits, as many advances under Obama that had been achieved through administrative action were reversed. Others, like DACA, might have been ended were it not for the sloppiness of the administration's campaign to terminate it. Legislation is the surest path to reduce fear *and* legalize immigrants. Congress should *not* follow the model of many earlier bills, which imposed burdensome conditions that would have made immigrants crawl over broken glass to navigate the path to citizenship. The explicit goal should be to help *all* 11 million undocumented people adjust their status quickly.

Trade-offs are inevitable. Congress is unlikely to pass a generous legalization bill without any negative elements. It is impossible to prejudge the concessions that must be made, but maximizing the scope of legalization and maximizing future flow through all channels (work, family, humanitarian, and diversity) should be top priorities. Accomplishing these two things will accelerate demographic change and activate the policy feedback loop described earlier so as to change the underlying politics of the country in irreversible ways.

In short, hard policy choices should be made with a focus on maximizing the potential power of pro-immigrant forces and eroding the power of nativist constituencies over time. By reducing fear and expanding legalization, a broad united front whose members disagree about the ultimate, long-term ends of immigration policy can nevertheless deal a decisive blow against white nationalist nativism.

Government should be mobilized to change hearts and minds in ways that lay the foundation for more ambitious policy change. To recover from the Trump era, a high-profile "Statue of Liberty Commission" modeled on South Africa's Truth and Reconciliation Commission should publicly acknowledge the human impact of family separation, caging children, turning away refugees, and other draconian policies. This commission should hear from affected families and be authorized to recommend criminal prosecution for those responsible and restitution to the people and families that are harmed. This is a matter of justice, but also of accountability and historical memory that will transform future policymaking. The state of California passed an Apology Act in 2005 for the expulsion of hundreds of thousands of Mexican Americans during the Great Depression, with a small commemorative marker in Los Angeles.[24] A prominent monument in the nation's capital should similarly acknowledge the grave harms done to this generation of immigrants. Restitution should also extend to policy, including a "right to reunite" for all of those unfairly removed from the country, so that they can rejoin family members in the United States.

Miller and his nativist friends weaponized the communications machinery of government to promulgate a false story about the role of immigrants in our economy and culture. A telling example is the elimination of the U.S. Citizenship and Information Services' official pledge to "secure America's promise as a nation of immigrants." Every act, study, and communication of the federal government should elevate the positive contributions of immigrants to the country. Worldviews are shaped not only by words but also by experiences. For example, a dramatically expanded AmeriCorps program could recruit young people from regions with few immigrants to work for immigrant community organizations, scaling up the bridging work that Azemun and Kruggel discuss in this volume.

Accelerate Pro-Immigrant Mobilization and Organizing

Third, the movement should accelerate political mobilization and organizing of immigrants, their U.S.-born family members, and allies. The advantage that U.S. pro-immigrant forces have, unlike their counterparts in nearly every other wealthy country facing growing nativism, is the potential political power of immigrants. That advantage, properly exploited, can break the back of white nativist nationalism. Even without further legalization, the potential voting power of immigrants and their U.S.-born family members is far greater than its expression to date. The voting coalition for pro-immigrant policies has a lot of room to grow, even as the number of older white voters is shrinking.[25] The political transformations of first California and then Nevada and Arizona were not inevitable.[26] In those states, community and labor organizers made long-term commitments to organize immigrants and allies and won the war, as Medina, Salas, and Taylor explain in this volume. In California and Nevada, there is no turning back: nativists have been reduced to fringe groups with little influence. Arizona is a work in progress but has been moving in the same direction ever since the fight against SB 1070, the "show me your papers" law. A faith-based vigil outside the state capitol in the days after the bill passed sparked community and youth mobilization that permanently transformed the state's politics. Many of the leaders from that movement now head key organizations and hold elected office.[27]

The tectonic shift of translating demographics into power, as these states exemplify, is already remaking American politics. This strategy should be turbocharged at the national level to prepare for the inevitable counter-mobilization in 2022 and 2024. Translating demographic advantages into durable political coalitions will sustain progressive policy changes.

This transformation can be accelerated by a pro-immigrant administration in Washington, just as it was retarded by the Trump regime. For example, Miller's policies doubled the wait time for naturalization applications.[28] Naturalization can be accelerated, both by reducing barriers and costs and by creating nudges in the immigration process that make it the default option for immigrants. Naturalization gives immigrants full political rights and creates a positive feedback loop that will sustain a pro-immigrant majority.

U.S. Citizenship and Immigration Services could also facilitate voter registration at naturalization ceremonies. As part of a national commitment to more effectively welcome new immigrants and strengthen the infrastructure of immigrant organizations, the new administration also could encourage immigrants to become members of immigrant civic organizations during the process of applying for various forms of legal status. Doctors, lawyers, and others are required to join professional associations as part of their licensing process. Why not give immigrants the option to join a civic or labor organization as one way to engage in democracy? The federal government also should scale up and fund community groups that help immigrants apply for various forms of legal status, including citizenship, and defray the costs for low-income immigrants.

Immigrant Rights as a Pillar of Economic and Racial Justice

Fourth, the immigrant rights movement should position itself as a key pillar in the broader movement for economic and racial justice. A bold immigration vision must go hand in hand with a broader vision of social justice. While tactical alliances with business groups or moderates will be important at times, the core partnerships will be with forward-looking labor unions, progressive whites, other communities of color, and, especially, Black communities. This coalition is more possible now than ever. One boomerang effect of Trump's draconian policies was to educate white urban middle-class people about just how broken the immigration system is. The immigrant movement has long collaborated at the grassroots level with other groups working for economic and racial justice. It should expand those efforts, not only to insist on the full inclusion of immigrants in agenda-setting but also to embrace a broader race-conscious working-class politics. There is a strong base to build from at the local level, including leadership from immigrant groups such as One America on climate policy, Make the Road New York on criminal justice and housing in New York, and on worker rights by the Coalition for Humane Immigrant Rights in Los Angeles, the Florida Immigrant Coalition, CASA de Maryland, and Voces de la Frontera in Wisconsin. Over time, immigrant communities can become the domestic social base for a more internationalist progressive movement that pushes for changes in U.S. foreign policy, including but not limited to addressing America's role in producing the conditions that lead to migration.

Immigrants' relationship to Black communities is pivotal. The success of that alliance depends on principled commitments by the immigrant movement to support the Black freedom struggle and specifically to address issues important to Black immigrants, such as TPS, refugee policy, and the diversity visa. Sustaining Black demographic strength and political power is a crucial goal, to avoid reinforcing the racial hierarchy that puts Black communities at the bottom. However, the greatest opportunity for forging solidarity may be not in the context of immigration but through a vibrant large-scale joint struggle, such as a campaign against Amazon or another low-wage employer. The "essential worker" frame created during the pandemic is powerful, making visible the role of both Black and immigrant workers in sectors such as care work and the food supply chain. Campaigns grounded in those identities and galvanized by common demands for unionization, living wages, immigrant rights, and racial justice could be politically transformative. Finding a concrete forum for joint, sustained action, in which relationships and deep political understandings can be forged and tested, is of central importance.

The 1965 Immigration and Nationality Act, mostly by accident, profoundly reshaped the nation's politics and culture. Today's immigration wars to sustain, improve, or reverse it are part of the long historical arc it created. President Johnson signed the 1965 act at Ellis Island with the Statue of Liberty as the backdrop. At the base of the statue is the famous poem by Emma Lazarus invoking "huddled masses yearning to breathe free." Fifty-two years later, Stephen Miller mocked a reporter for invoking the poem and denied its relevance to the country's identity. Given the reductions in immigration under Trump and the rise of nativist politicians around the world, we must be sober about the challenges we face. It's possible that we are at the beginning of a long night of restrictionism of the kind that began in the 1920s. But with a big vision and a leap of strategic imagination, the immigrant rights movement and its partners could be on the cusp of defeating white nativist nationalism, realizing the promise of Lazarus's iconic poem, and ushering in generations of progressive social change.

Notes

1. See Julie Hirschfeld Davis and Michael D. Shear, *Border Wars: Inside Trump's Assault on Immigration* (New York: Simon & Schuster, 2019).

2. Katie Rogers, "Before Joining White House, Stephen Miller Pushed White Nationalist Theories," *New York Times*, Nov. 13, 2019; Jonathan Blitzer, "How Stephen Miller Manipulates Donald Trump to Further His Immigration Obsession," *The New Yorker*, Mar. 2, 2020.

3. William Frey, "U.S. Foreign-Born Gains Are Smallest in a Decade, Except in Trump States," The Avenue (blog), Brookings Institution, Oct. 2, 2019.

4. William Frey, "U.S. Will Become 'Minority White' in 2045, Census Projects," The Avenue (blog), Brookings Institution, Mar. 14, 2018. Much of the demographic change is driven by higher fertility among U.S.-born people of color and the aging of the white population, rather than by immigration.

5. Frey, "U.S. Foreign-Born Gains" and William Frey, "The 2010s May Have Seen the Slowest Population Growth in U.S. History, Census Data Show," Brookings Institution, Jan. 2, 2020. If immigration levels were reduced to zero, the country would become majority non-white after 2060, rather than 2045 as currently projected.

6. Muzaffar Chishti and Sarah Pierce, "The U.S. Stands Alone in Explicitly Basing Coronavirus-Linked Immigration Restrictions on Economic Grounds," Migration Policy Institute, May 29, 2020.

7. Masha Gessen, "In America, Naturalized Citizens No Longer Have an Assumption of Permanence," *The New Yorker*, June 18, 2018. See also Katie Benner, "Justice Dept. Establishes Office to Denaturalize Immigrants," *New York Times*, Feb. 26, 2020.

8. Sarah Pierce and Jessica Bolter, "Dismantling and Restructuring the U.S. Immigration System: A Catalog of Changes Under the Trump Presidency," Migration Policy Institute Report, July 2020.

9. Hirschfeld Davis and Shear, *Border Wars*, 32.

10. Anand Giridharadas, "A Murder in Trump's America," *The Atlantic*, Feb. 28, 2017. And John Eligon, Alan Blinder, and Nida Najar, "Hate Crime Is Feared as 2 Indian Engineers Are Shot in Kansas," *New York Times*, Feb. 24, 2017.

11. McKay Coppins, "Stephen Miller: Trump's Right-Hand Troll," *The Atlantic*, May 28, 2018.

12. Leon Trotsky, "For a Workers United Front Against Fascism," in *The Struggle Against Fascism in Germany* (New York: Pathfinder Press, 1971).

13. See Alexander Hertel-Fernandez, "How Policymakers Can Craft Measures That Endure and Build Political Power," Roosevelt Institute Working Paper, June 17, 2020.

14. Stephen J. Russell, "An Introduction to the Overton Window of Political Possibilities," Mackinac Center for Public Policy, Jan. 4, 2006.

15. Abrahm Lustgarden, "Refugees from the Earth," *New York Times*, July 26, 2020; John Podesta, "The Climate Crisis, Migration and Refugees," Brookings Institution, July 25, 2019.

16. See Bruno Latour, *Down to Earth: Politics in the New Climactic Age* (Cambridge, UK: Polity Press, 2017).

17. Gilles Pison, "Which Countries Have the Most Immigrants?," World Economic Forum, Mar. 13, 2019.

18. Daniel Okrent, *The Guarded Gate: Bigotry, Eugenics and the Law that Kept Jews, Italians and Other European Immigrants Out of America* (New York: Scribner, 2019), 41.

19. See Jason DeParle, *A Good Provider Is One Who Leaves: One Family and Migration in the 21st Century* (New York: Viking, 2019).

20. Neil Irwin and Emily Badger, "Trump Says the Nation Is 'Full.' Much of the Nation Has the Opposite Problem," *New York Times*, Apr. 9, 2019.

21. Ryan Senser and Eleanor Morrison, "New Insights: Winning on Immigration," commissioned for Unbound Philanthropy, Oct. 2018.

22. Perry Anderson, *Spectrum: From Right to Left in the World of Ideas* (London: Verso, 2005), 320.

23. Hirschfeld Davis and Shear, *Border Wars*, 95, 135; Blitzer, "How Stephen Miller Manipulates Trump."

24. Erika Lee, *America for Americans: A History of Xenophobia in the United States* (New York: Basic Books, 2019), 327.

25. Steve Phillips, *Brown Is the New White: How the Demographic Revolution Has Created a New American Majority* (New York: The New Press, 2016).

26. SB 1070 made it a state crime to live in Arizona without legal status, to travel without immigration papers, and to transport or hire undocumented immigrants. It also allowed police to detain anyone they suspected of being in the country illegally.

27. Republic Staff, "SB1070: A Legacy of Fear, Divisiveness and Fulfillment," *Arizona Republic*, Apr. 23, 2020.

28. Hirschfeld Davis and Shear, *Border Wars*, 8.

ACKNOWLEDGMENTS

Many of the chapters in this book were presented in preliminary form at a webcast we organized, "Rethinking Immigration," sponsored by the CUNY School of Labor and Urban Studies, held on May 1, 2020. We thank the school, as well as the JPB Foundation and the Open Societies Foundations, for their support of both the webcast and this book.

CONTRIBUTORS

Mehrdad Azemun is Senior Strategist for People's Action. He has been organizing for twenty years. His roots are in the immigrant rights movement, community organizing, and electoral organizing. He ran the grassroots organizing operations for two national immigrant justice campaigns. He is an immigrant from Iran.

Deepak Bhargava is a Distinguished Lecturer at CUNY's School of Labor and Urban Studies. He is a longtime immigrant rights movement leader and previously led Community Change, a national social justice organization that builds the power and capacity of low-income people of color. He was born in Bangalore, India.

Justin Gest is Associate Professor of Policy and Government at George Mason University's Schar School of Policy and Government. His recent books include *The New Minority: White Working Class Politics in an Age of Immigration and Inequality* (2016) and *Crossroads: Comparative Immigration Regimes in a World of Demographic Change* (2018).

Marielena Hincapié is Executive Director of the National Immigration Law Center. For over two decades she has helped shape the movement for immigrant justice, in campaigns from DACA to the Muslim ban to Trump's immigrant wealth test. She has litigated cases impacting millions of immigrants, some of which set legal precedents protecting undocumented workers. The youngest of ten children, Hincapié immigrated to the United States from Colombia as a child.

U.S. Representative Pramila Jayapal (WA-07) was elected to Congress in 2016 and is a lifelong organizer for immigrant, civil, and human rights. She serves as Co-Chair of the Congressional Progressive Caucus and Vice Chair of the Immigration Subcommittee. She is the first South Asian American woman elected to the House of Representatives and one of only fourteen naturalized citizens in Congress.

Cristina Jiménez Moreta is a community organizer and cofounder of United We Dream, the largest immigrant youth organization in the country. She served as Executive Director of UWD for over a decade, leading pathbreaking campaigns to win expanded protections for immigrant youth, and is a leading voice for immigrant communities.

Amaha Kassa is the founder and Executive Director of African Communities Together, a national organization of immigrants from Africa and their families. He is a community and labor organizer with twenty-five years of experience, a licensed attorney, and an immigrant from Ethiopia.

Adam Kruggel is Director of Strategic Initiatives at People's Action and has more than twenty-four years of community organizing experience. At People's Action he helped to build the Rural and Small-Town Organizing Strategy, which has grown into one of the largest progressive rural organizing efforts in the country.

Penny Lewis is Associate Professor of Labor Studies at the School of Labor and Urban Studies at CUNY, and an elected leader of the faculty and staff union at CUNY. Her most recent book is *The City Is the Factory: New Solidarities and Spatial Strategies in an Urban Age* (co-edited with Miriam Greenberg,

2017), and she is co-author of the forthcoming *A People's Guide to New York City.*

Peter L. Markowitz is Professor of Law at Benjamin N. Cardozo School of Law and the founding faculty member and co-director of its Kathryn O. Greenberg Immigration Justice Clinic. He has published extensively on immigration and constitutional law.

Eliseo Medina began his lifelong career in the labor movement with the United Farm Workers. He later was on the staff of the American Federation of State, County and Municipal Workers and the Service Employees International Union, where he worked from 1986 to 2012, when he retired as SEIU secretary-treasurer.

Ruth Milkman is Distinguished Professor of Sociology at the CUNY Graduate Center and the CUNY School of Labor and Urban Studies, where she chairs the Labor Studies program. She is the author of *Immigrant Labor and the New Precariat* (2020), among other books.

Cecilia Muñoz is an immigration policy expert and activist who served as Domestic Policy Advisor in the Obama White House. She is a Vice President at New America in Washington, DC.

Mae M. Ngai is Lung Family Professor of Asian American Studies and Professor of History, Columbia University. She is the author of *Impossible Subjects: Illegal Aliens and the Making of Modern America* (2004).

Angelica Salas, a lifelong leader in the immigrant rights movement, is Executive Director of the Coalition for Humane Immigrant Rights (CHIRLA), a position she has held since 1999. She is also President of the CHIRLA Action Fund, the organization's political arm.

Saket Soni is a labor organizer who leads Resilience Force, the national voice for workers rebuilding America after climate disasters. He has testified in Congress and won landmark victories for workers. His writings have appeared in *Time*, CNN, and other publications. He was born in New Delhi, India.

D. Taylor is the International President of UNITE HERE, which has 300,000 members, many of them immigrants. Before being elected as the union's president in 2012 he served for many years as the secretary-treasurer of one of its largest units, the Culinary Workers (Local 226) in Las Vegas. His career with the union spans four decades.

Javier H. Valdés and **Deborah Axt** are the Co-Executive Directors of Make the Road New York; **Daniel Altschuler** is its Director of Civic Engagement and Research, and **Angeles Solis** is its Lead Organizer.